Cheaper Greener Cleaner

Ceiling to Floor Savings

Cheaper Greener Cleaner

Ceiling to Floor Savings

Carolyn Wootton
&
Dena Wootton

iUniverse, Inc.
Bloomington

Cheaper Greener Cleaner
Ceiling to Floor Savings

The recipes in this book are written in good faith. The contents of this book have been researched, although some of the methods may seem somewhat speculative in nature. The information we present should be used responsibly and at your own discretion. We cannot guarantee your results.

iUniverse books may be ordered through booksellers or by contacting:

iUniverse
1663 Liberty Drive
Bloomington, IN 47403
www.iuniverse.com
1-800-Authors (1-800-288-4677)

Cover photograph Green House Concept by Pablo Demetrio Scapinachis Armstrong.
White and Red Christmas Fireplace Interior photograph
by Pablo Demetrio Scapinachis Armstrong.
Change Ahead Sign photograph by Arkadi Bojaršinov
Photographs by Dena Wootton.

ISBN: 978-1-4620-6687-2 (sc)
ISBN: 978-1-4620-6689-6 (hc)
ISBN: 978-1-4620-6688-9 (e)

Printed in the United States of America

iUniverse rev. date: 12/01/2011

Also by Carolyn Wootton & Dena Wootton
"*Simply Centsational*"

This book is lovingly dedicated to Randy, Angelyn, Benyse and Ida Marianne; in loving memory of Benjamin, Cheryl, Ada, Bessie, Catherine, Eleanor, Esther, Ivy, Lillian Mary, Myrta Eleanor, and Sarah Amelia.

"Making the simple complicated is commonplace; making the complicated simple, awesomely simple, that's creativity."

Charles Mingus
American jazz musician, composer,
Bandleader and civil rights activist

Preface

There was a convergence of events and forces that brought about the writing of this book. It appeared as if the powers that be had been postured to unleash a well-kept secret which would liberate the spending bondage of today's consumers.

The long standing union between Madison Avenue and the industry cleaning and laundry giants have had such a chokehold on our spending habits. To make matters even more troubling they had been positioning themselves to entice us to give them even more of our hard earned money by way of the birth of the more expensive "green" products.

Having been a professional research/script writer for a media production company for many years, I researched a wide range of topics. Never did I think nor dream that this topic would have caught my interest and imagination. I thought I had finished that phase of my life until one day opportunity truly came knocking on my door. Yes, I realize this is a cliché, but it truly happened just that way.

My husband's mother, Ida Marianne Cowie Wootton, sent to us boxes filled with the Wootton family memorabilia. There appeared to be contents of drawers emptied into boxes that had been kept for over seventy five years. Knowing my love for research and knowledge, Mom gifted us these items as we later discovered were treasures beyond measure. What intrigued me were the poems from my husband's grandmother, Ada Dilworth Tracey Wootton and her recipes and ingredients for cleaning her home.

Once again I delved into intense research. Dena and I immersed ourselves into the pages, scraps of paper, and the ingredient labels. We pondered why she would preserve these bits and pieces, and then we understood. These were her cleaning staples. She had no other alternatives or conveniences. This was her way of life. We were awestruck with the simplicity of her cleaning recipes, and wondered about their effectiveness in her labor intensive tasks of that era.

These latest discoveries were not only enlightening about their lives but proved valuable knowledge for surviving in today's economy. With the advent of this information about some of our family during The Great Depression, we were intrigued to learn more and pondered the lives of past family members. The incentive to research and ultimately share our findings was based upon our innate characteristic of our frugality.

How far could we take this new knowledge? If we could replace a few of the highest cost items we had been purchasing, how about all the rest of the cleaning products that line the shelves? Feeling compelled to uncover as much of the mystery as possible and to truly make a difference more needed to be learned and shared.

After researching the material from Grandmother Ada, we went beyond ourselves to explore how the modern products affect the environment and we were hooked again! We became cheaper, greener, and cleaner in our own lives. Because we had so much fun, we decided to share with our family, friends, and neighbors. We even shared our newfound knowledge with shoppers on the laundry and cleaning aisles. Everyone could not believe that it was as easy as we were telling them, so we began demonstrating it to them in informal settings. They were astonished and grateful.

As consumers, we possess a great power, a power so strong that we are regarded by the industries as a vehicle to improve their bottom line. What would happen if we had an alternative to their high priced products? Could it really be this simple? Were we truly paying an enormous cost for our perceived convenience? Was this really something anyone could do while experiencing the same lifestyle? We would spend less, yes, yes, and yes!

After that, we began giving open workshops, showing how to become liberated from the high costs of retail cleaning and laundry products. In our workshops we demonstrated how we replaced hidden toxic chemicals from our homes. By actually making thirty recipes in thirty minutes we helped those that participated get past the preconceived notion that it took a lot of work and time. They were amazed and entertained! While saving so much money, we realized we were also helping the environment by going "green."

In our workshops, we demonstrate how to make thirty different cleaning and laundry replacements in thirty minutes. The most time intensive recipe is laundry detergent. This recipe can take as much as fifteen minutes and we still come in at thirty minutes. This is not labor intensive; this is easy at its very best! If these recipes didn't work, we would not be sharing them with you.

We wanted everyone to know how simple these well kept secrets were to master. "Going green" isn't anything new, it was green from the very beginning, the cleaning and laundry industry has turned it into the chemical mess we now need to clean up. What really makes all this possible is no one needs do anything other than "go green" in their own personal life at an affordable price far less than the industry giants are selling.

In our workshops, we share many of our family secrets. We have gotten ourselves into many interesting predicaments, and through each of them we have maintained a sense of humor even when we cringe at the failures. There are some we have vowed we would never tell on each other and somehow during all the laughter within the realm of the workshop moment some just slip out.

Another reason we wrote this book is our family can attest that we are always up to something. We have gotten in over our heads on more than one occasion. There isn't anything we can't do; at least we think that way. We are always looking for ways to save money, be creative, make it ourselves, and improvise.

It is now a standard joke in our family, if you are going to make anything, just start with a door. This came about when Dena and I got the bright idea we were going to make a dining room table. On a walk, we found a beautiful solid wood door which was abandoned in an alley. This door was in need of some repair work, but it was truly wonderful. We inquired about the possibility of buying this beautiful piece of wood and were told we could have it if we took it away right then and there. Procuring our prize, we proceeded down the street carrying it home. This was a sight to behold; two women lugging this big heavy door through the neighborhood. We ran out of steam and rested many times. A very kind man stopped and offered his truck, so we rode the rest of the way.

When he inquired if we needed help hanging the door, we proudly responded, “We are not going to hang it, we are making a table.” We thought he was going to crash the truck as he laughed so hard he was crying. At the moment, we were offended; we did not see the reason for his laughter. He did say he had to hand it to us for our resourcefulness, but how were we going to get anything like that to work as a table. Our instant response, “We are going to put legs on it, what else?” More laughter exploded as he just shook his head.

We were safely delivered home with our door/dining room table. We thanked him for his help and he left still shaking his head in disbelief.

With all the work involved, it did not bring about the grand piece of furniture we had envisioned. It was not sturdy; we hadn’t planned on that dilemma, next best thing, we put it next to the wall and didn’t move it, seating was limited, dining was cozy. Our next project was a desk - yep, we started with the door, after all we had lugged that heavy thing a very long way, we needed to put it to use in some fashion. By the way, these projects, while fun, did not last and our homes are not filled with furniture made out of doors.

With the disclosures of our varying successes, why would you be listening to us? What makes us think that these recipes are not going to blow up your house or turn your eggshell white walls green and orange? Well, for starters, we haven’t blown ourselves up. These recipes and tips are time tested and really work! We’re talking about saving money, something we are experts at!

Carolyn Wootton
Centennial, Colorado
November, 2011

Acknowledgements

Carolyn: I wish to express my sincere appreciation to my husband, Randy. You believed in me, you gave me the strength and courage I needed. I could never have done this without your constant support and input. Thank you for the hundreds of hours spent preparing, planning, proofing and keeping me focused and for all the times you took over for me to give me the time to see this to the end.

I truly appreciate all the tremendous effort you have given to our family and all that you have taught me. Your encouragement kept me going during my times of doubt. You taught me with strength of character and in turn gave me my strength to endure most anything, fed my faith and showed me the direction I wanted my life to take. You have always surrounded me with truth and more love than can ever be expressed. Our relationship is one of a true partnership; it just doesn't get any better than this on this earth. All my love to you!

Dena, this has been a wonderful adventure. We are truly dangerous together. We get these ideas and away we go. There hasn't been anything we couldn't do or at least thought we couldn't do together. I have loved working with you each day as we went through our successes as well as our failures. We have had so much fun researching, developing our recipes, our workshops, our chemistry "explosions" and varying messes. We have gotten ourselves into some interesting adventures. I cherish each and every one.

I am very blessed to have you for my daughter you have given me the honored title of mother which I truly treasure. You have honored Grandma and I know she would be very pleased with you and the mother you have become. My daughter, my best friend, I love you.

For my darling granddaughters, Angelyn and Benyse, thank you for your patience while Mommy and I spent so much time working on this book. You added humor in times when it was needed the most. You gave so much understanding even in your young and tender years.

Your experiments with our recipes, the bubbling mountains of froth, the exploding soda and vinegar and all the spills brought so much laughter we were in tears. You were always so willing to do whatever it took to research a new recipe. I particularly loved the crawling around on the carpet to test our carpet stain remover. I shall treasure these memories forever. I love you my darlings. Thank you for your sweetness of just being you! I love you. Grammie

My deepest appreciation to my dearest mother-in-law (my mom), Ida Marianne Cowie Wootton, your wisdom and insight through the years has greatly enhanced our lives. With a tremendous debt of gratitude I thank you for gifting us the treasured boxes, without this honored gift, I might never have taken on this project.

I would truly like to express my admiration to you for the example you gave to your children. You endured many challenges but never gave up. You taught how to turn weaknesses into strengths and lived by ethics of old. Most importantly I wish to express my love to you for the loving way you raised your son, my husband. A great husband was first taught to love, honor and cherish from his mother's lap. You opened your arms and heart to me when I entered into your family, treating me as if I had always been a family member. Thank you from the depth of my soul, you have helped me more than I could ever express. I love you, Mom!

My dearest Grandma, my memories of you are always with me, each one brings a smile to my face. So many times I have wanted to call you to get your help, wisdom or advice to again realize you have left this earthly state. I treasure all the times we spent together and recall how you lived your life and taught by your examples of moral principles. You were a tremendous inspiration to me, and a source of great comfort in my life. I wanted to always make you proud, never disappointing you.

I certainly wish to include a sincere gratitude to my husband's grandmother, Ada Dilworth Tracey Wootton. Without her efforts to preserve her family's daily history, none of this would have been possible. Finding her poems was an added treasure, she left us many glimpses into her life and helped us learn about the woman she was and the great life she lead. With great admiration I extend my deepest appreciation to her.

Dena: I wish to thank you, Mom. When it all comes down to it–"It's you and me against the world." We've been through a lot together. I have learned so much from you. Everything I am is because of your fine example. Our family is richly blessed by your example and your legacy will live on, just as those whom we admire from our past. We've managed to have a project that didn't involve any doors, odd looks from the neighbors, or anything else that would be "normal" for us. I've enjoyed hearing new family stories and learning to appreciate those whom helped shape us into who we are. This time that we've spent together is a treasured memory that I will have forever. Thank you doesn't do justice to what I am trying to say. I love you!

Thank you Dad, for encouraging me, you are a great sounding board and never let me get by on anything other than my very best. You always have stood next to our family motto, to do what is right. You have made such a difference in our lives. Thank you for being the level head, the guiding star, leading the way. You have influenced our lives so much. My gratitude to you is more than words can express. I couldn't do it without you.

Angelyn, my firstborn daughter; thank you for being you. You march to the beat of your own drum and do it proudly. You are an incredible person who has a lot of talents to share–share them! I have learned so much from you and how to conquer the challenges we have faced. Because of your sensitivities, I needed to rid our home of the harsh chemical cleaners that were making you sick. Follow your heart and aim for the stars and you will never go wrong.

Benyse, my spunky girl, you have given me much laughter when life seems very difficult. Thank you! Don't let others define who you are. Without your spunky spirit and willingness to try new things, I would not have had the courage to try a new life. When life is getting rough, remember that your talents are inside you and always stay spunky–life is too short to go through it without having fun. Search deep inside yourself, you will find the talents that you need when you need them most.

Dan, the other half of D^2, your support and encouragement as this project was nearing completion are worth the world to me. You listened to my frustration and helped lift me up when I did not see the light at the end of the tunnel in every possible way. Your presence in my life has greatly enriched it, and I am especially blessed to have you as my friend and my love.

"Mommy and Grammie you don't know how much I love you. You have no idea how glad I am this book is over. From your loving Daughter and Granddaughter, Benyse."

With our deepest gratitude to Deborah Geist, her contributions to this book are immeasurable and invaluable. Her ability to articulate, help in organizing our thoughts and strengthen our words made this book much better than we could ever have imagined. Thank you for the many hours you gave to us.

To Sara McDonnell, tremendous thanks for your patience and sounding ear. You gave so generously of your time and talents to help us gather our thoughts together to make this book a reality. Your insights were often sought and always appreciated.

Susan Tippetts, LeAnn Wheeler, Dyan Rupan, and Shannon Gish, we deeply thank you for believing in us. To all those too numerous to mention (and you know who you are) we wish to express our deep appreciation and thanks to all who encouraged the writing of this book after attending the workshops. Without your tremendous support and encouragement we wouldn't have taken this on. We also wish to thank everyone that have visited with us and shared with us their successes and experiences. We really love to hear how the recipes work and the money that is being saved.

To all the remarkable women from our past who have lived by the principles of patience, love, kindness, self sacrifice, perseverance and faith; we greatly love and admire them. We are grateful for their tremendous influence in our lives.

Introduction

I know that I am not unique in my desire to want the best for my family, as this is the very desire which defines "mothers" universally since the beginning of time. I want to give my family the very best. In this ever more confusing world with new products bombarding us every day and so much information from all sources (there's a reason we live in the "Information Age"), and scary reports of all the harmful products we use daily, I was lost. I'll admit the environment was not my first motivation to give this a try. I needed to save money any way I could in a very tricky economy. I found that by going back to basics, there were other wonderful benefits that came my way.

My daughter was diagnosed with Asperger's Syndrome (sometimes called High Functioning Autism) and bills for her various therapies began to mount. We faced (as so many other families in this decade) employment uncertainty and lay-offs. When the bills mounted and the income plummeted, we had to make a change. Enter a dusty old box from relatives. We found notes, home remedies and tips to do everything in a difficult time of the Great Depression.

What I never would have expected was the benefits to our life beyond the family budget. I began to see a global change in myself and my children. We saw life through a new lens and became more adventurous, more self-confident, and more self-reliant. My children began to take more initiative (sometimes a bit too much) in being responsible for their messes. (We still have a long way to go sometimes!) They began to see that all around them advertisers were trying to "trick them out of their money" and make wiser choices, not needing every little fad that came along.

They began to make their own products with great pride and gusto. They have their own recipe that they developed in this book,

"Sweet Dreams Spray." This they have tweaked and customized so that it is the exact mixture that they like.

Imagine seeing your children express themselves in such a personal fashion. Not only does it give you an insight to their feelings and likes/dislikes, you see them able to work to express it. As a mother of a child on the Autism Spectrum, this became so dear to me as I learned that there were scents in the house that actually were causing her to shut down because they were overwhelming her.

I can't say with absolute proof that ASD (Autism Spectrum Disorder) is caused nor affected by the chemicals in our home, but I can say that for us, it seems to have helped in the day to day life of a family affected by ASD. We have fewer days with those stressful high anxiety worries that plagued her, fewer headaches (for all of us) and generally an easier time.

Headaches in our family can be triggered by chemical sensitivities and greatly impact our lives. We still have many problems outside our home, but at least we have a refuge and our home is one that we can be in without the pounding pain in our heads. Again, I'm not a professional, but I can tell you that it worked for us.

We not only had headaches that lessened, we had allergies and skin conditions that seemed to diminish as well. Both my daughters suffer with eczema each winter and one of my daughters has a chronic skin condition known as keratosis pilaris, making her skin rough and bumpy, which is irritated if her clothes were not adequately soft. Adding to my concerns was the fact that with my daughter's ASD, her clothing needs to have enough softness to not cause her sensory issues to present themselves and make her uncomfortable.

I thought we were frozen perpetually into buying the allergy free, dye free products that were so expensive. The one thing that I did not like was that these products seemed to lessen in their effectiveness over time and I added more and more to the wash loads to get my desired results. By adding more, the end results would improve for a while and then plateau and finally dive. The answer, use more again. It had gotten to a point that I was using a full three times the amount recommended.

I was skeptical to using such a small amount of any product, and using less created a learning curve that at times was downright uncomfortable! I can say that it is easy now to have the discipline to do so. Before this new lifestyle, I needed fabric softener at least once each month. This was probably the hardest purchase for me to give up. My family needed soft clothes for their skin, and I was somehow judging myself as a mother based on how fluffy my towels were! Silly to see in black and white, but revealing as to how pervasive the messages on commercials can be!

Not only did my children have skin conditions, but allergic reactions of unspecified origin have always been a problem of mine. Every few years, I would have a full body case of hives and very infrequently, we would find the trigger. Most often, I would rotate products that I had been using on my skin, and I would get relief. I've not had any problems with this in all the time that I have been making my own. It is a freedom for me.

Mine and my daughters' skin challenges have all but disappeared by the simple elimination of the very product that I thought was the answer to the problem. Ironic, isn't it? I can't promise that this will be the case for you, but I can say it works for us. Believe it or not, fabric softener that works for us the very best is the most simple, quick and fast of our recipes, "Simple Fabric Softener!"

I imagined making my own products as an enslaving process. Rather than enslave us, it empowers us. By buying what I need to make my own, I am simply able to do this on my own time, when I need it, rather than run to the store every time I have forgotten window cleaner, etc. (I'm sure you have never forgotten to pick something up at the store and then realized that you need it, but I have, more times than I care to admit!) This is convenience at its purest and most basic way.

I love "boycotting" entire sections of the grocery stores! Sometimes I go down the cleaning aisles just for a reminder of what my life used to be like. I shudder as the squeaky buggy goes through a maze of products, feeling bad for those who just buy "because they think they have no other choice."

Since I was seeing so many benefits financially, physically and emotionally, I began to realize that my home was less a collection of rooms and "stuff" and view my home as a miniature eco-system. By keeping it in balance with natural products, we benefited economically as well in our health.

Extrapolating the global environment from a home eco-system, I began to view the world almost as a living organism, and one that can be affected by what we are doing, putting into the air and water and saw that we can make a difference.

At first, I fell into the old trap of feeling a bit small and helpless, "What can one person do to make a difference, really?" Then I remembered a story I heard once about women in a poor village. None of them could do much to help others, but they wanted to help each other. Each day when they prepared their rice, they took a small amount, even a spoonful and poured it into a separate container. This small amount accumulated over time and the women combined each of their small efforts to give to one who was in need. We can achieve great things as a small army of doing our small part.

Please join in by making a difference in your lives, whatever the reason you felt the need to pick up this book, there are small and simple steps that you can take to make a difference in your life, in that of your family, improve your home eco-system, and the global environment.

This is not your average run-of-the-mill recipe and or how to book. Inside we share with you hints and quick references to not only tell you what works, but the background of why it does. We also give you the background in chemistry of all the ingredients included in our recipes. We want you to experiment to tweak the recipes to fit your needs and tastes.

The savings illustrations show you how much you can save. The prices that were used from shopping trips in 2009-2010, and all are at the lowest prices that could be found.

Also, just a reminder when you are looking at the recipes and the savings illustrations as well as the estimated cost which are included in all the recipes, remember that $.03 means three cents. The "cents" sign is strangely difficult to find on the keyboards and character maps, it is oddly obsolete! We're here to say that spending cents for things is not obsolete, and is certainly possible.

Not only does following the Cheaper Greener Cleaner recipes mean a "Ceiling to Floor Savings in Thirty Minutes or Less," as shown in the workshops; it means that you become more knowledgeable in chemistry and the smaller numbers; you also get a chance to realize large number savings on everyday purchases. For example, in one illustration you can save 683%. What does that mean exactly? Without going too far into mathematics, you move the decimal point to the left two places. What this means is simply that the traditional cost in the example is 6.83 times more than our cost saving example. Now which one of us would cut out a coupon that we could take to the store and buy **one** for the price of **seven**? Yep you read it right, that's what most of us are doing.

As a society, due to the rampant high prices of everything, we've forgotten how to work with the really small figures.

This book was written to show you how to live a modern, convenient 21st Century life paying a 19th Century price.

Dena Wootton
Centennial, Colorado
May 2011

Cheaper Greener Cleaner, Ceiling to Floor Savings has many uses. What you decide to do is totally up to you. You can use the recipes to replace the retail store purchased laundry and cleaning needs or just to replace a few items. You don't have to spend hours to save pennies. You spend minutes to save dollars, no kidding. Decide which of the many recipes work best for you. Customize your cleaning to fit your needs. Most importantly you set the price you pay for the laundry and cleaning products you use. When have you ever been able to name your price?

Whatever you determine, you will save money with very little investment of time or money. Remember, the more cleaning items you replace with these recipes, the more money you will save. We make thirty recipes in thirty minutes in our workshop. We are not suggesting that you need all thirty recipes to clean your house and do your laundry. We have included a variety of recipes to suit many different cleaning preferences. We are confident you will find many which will fit your needs.

You will discover that you can use the same recipes for many areas in your house. You are reading this book for a reason, either to save money, improve the environment by removing hidden toxic chemicals in your home, or you are just bored.

Chapter One Trash or Treasure gives you a new perspective on our **DNA** which we wish to share with you. Discovering Natural Alternatives is throughout the book. The recipes included will truly replace all cleaning products that you have been buying. Have some fun keeping track of your savings.

Use the notes section at the end of each recipe to keep track of your ideas, customization or what you did or didn't like about each recipe. Experiment, have fun remember this is all about you and your personal needs, this is not a one cleaner fits all. You might want to use the notes section to record some of your successes as well as some of the things that did not go so well.

We share some of our family secrets in our workshops and want to share them with you. What we considered as being conscientious CFO's chief financial officers of the household budget has now been redefined by our family.

We have always liked to save money. We like the thrill of a deal. We love to get more for less. When we need to comparison shop, we do so. We will always look for a way to spend less. It is a personal challenge of ours to seek another way to have something for less than we are willing to pay. We would like to say this as complementary as possible but the simple and plain truth is we are cheap.

We learned early on that cheap was our destiny and resistance was futile. Our family has even put into place a coveted position in our family's hallowed halls of "Best Found Bargain Award." We began competing with family members for the longest and best standing record of bargain savings. The bargains were always left to the females until one day we recruited Randy/Dad. That was our greatest victory; if we could win him over we could win anyone. He admitted he never really thought we were quite accurate in our money savings reports. The savings were just too good to be true until he was the recipient of a great bargain, he was now a true believer; he got the taste of extreme savings and he was hooked. He has really gotten the spirit of savings, he gets really excited when he reports to us how much he saved, and he is pleased to be a contender in our family's the "BEST BARGAIN OF THE YEAR AWARD."

If you want to just dive in and get started, you can begin with any chapter that is of interest; the recipes are easy to follow. **Just remember never use ammonia and bleach or products containing bleach with ammonia, a deadly chlorine gas may be produced.**

We have broken down the chapters by rooms in your house. You can use bathroom, general cleaning and kitchen recipes in any room of your house. Though there are many recipes, use those that appeal to you. If you are unsure, start small with a really quick, easy cheap one. Try a recipe which you already have all the ingredients.

You don't have to submerge yourself at the beginning. Let your successes and the money you save tempt you into expanding your adventure into making your own cleaning items. Once you get a true taste of how quick and easy this all really is, you just might become hooked.

If you want additional information about all the Fantastically Frugal Fifteen, go to **Chapter Eight Cleef's Notes.** (Remember those yellow and black paperback books we would read to help us pass tests when we didn't read the book assigned.) **Chapter Eight** was written for those of us who might have lost, misplaced or burned our high school basic chemistry notebook. If you are like most of us, who would have ever thought there was something of importance in that beat up old thing.

We do not recommend that you make different recipes for each room. Find an all purpose cleanser, disinfectant cleaner and use them throughout your house. Make notes in the note section as a self reminder.

Make changes as you go, recreate your own recipes, experiment and above all have fun. This is not meant to make more work for you, quite the opposite. This is to give you choices you never thought you had, drastically reduce the amount of money that you have been spending, helping rid your home of any possible hidden toxic chemicals from the products you have been purchasing and help the environment all at the same time. This is a Win, Win, Win solution!

Now before you begin on your DNA journey take a deep breath, recite to yourself, I can do this! This is really so simple, if I can measure, mix, stir, pour, chop, cut and grate I have conquered the hardest part.

Carolyn Wootton
Dena Wootton
Centennial, Colorado
May 2011

The dictionary defines frugal as costing little. Thrift is defined as wise economy in the management of money and other resources.

You can call it frugal, frugality or thrifty; it all comes down to getting more, much more for your money!

In today's economy, more than ever, it's not just what we make; it is what we are able to do with what we make that determines to a large extent our quality of life!

Table of Contents

Chapter One

Trash or Treasure?

Glimpses of the Past

"One woman's trash is another woman's treasure," has been stated many times in different ways regarding a variety of topics. Many lost treasures have been found because others have realized their importance, or looked for the unseen value. The earliest crediting we can find referring to "One person's trash is another's treasure," dates back at least to 1916 where this axiom appeared in the book, Speaking of Home: Being Essays of a Contented Woman, written by Lillian Hart Tryon. What a profound statement this is for us because what we found in one's trash was certainly our treasure.

My very wise and generous mother-in-law, Ida Marianne Cowie Wootton, had kept all that she had of family members from the past. She had in her possession numerous items for over sixty years but alas the time came when she needed to reduce the items from her home. Many family members wanted an antique trunk, but no one seemed to want to go through the contents which she had saved. It was the general consensus to throw the loose papers and such into the trash. She was determined to save her valued treasure of unknown worth. Determined not to allow family members to throw away the contents, she cleverly placed the items into boxes and placed our name upon them.

Shortly after the family members left with their chosen items, we received a phone call telling us of the boxes we were given. Now some might think we were on the short end, this would depend on what or where one places value.

When the boxes were received, it was a bit of a shock as the boxes were opened for it did indeed look as though it was just trash. Knowing Mom, there had to be a reason she loved and cherished these crumbled and tattered paper pages and scraps for all these years. To our great delight, we uncovered treasures that others could not behold. We found many items inside the box which we will be donating to the historical society. Certainly we found treasure instead of the trash which was perceived by others!

There were numerous recipes for food, home remedies, health tonics, and cleaning items on scraps of paper along with valuable information. We found bank receipts, signatures from my husband's late grandfather and grandmother, stock certificates, grocery lists, business journal, pictures of great grandparents never before seen, and numerous handwritten original poems no one knew existed. These were written by his grandmother, Ada Dilworth Tracey Wootton, whom he never had the privilege to meet. She passed away before she could impart her wisdom, talents, and gifts to her family.

These poems gave us so much insight into this great woman and her earthly trials. We learned of her heartache as she said goodbye to two of her young children that were taken in death. We read about her life, the trials, tribulations, and her complete devotion to her husband. Through her poems she gave a bittersweet experience to our family for never having the opportunity to know her. Somehow we needed to do something to acquaint her to her family.

We learned that one of her poems was published in an anthology of poetry for the 1939 World's Fair. We also found an issue of "Peterson's Ladies National Magazine" dated August 1882, that belonged to her mother. This was a great discovery. My daughter and granddaughters were delighted to look upon a magazine similar to what they had read about in the "Little House" series, by Laura Ingalls Wilder.

Considering her life during the Great Depression, we studied each scrap of paper that held wisdom and insight into this woman's life. So many pieces began to fit into place much as working on large a puzzle. Her writings were found on anything she could use to write on. We presumed that paper was a choice commodity during this time. We even found that she used straight pens to put pieces of paper together to continue with her poem versus when she seemed to have run out of paper. She must have been very resourceful and yes, completely frugal.

Our family talked about these grandmothers, and we wanted somehow to bring to life the grandmother we only knew by name, her poems and items in the boxes. We carefully transcribed her poems with the chance to know more about her and to help us make her life come alive for us using the vehicle of her writings to explore her life.

When finished with the poems, we discovered a nearby outdoor museum with a historically accurate farm-house from the 1890s. On a family outing we went to try to get a glimpse of her life. As we walked about the home, we talked about this grandmother and how she lived and cooked and so forth. This was originally planned for the grandchildren, but we quickly became lost in our own thoughts of her life. As we explored the house, to our surprise, we found some of our grandmother's cleaning ingredients on the pantry shelves. We became intrigued and began to diligently study her ingredients. We wondered how well these cleaning items worked.

We decided to try Grandmother Ada's ingredients. We didn't know what to expect. We thought nothing could compare to what we have available today. All the products with their fancy containers supposedly cleaned far better than anything ever before, or so we thought. To our amazement, we had marvelous results! Indeed we had discovered a great treasure among the many pieces of paper.

Not only did we get our clothes and house clean, our chemically triggered health concerns were reduced. Could there be something to this? The serious research started, many hours spent learning about Grandmother Ada's ingredients.

Our thoughts then took us to those of our own grandmothers and the many fond memories we had of times spent with them. The path down memory lane took us back to many happy visits to our grandparents' farm. We found ourselves smiling and crying at the same time when a new memory flooded the minds and filled hearts with emotions. Although from differing backgrounds and geographical regions, we found so many similarities between these women, during the same span of time during the Great Depression. The more we delved into the boxes, the more insight we found into a past long forgotten.

We then remembered an incredible illustration of trash versus treasure when our paternal grandmother's Colonial Mansion burned down. Grandma Bessie went to help out to provide any comfort and assistance that she could give to her daughter's mother-in-law. She gathered all the torn down draperies, banquet tablecloths, and other linens which had been removed from the house in hopes of saving as much as possible. All these were covered with soot and smoke, while some were charred and wet from the fire hoses. This dear little lady was trying so hard to recover anything that she could for my paternal grandmother. She dragged these heavy fabrics over to the neighbor's yard to use their hose to rinse. She wrung out the excess water as best she could and went to report that she would take the items home to wash and restore what she could and return the items to this in-law.

This was an embarrassment to the in-laws' standards. She was told to just let it be for it was nothing but trash. As if an afterthought, she was told she could have anything she wanted. Grandma Bessie then asked if she could have all that she had collected and anything else she found. She was granted permission to have any and all things that she wanted.

Grandma toted home all that she could find and began her labors. She soaked, washed, bleached, sun bleached, and aired out the fabric until there was not a trace of soot or smoke odor in any of the fabric.

Many of the tablecloths became the batting substitutes, or the backing to her quilts. She remade the draperies to fit her windows in her farmhouse. The amount of quilt pieces she was able to make and use was remarkable, not to mention some of the furniture she was able to salvage. I have one of the many quilts which she had placed the table linens from the fire inside as the batting.

It was not until shortly after the death of my grandfather, Bessie's husband, which the family realized this was not the poverty stricken relatives who everyone thought they were. Everything unfolded to what had been their financial practice throughout their over fifty years of marriage. By their frugality over their lifetime, these wonderfully disciplined grandparents had investments and savings that gave Grandma Bessie financial support for herself to last her lifetime, gift to her children, and support a daughter and a grandchild with severe special needs.

Contrasting this with the paternal side of the family, who happened to look down their noses at the frugal and simple lifestyle of the farm family, had that expansive Colonial Mansion, (which had burned to the ground) the best of everything, and tons of debt. She spent her money on the best luxuries designed to make her every day better. This Grandmother, upon the untimely death of her husband, spent her forty plus remaining years living in the home of one of her sons and drawing her meager Social Security. We give these examples to illustrate the polar opposites that existed in our families.

What was the common thread with these great women from our past? As we pondered the varying backgrounds, from farmers, merchants, and an heiress, we began to realize a common paradigm. These were women who did all that they could and then more. They were women of strength and principle. They endured hardships beyond anything we could ever imagine. They gave their children strength of character, truth and ethics. There were no excuses, for excuses meant failure, and failure could mean death in some cases.

As it turned out, we learned a lot about basic household chemistry. We began to feel empowered and questioned the myth that was set forth by Madison Avenue–and began a journey of self-education and self-reliance. We broke away from the bondage of needing what the ad agencies told us we needed. As a result, we began removing hidden toxic chemicals from our home environment and we began seeing noticeable changes within our family's health.

We decided if we couldn't pronounce an ingredient on a label, it didn't belong in our homes. We have easily removed chemicals from our homes and the air we breathe. Best of all–the money savings is incredible!

We have added touches for today's home and woman. We live in a time that is a marvel, just think about it! In a relatively short time, it is similar to going from caveman to space traveler. We have instant information at our fingertips, on-demand entertainment, GPS that tells us how to go wherever we need to go, and every product available to make our lives simpler. From calculators to computers, we have it pretty good. The trade off for this ease of lifestyle seems to be the lack of confidence in ourselves and looking for easy answers elsewhere. There are products for everything, from washing machine cleaners to special wipes for stainless steel. Break free from the dependence on others and give yourself credit for the gray matter between your ears. You can do this!

From ceiling to floor, we loved the results and rejoiced over our newly found time-tested, home-made, green and inexpensive cleaning and laundry recipes.

As for the quality and benefits of this lifestyle, all we can say is **wow**! We were amazed to realize just how effective these homemade recipes really worked and many times out-performed the modern pricey products. Talk about quick, easy and convenient. All it takes is a trip to another room in our house to get the cleaning items needed to do a cleaning chore. No more running to the store for window cleaner or laundry detergent.

Without the great care and concern of my dear mother-in-law for preserving these precious items, we would never have had the insight into the life of Grandmother Ada. Without the example of Grandma Bessie, we would never have had the courage to take on this project. It is our sincere desire to honor these great women from our past with a loving and respectful thank you for being the women that they were.

**"Where there's a will,
There's a way."**

Old English Proverb
(This was one of Grandma's favorite sayings. I can honestly say, she meant this earnestly and lived by it all her life.)

What Does Green Mean to You?

Thirty minutes is all it takes to go green.

As we began our adventure, it was for the purpose of saving money during the past few tough economic years. That was the sole purpose. We didn't really think that our little effort and our experimentation would have any impact on our environment let alone help us to "go green." We soon learned otherwise.

We never realized what we were spending per use of any of the products we used. To have a frame of reference as to how much we could save, we needed to do some math. This became my great challenge. Math was not one of my better subjects; the mention of math problems could conjure cold sweats from the memories of trying times in school. At this point having suffered total humiliation in this subject, resistance was dominating all rational thought. A change in paradigm was the only way to conquer this demon. The focus now became a quest to solve not a math problem but a need to resolve the never ending enormous laundry expenditures.

As Dena mentioned in the Introduction, she was using far more laundry detergent and fabric softener, trying to get the softest clothes possible for her family. When we started to analyze her usage and the costs involved this became a very big deal for her budget. The simplest solution was to use less and buy the generic or house brands. This would not work for her, due to health challenges from allergies to fragrance and dyes added to all but the most premium products. She was using or over using to a great extent her high cost fabric softener to help her daughter with sensory sensitivities.

We discovered Dena was spending $1.50 per load on laundry. This was outrageous; now the work began. Family needs outweighed math chills and we broke down everything that was purchased. We were completely shocked at the amount of money that could be wasted needlessly.

Our first homemade replacement was laundry detergent. More money was being spent than should be necessary. We were victorious! With the results we experienced we decided to replace something else which was high priced. Fabric softener was our second victory, so why not try all other laundry needs? We scored another victory the laundry cleaning industry giants, experienced their first casualty. Right away in the laundry room, we saw huge savings of 531% in detergent, 2,855% in stain removers and 704% in fabric softener, without sacrificing our convenience, quality or TIME.

The laundry products that we replaced can be made in less than thirty minutes, no kidding! We were hooked! After this savings we were encouraged and emboldened to try more. After all, when you get these types of results, why not try to save more? Where to go next?

As homemakers with the constant battle fighting dirt and germs, we are unknowingly exposing our families to hidden toxic chemicals. These are present in the clothes we wear, the air we breathe, the surfaces we touch, and on the dishes from which we serve healthy meals. There is very little to do about it, right? No, not quite. You hold in your hand a solution to removing these substances from your lives and homes. Not only can you remove the hidden toxic chemicals, you can do it with little time commitment and virtually no change in your convenient and modern lifestyle. You will save yourself a lot of money in the process. We'd like to invite you along on the adventure.

We discovered the hazards of the chemicals which are in our bodies and our homes, originating from the products which we use. We are surrounded by laundry and cleaning products. We can't go anywhere without being exposed to commercial or industrial cleaning products laden with hidden toxic chemicals. In our society today we value the cleanest of homes, clothes, surfaces, establishments and the freshest air. Unfortunately the products we use clean the surfaces, but in most cases make our environment worse. This is not only our water and air, but many times our physical health may be affected.

To "go green" by our way of thinking can also refer to increasing our own "green," our money. As consumers we are courted and enticed to separate ourselves from our "green" at every turn. Is there anything anywhere that gives us direction how to keep it? It has been stated many ways, don't spend more than you make, this is indeed wise advice. Now that we said that, who is helping us to be strong and not fall for the habits we have made? What alternative do we have? We go to the store; we look for the least expensive price, yet, is that the best we can do?

We think not. Rather, we know that it is not. We hope to inspire everyone to broaden their vision, step into new habits that are fun, exciting, and empowering. Do something you have never done before. Look for alternative ways to get the same or better results. All it takes is an open mind and a willingness to try.

"Going green" did not conjure up any desires to leave the comforts of our modern home for a yurt, (a portable, felt-covered, wood lattice-framed dwelling structure traditionally used by Turkic and Mongolic nomads). It also doesn't mean hitching up our children to plows to plant our food, or harvest our crops. Standing over boiling cauldrons stirring lye and ashes making our own soap, or shearing sheep to make our own wool yarn is not what we had in mind.

You don't have to build your own new green home made from egg cartons or another's garbage. It doesn't mean candlelight reading, or peddling your little legs out to crank enough electricity to flicker a wee nightlight let alone enough energy to power your laptop. Most especially it doesn't mean selling your car to build a covered wagon to do your carpooling, shopping, and run errands.

Yes, these were lifestyles of the past when our ancestors left a minimal carbon footprint. But must we go back to this way of living today? No, we say "going green," does not have to be about spending more money, more work or extra time consuming tasks. It can be as simple and as painless as following a cake mix recipe.

We are hearing about the need to clean our environment, we all need to do our part to protect our earth. We completely agree, just not at the cost that the giant corporations want us to make. Since "going green" has become so popular, just about every manufacturer either is trying or has found a way into your pocketbook. These products are usually more costly, and often times not as green as claimed. We all want to do our part but without such a high price tag.

With the birth of the "green" products, it was a guarantee that numerous products would hit the market hoping to gain a percentage of the market share. Of the "green" products which line the market shelves, four and one half percent are really "green" while ninety five percent are really self proclaimed as being "green." (TerraChoice Environmental Marketing 2010)

We want to share with you something we found on a highly recognized commercial product that claims to be a "green" product. You be the judge.

This is a list of ingredients found on the back of a leading

Liquid Laundry Detergent 2X Ultra Concentrate (marketed as being eco-friendly) is as follows:

"Aqua (water),sodium laureth sulfate, coceth-7 and glycerin (plant-derived cleaning agents), sodium citrate (water softener), oleic acid and glyceryl oleate (plant-derived anti-foaming agents), sodium hydroxide (alkalinity builder), sodium borate (alkalinity builder and soil dispersant), amylase, cellulase and protease (enzyme soil removers), calcium chloride (cleaning enhancer), essential oils and botanical extracts* (lavendula angustifolia, lavendula hybrida, eucalyptus dives, eucalyptus radiata, eucalyptus ploybractea, pinus sylvestris), hexahydro-1,3,5-tris (2-hydroxyethyl)-s-triazine (preservative). Trace materials are commonly present in cleaning product ingredients."

When researching the contents of this product, (available in nearly every local area market) we found the following additional information, to provide a breakdown of what the aforementioned ingredients actually are. See if you think the ingredients are "green."

<u>Aqua (water)</u>

<u>Sodium laureth sulfate</u> and its cousin, sodium lauryl sulfate, are very dangerous, highly irritating chemicals. Far from giving "healthy shining hair" and "beautiful skin", soaps and shampoos containing sodium laureth sulfate can lead to direct damage to the hair follicle, skin damage, permanent eye damage in children, and even liver toxicity. Although sodium laureth sulfate is somewhat less irritating than SLS, it cannot be metabolized by the liver and its effects are therefore much longer-lasting. Sodium laureth sulfate is also absorbed into the body from skin application. SLES also dissolves the oils on your skin, which can cause a drying effect. It is also well documented that it denatures skin proteins, which causes not only irritation, but also allows environmental contaminants easier access to the lower, sensitive layers of the skin."(National Health Information Centre 2002-2008)

<u>Coceth-7 and glycerin</u> (coconut derived cleaning agent) may cause allergies and hypersensitivity to persons allergic to coconut and coconut oils. (Environmental Working Group's Skin Deep Cosmetic Safety Database 2010)

Sodium citrate (water softener) sodium salts of citric acid contact with dry citric acid or with concentrated solutions can result in skin and eye irritation. (American Tartaric Products, Inc. 2004)

Oleic acid and glyceryl oleate (plant-derived anti-foaming agents) can cause minimal to moderate eye irritation. (The Personal Care Products Council, 2004) need date

Sodium hydroxide (alkalinity builder) also known as lye or caustic soda, "sodium hydroxide is a manufactured chemical. It is present in several domestic cleaning products. Very low levels can produce irritation of the skin and eyes. Exposure to the solid or concentrated liquid can cause severe burns in the eyes, skin and gastrointestinal tract which may ultimately lead to death. This substance has been found in at least 49 of the 1,585 National Priorities List sites identified by the Environmental Protection Agency (EPA)." (Agency for Toxic Substances and Disease Registry 2002)

Sodium borate, sodium tetraborate decahydrate, (alkalinity builder and soil dispersant) or Borax™ "can cause eye irritation, not to be ingested." (Bonincontro, 2010)

Note: We use Borax™ in our recipes, and it is generally considered safe, use all ingredients with wisdom. Rather than identify this ingredient as something we can buy easily, it is masked by its chemical name. See the detailed information on Borax™ for more information on how, when and why to use it.

Amylase is a protein (enzyme) which is added to increase chemical reaction to remove resistant food starches, often used in dishwasher detergents. (Hasan et al. 2010, 4837)

Cellulase (enzymatic soil remover) is used in biological fabric softeners. (Hasan et al. 2010, 4837)

Protease (enzymatic protein dissolver) is used to remove protein stains from clothes, often to pre-treat or to soak. (Hasan et al. 2010, 4837)

Calcium chloride (cleaning enhancer) contains acidic properties and as with many chemicals, exposure may pose health risks. Inhalation: respiratory tract irritation, coughing, shortness of breath, chemical bronchitis. Ingestion: internal bleeding, possible perforation of esophagus, severe pain, vomiting, diarrhea and collapse. Eyes: severe irritation, pain, ulceration, blindness. Skin: is an irritant, particularly on moist skin burns, blistering. Chronic exposure: dermatitis or severe irritation to skin. (International Occupational Safety and Health Information Centre 1995)

Essential oils and botanical extracts (lavendula angustifolia, lavendula hybrida, eucalyptus dives, eucalyptus radiata, eucalyptus ploybractea, and pinus sylvestris) are not for ingestion. While essential oils are generally considered safe, there are some that are not recommended for use during pregnancy. (None of these are on that list.) See **Chapter Seven A Little Drop Will Do Ya'** for more information.

Hexahydro-1,3,5-tris (2-hydroxyethyl)-s-triazine (preservative) or "hexahydrotriazine is an antimicrobial agent that acts by releasing formaldehyde. It is used as a material preservative and machine cleaner to control microbial activity in metalworking fluids and on machine surfaces. It is also used as an in-can material preservative in water-based products such as paints, adhesives, resin solutions, printing inks, stuccos, joint compounds, cleaners, liquid detergents, fabric softeners, floor finishes, and liquid polishes." (Health Canada 2010)

Trace materials are commonly present in cleaning product ingredients.

We assumed that a much safer list of ingredients for a "green product" would have been listed.

Once again, we are expected to believe what the industry wants us to believe. By making your own, there are no surprises, no mystery ingredients, and nothing that you can't spell or pronounce! You can't be fooled by marketing tricks.

Our successes gave us the confidence and the courage to do more and more until here we are. We never imagined ourselves singlehandedly taking on a seventeen billion dollar industry nor teaching the masses to wage war on the myths of Madison Avenue. (First Research 2008)

We have figured the costs per use or per ounce price with each recipe. We have comparison costs from commonly used brands readily available in stores. The savings as well as the percentage saved are also listed. There is no guesswork in realizing what you could be saving.

The amount we have saved by using these inexpensive alternatives is staggering. Our homes are just as clean; we believe cleaner because we have removed the invisible toxic chemicals that lay about in our carpets, on our furniture, floors, and the air we breathe.

You don't have to use all the recipes to realize gigantic savings. Pick out the ones which you want to try. You never know, the bug just might bite you as it did us and you will want to try more. We certainly did.

We are not professing to be health care providers nor do we state that you will have fewer health challenges by making your own cleaning products. As for our family, we have had far fewer challenges since changing our personal environment to all green cleaning.

Make your own products with easy recipes and you can even customize your cleaners. Your home will look, smell, and feel clean, because it will be. (Disclaimer–we can't actually do the cleaning–but we can help make it safer and easier.)

You Might Be A Frugalista If...

You know how to get a good deal without looking like this!

We start off our workshops with an easy, quick, and fun quiz, to get ideas flowing. The questions we introduce are a few of the topics we will be addressing:

If you do laundry
If you clean your home
If you compare prices
If you want to save money

If you have too much month at the end of your money
If you look at sale ads
If you want to avoid buying many high priced products
If you have ever clipped a coupon
If you have ever gone to a garage sale
If you buy store brand products
If your children don't know that cereal comes in boxes
If you enjoy getting a bargain
If you know the best price for milk, bread, and gas in your neighborhood

If you answer yes to nine or more, you are a Frugalista. If you answer yes to six to eight, you are a Frugalista in Training. If you answer yes to five or fewer, you think that a Frugalista looks like the picture above.

Things really get rolling and the laughter is explosive when we share this photograph with our audiences. *This is not what thrift store or second hand clothes shopping needs to look like! (Thanks, Angelyn and Benyse, for being great sports and allowing us to use this picture taken at a "Tacky Day" activity.)*

For the record, Angelyn (older) is sporting a lovely Jack-O-Lantern orange turtleneck, topped with a bright lemon yellow short sleeved shirt. She chose to complete this ensemble with cotton candy pink flared leg culottes over a royal purple knit legging with a slight paisleyesque pattern. Benyse (younger) is modeling a lovely hairstyle with every color of the rainbow as hair ties. Her outfit is also a trendy, layered look. The turtleneck is a classic white, topped with a Kelly green Saint Patrick's Day shirt (in January). Her bottom layers consist of pale pink bike shorts over white floral leggings, which are two inches too short. Ever daring, she donned a red and green Christmas sock and a baby blue and royal blue snowman sock.

In our workshops, we are often asked for the next step to become Frugalistas. The list is quite long and there are ways to save money everywhere you look. One of our favorites is to go green with our clothes, household goods, and toys by hitting the thrift stores. We always show the picture above to get folks' attention. It always does!

The workshop then includes a little game called, *Guess the Right Price*. We show some of our great finds and have contestants guess what we actually paid. We have had some amazing finds. Once, we found a brand new Ralph Lauren sport coat, tags still attached. Checking over every possibility of what could be wrong with this coat and finding nothing but perfect condition, it was purchased. To make the find even better, my husband had been shopping at the mall and he had tried on a very similar coat. Knowing he wanted it, I was feeling on top of the world. I couldn't wait to give it to him. When he tried it on, everything was perfect, the fit was as if custom tailored just for him, and then he buttoned it. "Here is your reason, it was donated," he stated as he stood there with the sides uneven by about six inches. My jubilation was dashed within seconds; he was laughing. Not believing what I was seeing, he joked, "You don't expect me to wear this do you?" What to do, how could I have overlooked something so important, had the thrill of the find caused me to miss the mismatching of the plaid? I had to fix this; my standing of the best bargain up to this point was on the line. As I unbuttoned the coat, the answer was presented. The buttons were sewn on at different levels than the buttonholes. Needing a quick fix, the problem was solved by removing the buttons and sewing them on again in the proper alignment, perfect coat, perfect record. This was a $495 sport coat, I paid $14.99. This entitled me to the family award, best find of the year.

Once you have been bitten by the green bug, there seems no way of going back. Saving money is catchy and exhilarating. It seems to take hold and you might be transported into a whole new place.

There are real treasures at thrift stores to be found, especially for items that you know will be used for a short time and outgrown. (Hopefully it is the kids that will be quickly growing out of their clothes, rather than their parents!) When you go to a thrift store, realize that while you are potentially saving a lot of money, you must be ready to spend the time to make sure you know what you are getting. Take time to inspect each item for stains, grease spots, broken zippers, etc. Taking a little extra time can prevent you from spending money (and getting a bargain) on something that is mismarked, stained beyond help, or needs altering that you can't or won't be willing to do.

Items can be repurposed to meet other needs. We found a new beautiful gold (yes, gold) cloth shower curtain at our favorite thrift store. While we tried to imagine the bathroom design, we saw that it would be wonderfully repurposed as a Christmas tree skirt. To buy the fabric would have cost ten times the cost for this curtain. It looks lovely as a Christmas tree skirt.

Become a Frugalista by visiting garage sales, shopping with coupons, trading with friends, rebate shopping, gardening, you name it. We can't go into all of this since it is beyond the scope of this book, but we hope to inspire you to look for ways to boost your own budget.

Shopping after the holiday, usually nets tremendous bargains. This may take a little planning if you are shopping for the next year but sometimes spending 10% of the purchase price on holiday décor is well worth the time, effort, and storage space. We completely redid our Christmas theme for a fraction of the cost by waiting until the after holiday sale.

When we shop for back to school clothes, we buy from the clearance rack, why? It is too warm to wear the fall and winter clothes at the beginning of the school year. Summer clothes are still needed. We started to school with new clothes; we were more comfortable than those who wore their wardrobe ahead of the weather change. This trick was explained to me as a child. My father was a general manager of a large department store chain. We always had the very nice clothes but we only paid a small fraction of the price.

In our workshops, we set our timer and we show how to make thirty different cleaning and laundry replacements in thirty minutes. The most time intensive recipe is laundry detergent. This recipe can take as much as fifteen minutes and we still come in at thirty minutes. This is not labor intensive; this is easy at its very best! If these recipes didn't work, we would not be sharing them with you.

We have tested and used every recipe that we have placed in this book, even if it meant soliciting help from friends. ("Is your leather couch dingy? Can we come clean it?") We are happy to say we still have those friends and thank them for their support and laughter.

You, the reader, are at a slight disadvantage. You are not able to see firsthand, just how easy this is. You might think, just as we did, that this is something so hard and complicated that there is no way you want to take on this time consuming task. You might think that the immense amount of work and education required to tackle the production of chemical cleaning products is something you just don't have time.

Sometimes in our workshops we come in under our thirty minutes and take a water break. We have a great time laughing and joking about our mistakes and successes. We share our secrets of what works and what doesn't. If you have found yourself smiling in any of our notes, this is probably something we shared in our workshops.

When our workshops are over, everyone is so excited to begin the creative adventure of making their own cleaning solutions and saving a ton of money in the process. We have had so much fun teaching others the simple way to help reduce cleaning and laundry expenses, make their homes safer and going "green" in the process.

Here we are eighteen months later, and sharing this wonderful information with you. We hope you enjoy it.

It has been a great privilege to meet so many wonderful women at our workshops. It is so renewing to hear how Cheaper Greener Cleaner, Ceiling to Floor Savings has helped so many. We really love to hear the stories. We wish to thank all of you who have taken time out of your busy lives to share your stories of successes and savings.

We would like to share with you excerpts from some of the wonderful letters.

I am writing to tell you of my experience with my daughter and granddaughter. I sat with my three month old granddaughter a few days ago and when I went to change her, I found a terrible set in stain on the back of her outfit. From stem to stern the outfit was discolored in the bright mustard yellow of baby poop. It really bothered me that she had stained clothes, and I asked her mother about it. My daughter replied that she'd missed soaking the outfit and it had been dumped into the wash in hot water, dried on high. When she was folding the clothes, the stain was discovered. She tried all her arsenal of spot removers, washed it again several times and had given up. She did not like that the stain was there, but loved the outfit and had paid a lot for it, so as it was on the inside she was consigned to it.

I remembered your comment in the workshop and went to get my materials. I asked my daughter if we could try one more time and we decided that it couldn't hurt.

We soaked the little outfit in ammonia and washed it the next day. When I was getting ready to start the load, I was amazed since the stain was almost gone. When it came out of the washer, it was as good as new.

Thank you so much for your help.
A Grateful Grandmother

Wow, I can't believe this at all! I've always prided myself on saving money. You've given me so many more ways to save. Within a week and a half of attending your workshop, my family's finances changed drastically. I didn't have to purchase all the costly items I was out of. Replacing my laundry needs saved so much money. I was so excited to have the tools you'd given me, to say the least.

The prospect of saving a lot of money always gets me excited, but this change in lifestyle made me jump in with both feet. I never was much of a cleaner before, and did not have a product for each "problem" in my home. I'd heard to use vinegar and it worked well and saved money, but I would never have believed it. I love how your recipes are so easy to follow. I saved a ton during this financial hardship.

Thanks!
A Frugal Fannie

"I didn't want to spend more time and money that I didn't have for something that feels as though it is only benefitting the big companies. I wanted to be more environmentally responsible, but really, what could one family do to make a difference? That's what I thought before going to your workshop Thank you for your quick and easy recipes. I feel inspired to do more since you've shown just how much can be done without the high cost and great effort."
Busy Bea

We know what you mean. We all can feel as though our efforts and lives could be insignificant on a global scale. We are very pleased that we have had this opportunity to make a difference. It has been our sincere desire to leave the world in a better place, one family at a time. Thanks to so many of you who have greeted our ideas with such gusto and helped us to reach even higher than we ever thought we could.

Gimmicks, Tricks, and Trends

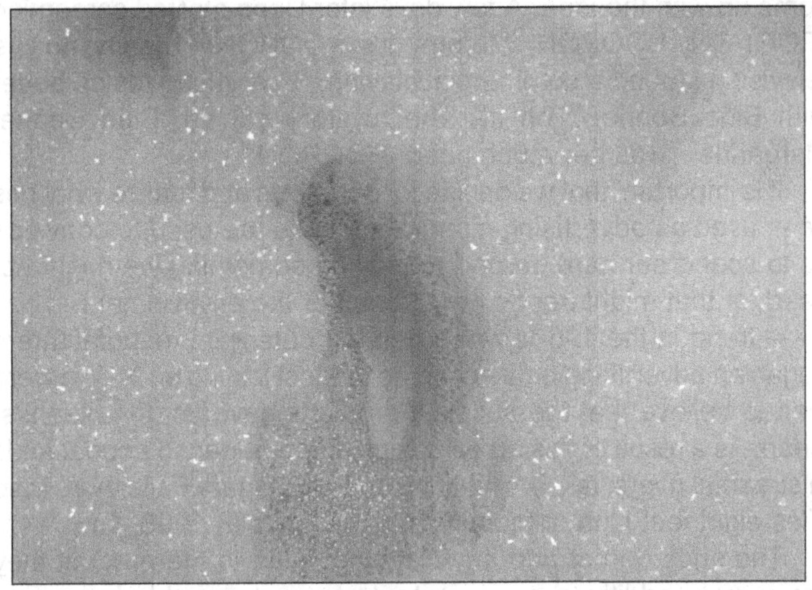

What do margarine and soap suds have in common?

We have been trained very well on how to be consumers. It seems Madison Avenue advertisers don't want us to think or do for ourselves. Advertisers have jingled, catch-phrased, convinced, warned, misled, frightened, enticed, and everything else imaginable to influence us as consumers to buy that which they are selling.

The United States soap and detergent manufacturing industry has about seven hundred companies with the combined annual revenue totaling seventeen billion dollars. (First Research 2008) It wasn't hard to understand how much they need to keep us under the guise of needing their products. To do this they use the advertising jingles and gimmicks that "Madison Avenue" has made famous.

A perfect example of having the advertisements persuade our purchasing for us reminds me of a time when I was a young mother crazily going up and down each grocery aisle searching for "Poopon." Dena was two years old and adamant that she needed "Poopon!" Everything I presented was wrong she continued to repeat she wanted "Poopon." I could not find what she wanted anywhere in the store. We left the store, Dena was tearful and I was very puzzled as to what "Poopon" was and where had she come up with the idea. A few days later Dena started screaming "POOPON, POOPON, Mommy it's POOPON!" running to the television I found a commercial playing, "Everything tastes better with Blue Bonnet™ on it!" The mystery solved, Blue Bonnet Margarine™ was her much need "POOPON."

It is important that we decide for ourselves and realize what has been used as advertising gimmicks. These are used to convince us to spend our hard earned money on something we might not need, or that might not be good for us or the environment.

A trend in the 1960s was when the detergent manufacturers began an advertising battle over the longest lasting suds. We were lead to believe that the sudsiest products gave us, the cleanest clean. As a result of this ad campaign, there began to appear suds in streams, rivers, lakes, and at the foot of Niagara Falls there rose piles eight feet high of foaming suds. (Outwater 1996, 155)

The suds do not add any cleaning value to the product they are merely additives or surfactants to portray added cleaning power. Suds are pretty to look at and fun to play with, yet we were tricked into believing we needed the mounds of foaming suds to get our dishes and clothes as clean as possible.

Remembering my grandmother washing her clothes in her cellar brought back long forgotten time spent with her. She had an old wringer. She would fill her wash tub with hot water, rub the heavily soiled clothes with a strange bar of soap and begin to scrub her clothes on an old washboard. There were never any soap suds in her wash tub.

Now, not being that ancient, no matter what my little granddaughters might think, there really were electric washing machines when I was a little girl. My grandmother was just very frugal. She knew her way of washing was the cheapest and she did get our clothes much cleaner than my mother. No matter what we got into, we never left with any stains on our clothes and we did get mighty dirty on her farm.

As the research developed, I understood why my grandmother's laundry was always brighter than my mothers. She didn't pay for nor have any additives, chemicals, fragrances, or dyes in her laundry soap. She used plain, simple and inexpensive soap, Borax™ and washing soda. She didn't have the mounds of suds which ran into the rivers.

Now as the cleaning industry takes us into the "go green" and protect the environment era, we are undergoing a new learning curve. We are going to H.E. (high efficiency) washing machines, which require low to no suds detergents. Wow, no wonder some of us are so terribly confused! Will these "new green" products work as well as the old ones?

We are expected to fall for the advertising gimmicks once more. Why should we really place much faith in this industry because of their practices and abuses in the past?

They also do not disclose all the ingredients in their products nor do they tell us the plain truth about just how easy it would be create our own. They are now leading us to believe that these new products are premium and deserve a premium price. What they have failed to tell us is we never needed the coveted suds in the first place! We polluted our waterways for the benefit of the profits of the cleaning and laundry industry.

A leading authority in market research and analysis states that the soap and detergent industry's marketing strategy may be for accelerated growth and highly profitable sales. This would be in the higher-end, eco-friendly products, referred to as "the sweet spot," targeted to consumer's desire for easy use and convenience. (Packaged Facts 2008)

Once again, the consumer is regarded by the industry as a vehicle to improve their bottom line. It would be really refreshing for the industry giants to think of our bottom line in the same way they think of theirs.

In another report by the same leading authority, it states that the retail sales of green cleaners in 2009 totaled five hundred fifty seven million dollars. This was split between three hundred thirty nine million dollars from green household cleaning products and two hundred eighteen million dollars from green laundry products. (Packaged Facts 2010)

The industry is so confident that as the green marketers are better connected to their products and to consumer preferences, the trend will continue to move into mainstream and ultimately approach two billion dollars in sales by 2014. The trend to "go green" by becoming eco-friendly puts a whole new meaning to the soap and detergent companies. They are charging us more for these products and certainly greening up their bottom line. (Montuori, Packaged Facts 2010)

It is very apparent that trend spending is expensive. Once a trend catches on, everyone wants a percentage share of consumer spending.

"As you've probably noticed, the latest twist in detergent is to sell us less product at a higher price with "ultra-new-and-improved" concentrates."

Do-It-Yourself Laundry Detergent
Money Talks News
Stacy Johnson 2010

One Billion Dollars Down the Drain

Why pay more when it is not necessary?

One of our family's favorite movies is "Father of the Bride" starring Steve Martin and Diane Keaton. We identify greatly with the scene in the grocery store when George Banks (Steve Martin) has a consumer nervous breakdown over hot dog buns. For those of you who haven't seen the movie, George Banks is the father of the bride and is paying for a lavish wedding, (complete with swans) and has virtually no say in how his money is being spent.

He is sent off to the store to buy dinner for the family and begins to rant about eight hot dogs vs. ten hot dog buns per package. He goes into the bakery aisle and begins ripping buns out of the bag and putting them back on the shelf, ranting about the hot dog executives and hot dog bun executives in a massive conspiracy to rip off the American consumer. (Too Many Buns. Father of the Bride, 1991)

The examination of the scoop or cap sizes in or on laundry products, brought about a mini "George Banks" moment. Was this a convenience for consumers to add more if they desired? The mindset that the larger scoops in the containers are not for our benefit, just theirs brought on new and unanswered questions. Based on the assumption that the oversize was by design and to entice the consumer to use more seemed more viable, or should we say more profitable.

Thinking that there might be something to this, delving deeper into the industry would hopefully bring about some answers. Being committed to find out as much as possible about the added benefits for the major laundry detergent giants was astounding.

Using more laundry detergent than needed is very common, as the manufacturers must have been thinking when they designed the oversized scoops or cap cup. (*Wall Street Journal*, 25 January 2010, D8) Think about it, if you use more, you buy more and who is that really helping? Certainly not your pocketbook! Just about every product on the laundry aisle contains a scoop or measuring lid. One of these products gave included a scoop holding about 1 1/2 cups. If you read the label, it recommends adding 1/3 cup to every load. Is the scoop clearly marked for 1/3? No. Do most people treat their laundry with the precision of a recipe, usually not!

You might be thinking, "How does this really affect me?" We are a large or biggie size mentality consumer. More is always better, right? Wrong, if you overuse detergent you will now need to buy yet another (and expensive) product to clean out your washing machine. You guessed right, this product is made by the industry giants. This cleans out all the extra chemicals that build up in your washer. The washing machine manufacturers state that a regular cleaning is needed to prevent damage to your machine.

The research proved fruitful, a study was done which stated that 53% of consumers do not use the recommended amount of detergent per wash load. Consumers were guessing or just filling to the measure. This practice will take you back to the laundry aisle twice as fast and substantially increase your spending. (Method Products Inc. 2010)

To illustrate this concept, I conducted a little psychological experiment which was unknown to my family. It is common knowledge that we only need a tablespoon of our laundry detergent per load. By removing the correct measuring scoop in our detergent and replaced by a larger scoop (which was received from a prior detergent purchase), having various level markings on it what would we do?

This was just amazing! None of us, (not even me) used only the one tablespoon required on a consistent basis. Being in a hurry to get the task done and fell for the psychological crutch to just pour in the amount of the measure provided. "It is only laundry detergent and money already spent." We used up the detergent in record time and wasted money, all for the want of saving a few seconds and not wanting to measure correctly. The tablespoon scoop in the laundry room was replaced and we will not be without it again.

To better understand the magnitude of this practice, it is necessary to inform consumers that according to an industry giant 1,100 loads of laundry in the U.S. are started every second of every day. This equates to over 500 million pounds of laundry detergent going down the drain and into our waterways every year. (Method Products, Inc. 2010)

This is common knowledge in the laundry industry. Now factor in the findings of Method Products Inc. that if 53% of consumers use twice as much as needed or completely fill up the provided cup or scoop, 33% of all laundry detergent purchased by you, the consumer in the United States, is just wasted.

It doesn't stop there, since $3 billion of laundry detergent is purchased each year the detergent manufacturers could be making $1 billion a year on unnecessary overuse of their products. This is an extremely costly practice which we have fallen into.

Realizing the answer to my query of why a much larger measurement is provided, it comes down to sales/profit. Is it so hard to believe that the $1 billion is only for the profit of the industry? Do we really believe that they provide the larger size scoop for our convenience to use more if we desire? Our measuring habits of overuse are only benefiting the industry, not the convenience or the pocketbook of the consumer.

If the manufacturers would resize their caps or scoops, they could save millions on the plastic cost. It doesn't take a genius to understand the difference in their bottom line, saving millions or making billions from our undisciplined overuse habits.

Would you be willing to pay an additional 33% usage charge on your laundry detergent? Of course not! Why even ask such a question, you might think. I have a great reason, you already are doing so if you use more than the recommended amount needed! This sounds unbelievable, I understand, I find it so outrageous I want everyone to know the profits which the laundry giants are making because of misleading measuring sizes to promote intentional waste.

"Waste is worse than loss...
The scope of thrift is limitless."

Thomas A. Edison

You Want Me To Do What?

You're going to love it!

Why does it seem that everything good for the environment is really bad for the budget? We have a solution. Make It Yourself! Now is where you will want to yell, ***"YOU WANT ME TO DO WHAT?"*** Yes, we are saying that by making your own cleaning and laundry products it is the greenest, quickest, easiest, most inexpensive way to reduce your carbon footprint.

With your busy schedules you are probably wondering where will you ever find the time? We thought the same thing until we tried just the laundry detergent (which is the most time intensive of all). We really enjoyed the experience and got into this new endeavor. We discovered it was faster than a trip to the store.

Let's imagine that you are doing your laundry one Saturday morning, and realize that you do not have enough to do the job.

(Which is not too big a stretch, is it?) You put the load in, grab your checkbook, phone, sunglasses, inspect the house for anything else you might need at the store and head out the door.

If you are anything like us, you probably get into the car and realize you needed to use the restroom, forgot your list or car keys. You go back into the house, shake your head and then drive to the store. You find yourself waiting for the road work ahead of you to allow you to pass by and finally arrive at the store. After finding a parking place in Outer Mongolia, you enter the store, and realize that there are no shopping carts. You go back into the parking lot and rescue an abandoned cart and begin shopping.

As you begin to steer your cart, you quickly find that it is one of "those carts," you know, the ones that have one wheel that wobbles and makes a sound like a few dozen cats caught under a fence. It also lists to the left, so you feel as though it is deciding where you should go, rather than the other way around. You find yourself in a maze of people, everyone going their own way and making the German Autobahn look tame.

On the way to the laundry aisle, you get the backs of your heels run over by an unruly child (hopefully not yours) and you get what you need. When you get to the checkout line, it stretches almost all the way to the dairy section. You see the light flashing in front of you as there is a problem ahead, indicating the need of a price check or something of the likes.

When you finally make it to the front of the line, you are assaulted by many tabloids and you learn far more about some celebrity's life than you care. You pay the equivalent of a movie/dinner date and head back out to Outer Mongolia to load the car. You remember that you forgot your sunglasses in the store and trek back inside.

An hour later, you return home, ready for a break rather than the work of your laundry. Why did you do this? It's convenient and what other choice do you have?

You absolutely have a choice and we are sharing it with you. Now imagine a different scenario. You see that your laundry supplies are running low, so you take out your soap to dry a week or so ahead of time. When you have a few minutes during the week, you chop it into pieces. You mix the other ingredients and pour it all into the food processor. You take a moment or two to have your favorite beverage and look at a magazine while the machine does all the work. When it is done, you put it all in a gallon sized zipper bag knowing that you saved yourself enough to go out for a movie and dinner.

There is nothing more convenient as having everything you need right in your own home. Which brand of convenience do you prefer?

The convenience of making your own recipes goes beyond just saving money or making the environment of your home safer. You can customize your own line of products. You are in charge. Do you prefer a favorite scent to your fabric softener? Now you can make it! Do you want a chlorine bleach free home, without giving up the disinfecting? Now you can! Do you still want all the conveniences of the high-priced, special laundry products? You can still have them! Do you want to remove the harsh and hidden toxic chemicals your family can be or are exposed to with your current commercial retail products? Does your family suffer from allergies and are you stuck paying high prices for hypoallergenic dye and fragrance free? You are holding in your hands the answer to your challenges.

By making your own, first you are not creating any additional production pollution to the environment. Second, you remove hidden toxic chemicals from your own personal environment and this helps reduce the impact on Mother Nature. Third, we have improved the air we breathe, the waterways from which we drink, and reduced the amount of natural resources required for packaging and delivery. All of these benefits are worthwhile, and the final benefit is realized by removing the high costs from your cleaning and laundry budget and keeps the once spent money in your own pockets. The once high costs are now turned into money saved.

We make our own cleaning and laundry products, and yes we still live in a modern home, have indoor plumbing, have all the same conveniences, the demands on our time, and we use an automobile. We have realized the money we spent unnecessarily, so much so, that when income was limited due to employment cutbacks, the reduction was far more manageable when the outlay was so dramatically reduced.

We have also liberated ourselves from advertising enticements, overpriced products and created a more effective and convenient way to meet our cleaning needs. We no longer labor over decisions to make regarding which brands to buy, and cost comparisons in the cleaning and laundry aisles in the store.

You will be amazed just how quick and easy you will remove hidden toxic chemicals from your home for pennies. Sounds too easy, give it a try, what do you have to lose?

Making your own laundry detergent isn't the arduous job our great-great grandmothers experienced! There is not the cauldron boiling with the hot lye mixture.

Prior to receiving Grandmother Ada's recipes, Dena had entertained the idea of making laundry detergent. On the other side of the debate, my position was unmovable. I was very opposed to this, having only the preconceived notions of the back breaking labor intensive chore. Each time Dena would say, "Mom let's start making our own laundry detergent," I would counter with "**NO, we are not going do this,"** I just knew I would never survive this adventure. I was so close minded I didn't even give her idea a second chance. When we found the recipes, I was astounded, and ashamed that I so stubbornly opposed Dena, could it be so simple?

The process is quick and easy. It is simply grate, measure, pour, and stir. If by chance you don't get the exact results you are looking for, don't give up! Try adding more soap or whitener, Borax™, washing soda and/or baking soda to adapt to your specific needs. Be creative; you will be amazed at your success!

All of the laundry detergent recipes work great in the new High Efficiency (**H.E.**) machines due to the low or no suds formula. Remember to keep in mind that more soap suds in no way means cleaner; they just take up space in your washer or cascade down your washer and onto the floor. We have again been led down the high cost golden brick road by laundry detergent companies.

Most people are not aware that soaps and detergents work differently based on water chemistry, hardness, and even the time of year. (We live five blocks from each other and have different tweaks that work for us.) If you don't get the exact results that you are looking for, there is no need to throw out your newly made detergent mixture. Adjust as you go. When you come upon the right mix to fit your specific needs, then simply adjust the entire batch. Use the "Notes" space at the end of each recipe to record, make changes, suggestions to yourself and quick reminders of what you liked and what you changed based on your water chemistry.

You can have the results you want for your laundry needs without paying the high prices for all the costly additives. Remember, your water is probably the clue. First try the water softener recipe to assist you with your wash. If you think your clothes are dingy, you probably have hard water.

Hard water is the presence of dissolved mineral salts, calcium, iron, and manganese. As hard water evaporates, the mineral deposits are left behind, causing this mineral build up to increase over time.

These minerals can reduce the effectiveness of the soap in laundry detergent. Clothes washed in hard water fade faster, can appear dingy and feel stiff when they come out of the dryer.

Don't despair! We have a quick, inexpensive, and easy solution. You can purchase a leading brand water softener or make your own for a fraction of the cost. You will have a solution for whitening your whites beyond their imagined potential!

For optimum cleaning, use powdered laundry detergent with hard water and liquid detergent with soft water. Most people have hard water rather than soft.

Ok, let's admit it, doing laundry probably ranks right up there with having a root canal for many folks. Well, maybe not that bad, but it is a chore that is a never ending, time consuming, but absolutely necessary for the smooth running (and socially acceptable smelling) family. There is a real rush to completing my laundry. I love the way that it feels for the brief and shining moment that I have it all done. Of course, we always realize that there is yet another load coming.

Developing the recipes for the laundry was a personal favorite. It was the largest monetary outlay for the housecleaning chores. More money was spent on products, getting the least favorable results and wanting to see the most savings. Plus, the quality of the product actually improved!

In making the laundry soap, the recipes were tried and tweaked for many varieties. Our personal favorite for cost effectiveness, ease of preparation, storage and effectiveness is the **Extra Plus H.E. Laundry Detergent.** It replaces the need for additional laundry boosters most of the time (see notes and tips on hard water and seasonal changes in water quality). It is so simple, making a few batches at a time is even more time efficient.

The "More is More Club" is what we dub those who think that more is always better. This is a difficult habit to break. All logic indicates this to be a truth, but more is not always the best. More in many cases can just be more wasting and more money spent needlessly. More does not guarantee more clean when referring to soap.

If you are a member of the "More is More Club" (Dena, a recovered member, has gone through rehab and has been clean now for some time) remember with most of the recipes, a single tablespoon is all you really need. For cleaning those heavily soiled loads (think rolling around with pigs), two tablespoons may be used.

My husband (another recovering member of the "More is More Club") was a skeptic about whether a tablespoon would really work and was using one cup to a one and a half cups of the detergent per load. Not only did we go through the detergent much faster, but the washing machine got a nasty ring around the tub (it was terrible) proving that more in this case did not mean "more clean;" but more money, more waste, and more work.

DNA Cleaning
Discovering Natural Alternatives

Elegant Simplicity

Have you ever thought that DNA and cleaning having anything in common? Probably not, so we want to introduce you to our DNA. Discovering natural alternatives (DNA) is easy and far more cost friendly than the high priced items you are probably now using.

Keeping our families safe, secure, and healthy is a full time responsibility. We need all the help we can find to provide a hazard free environment for those we love. Removing hidden toxic chemicals from your home by replacing the harsh household cleaners with green cleaners is the first step in DNA cleaning. How many expensive, potentially toxic chemical cleaning products do you have in your home?

The Center for Disease Control and Prevention reported in 2009, "Everyday, three hundred seventy four children in the United States ages zero to nineteen are treated in an emergency department, and two children die, as a result of being poisoned. It's not just chemicals in your home marked with clear warning labels that can be dangerous to children. Everyday items in your home, such as household cleaners and medicines, can be poisonous to children as well. Active, curious children will often investigate—and sometimes try to eat or drink—anything that's left out and within their reach."

As a toddler, my mother-in-law was a curious child. Her father brought home an acid to apply to her brother's warts to burn them off. Her mother took the acid from off the top of the china cabinet from where it was placed for safe keeping, to dust. She placed the acid in the middle of the dining room table, never thinking that her small child could reach it, nor could she climb to that height. As many parents can attest to, she could and she did. Mom drank the acid, being so dainty and neat to not get a single drop on her face. She suffers to this day with a badly scarred and extremely narrow esophagus causing frequent choking and emergency dilation.

After one of our workshops, a young mother came up to share her story with us. This really touched us because in our family we too had one of these little darlings that sent many frantic phone calls to Poison Control, and speedy trips to the Emergency Room; her story went something like this.

She explained that she had spent a lot of time at the Emergency Room. Her daughter was determined to give her mother gray hair and did as many things to worry the poor soul to death that she could. Her speed dials were changed to the Pediatrician's Office, Poison Control, and Ask-A-Nurse.

She shared a scary moment she had in her bathroom with her eighteen month old daughter. The child was playing on the floor of the bathroom while she showered. Between the shampoo and conditioner, the little one found an old and empty canister of toxic toilet bowl cleanser. The small one was licking the top of the lid as she jumped out of the shower to snatch it from her.

Without thinking, she stuck out her tongue and licked the top of the canister herself to see if she could get an idea of what her daughter had gotten as far as ingestion of this horrid product. Quickly reading the label she panicked, then called poison control to report what they had both done.

She quickly wanted to change the environment in her home to make it perfectly safe for her daughter. She loves that she is saving money, and having greener cleaners that are safe for her home and small children.

Vinegar and baking soda don't taste wonderful, but they beat the taste of that nasty stuff that she and her daughter licked! The safety of household products gives her peace of mind. We're glad to help since we've been there ourselves, although we can say that we never licked the top of a nasty toilet bowl abrasive cleaner.

Hidden Toxic Chemicals

vs.

Fantastically Frugal Fifteen

Ceiling to floor savings, nothing hidden, and nothing you can't pronounce.

We seem to live in a day and age where there seems to be warnings about virtually everything up to and including the air we breathe and the water which we drink.

Unfortunately, we are aware of a case that involved a person who was reckless and caused their own fatal injury misusing a perfectly safe food product. It is the lack of common sense and reason that is always the threat. A wise friend once said that, "Life is dangerous in the hands of the wrong people."

Good sense is not something you can control with a label; we have provided those elements that have survived time and conditions for your productive use and good health.

There are many toxic chemicals (just for clarification, a chemical is anything made of matter, a liquid, solid, or gas; water is even a chemical) in cleaners such as; for bathroom disinfectants, window cleaners, furniture polish, drain cleaners, oven cleaners, dish detergent, kitchen surface cleaners, carpets and floors, and car waxes.

These chemicals to which we are referring are contained in our everyday cleaning products. Federal law generally doesn't require manufacturers to disclose which chemicals are used in household cleaning products, though companies must include on labels any emergency warnings and instructions for first aid. The passage of the "Safe Chemicals Act of 2011" would require the Environmental Protection Agency to determine what minimum data would be required for each class of chemical to meet a safety standard.

The following is a small sample of some of the chemicals and their potential health hazards which are commonly found in many of our daily household cleaning products. At the time of this printing, manufacturers are still not required to use full disclosure of chemical contents in the products which they produce for our purchase. How are we to protect ourselves while cleaning and our family from exposure when we don't even know what we need to protect ourselves from?

Chlorine, in dry form, is highly concentrated. It irritates the skin, the eyes, and the respiratory system, and the number one cause of child poisonings.

Hydrochloric acid is a highly corrosive irritant to both skin and eyes that can damage your kidneys and liver.

Petroleum distillates, are chemicals that can cause skin and lung cancer; entry into the lungs may cause fatal pulmonary edema.

Perchlorethylene, is a known carcinogen.

Ammonium hydroxide, is a corrosive that's damaging to eyes, skin and respiratory passages.

Sodium hypochlorite,is a corrosive that irritates or burns skin and eyes, and causes fluid in the lungs, which can lead to coma or death.

Formaldehyde, is a highly toxic known carcinogen.

Trichloroethane, is an eye and skin irritant and nervous system depressant; it can also damage your liver and kidneys.

How about using safer, self selected chemicals? What if we chose what we would and would not accept in our homes? What if we knew how safe our cleaners really were, with no hidden ingredients, and remove all the guesswork?

It is impossible to remove all harsh chemicals from our environment, yet we can certainly pick and choose the ones we know about and feel safe using.

Below please find our Fantastically Frugal, Fifteen items we use from our DNA (discovering natural alternatives) research. We use our new found DNA to make all the recipes contained in this book. There are no surprises, no extra ingredients just these fifteen common items. These simple and inexpensive items are readily available and are just as effective. By making your own eco-friendly products, you will be amazed at the low cost as well as the ease of the task at hand.

Ammonia Inhalation can cause coughing, and nose and throat irritation. It can be a harsh or even toxic chemical if it is not used properly, if used in a very concentrated form, used with chlorine bleach, and without caution.

Baking Soda, there does not appear to be any health hazards or warnings

Borax,™ or sodium borate, is a naturally occurring alkaline mineral. It is usually a white powder consisting of soft colorless crystals that dissolve easily in water health effects such as oral and skin toxicity, as well as eye and skin irritation harmful if ingested.

Citric Acid, avoid contact with the eyes, citric acid can cause a burning sensation. When ingested can cause heartburn.

Cornstarch the dust may be an eye irritant and it may be irritating to respiratory system (noses and lungs).

Cream of Tartar, avoid direct contact to the eyes, mild to moderate irritation such as redness and swelling can occur.

Glycerin, no known adverse health hazards to using glycerin in household cleaning. Side effects of glycerin enemas and suppositories include anal irritation, burning sensation, diarrhea, gas, nausea and stomach cramps.

Hydrogen Peroxide is mildly irritating to the skin and mucous membranes.

Isopropyl (Rubbing) Alcohol, to avoid the risk of improper inhalation use isopropyl alcohol in a well-ventilated area. Not for internal consumption.

Lemon, avoid contact with eyes, can cause irritation.

Olive or Vegetable Oil, there are no known health hazards.

Salt, no known health hazards associated with salt.

Soap, not intended for internal consumption.

Washing Soda, may be harmful if swallowed or inhaled, a severe eye irritant, and a moderate skin irritant.

White Vinegar, there are no known health hazards for using or exposure.

The ingredients listed above are all inclusive. You won't need anything else to make any of the recipes.

When you compare and consider the list of chemicals we have put together above, along with the information and safety precautions for the Fantastically Frugal Fifteen, we invite you to make the choice which you feel safest with for your family. We believe that this choice is simple. Which option do you feel more comfortable using? Also keep in mind, when you make your own cleaning and laundry products you do not add any hidden ingredients. You know exactly what you are using every step of the way.

To Use Ammonia or Not:

Ammonia is a cleaning agent that has been used in the home and in restaurants and many other public locations. What most people may find surprising is that ammonia is a base ingredient found in many of their cleaning products. Using ammonia has been an inexpensive alternative to high priced cleansers and can be safe as well as effective.

Ammonia is also commonly used in commercial and household cleaners. In industry, ammonia is used in petroleum refining, to manufacture pharmaceuticals, to disinfect water, and as a refrigerant. In agriculture, ammonia can be used for crop processing, fertilizers, or as an anti-fungal treatment for citrus. Ammonia can also be produced naturally when stored materials such as manure, compost, or other materials break down.

To prevent overexposure to ammonia, know the amounts, concentrations, and properties of the materials that you are using.

Ammonia can be used full strength as well as diluted with water. Ammonia is excellent for cleaning and disinfecting kitchen surfaces, including wooden cutting boards as well as stainless steel. Its properties work well in cutting through grease and degrease buildup.

Ammonia is also an excellent cleaner in the bathroom. It is great for removing soap scum and cleaning tile and porcelain.

You can even use ammonia full strength for the stubborn water stains in the tub.

Before using on carpet and upholstery, blot on in an inconspicuous area to check for colorfastness and fading.

It is always important to remember whether you are using ammonia diluted or full strength, to use in a well ventilated area. **And NEVER MIX AMMONIA WITH OTHER HOUSEHOLD AGENTS, SUCH AS BLEACH.**

According to a statement made by the Public Health Service of U.S. Department of Health and Human Services,

"You can reduce your risk of exposure to ammonia by carefully using household products and by avoiding areas where ammonia is used or produced. At home, you can reduce your risk of exposure to ammonia by careful handling of any household products that contain ammonia. For example, some cleaning products contain ammonia; so when you use them, you should be sure that rooms are adequately ventilated during the time you are using them. Avoid ammonia-containing products in glass bottles since breakage could lead to a serious exposure. You should wear proper clothing and eye protection, because ammonia can cause skin burns and damage eyes if it is splashed on them. To lower the risk of your children being exposed to ammonia, you should tell them to stay out of the room when you are using it. While use of ammonia by a child is not recommended, any use by a child should be closely supervised by an adult." (Public Health Service of U.S. Department of Health and Human Services, 2011)

We certainly want to express our concern for your safety when using ammonia. When cleaning with ammonia solutions, use every precaution to ensure a safe environment. Use in a well ventilated area, and do not use more that the stated amount without increasing the water content. Remove direct or indirect contact of ammonia use around children, the elderly, and persons with lung diseases such as asthma or emphysema may be especially sensitive to ammonia. Avoid continued ammonia exposure with this population.

We have added precautions from the U.S. Department of Health and Human Services Public Health Service. If you use ammonia use the recommended precautions.

Please note we have not included chlorine bleach in our list or in any of our recipes. Chlorine bleach a corrosive chemical, sodium hypochlorite is an eye, skin, and respiratory irritant. It is especially hazardous to people with heart conditions or asthma, and can be fatal if swallowed. It may be a neurotoxin and toxic to the liver. Found in a wide range of household cleaners. All our recipes are made without the use of chlorine bleach.

As you discover your new DNA you will be "going green" in the easiest and least expensive way imaginable! Your environmental movement will be started right in your own home with increased benefits for your family first.

The media has repeatedly reported the environmental issues facing us. Earth Day 2011, a theme was adopted, "A Billion Acts of Green."

To date, over one hundred and two million people have pledged to "go green." These include an array of activities from the very simple ways to save water to growing gardens. There is encouragement to do something big or small to help make a healthier environment.

With millions of people already desiring to take an active role in creating a healthier environment, why not start in your own personal environment first? By each of us removing the hidden toxic chemicals in cleaning and laundry items used in the home we will be cleaning the air we breathe, the waterways we use, and reducing toxic chemicals from the earth itself.

We are not suggesting you set up a chemical factory in your home. Read on, all you need is a small work space, containers, measuring cups and spoons. This is so easy your children can help with many of the recipes. DO NOT USE ammonia recipes around children. This is one ingredient that we keep away from the children when we are making our supplies.

In **Chapter Eight, Cleef's Notes**, we will tell you more than you probably want to know about these simple household substances. We also have included a section on the classification of cleaning products to better assist you.

We have really enjoyed customizing and tweaking the recipes to fit our needs. If we need a stronger cleanser, we know which of the Fantastically Frugal Fifteen we can increase to meet our requirements. Another great feature about making your own laundry and cleaning items is you can personalize everything you make and use.

Chapter Seven, A Little Drop Will Do Ya,' in the Holiday Cleaning section, more detailed information is available. Essential Oils are mentioned in some of the recipes and their use is completely optional. These oils have some amazing properties but are not required for the performance of any of the recipes. We personally use a few of our favorites in various recipes to fit our personal choices.

If you choose to use Essential Oils please read **Chapter Seven, A Little Drop Will Do Ya,'** to view the list and any precautions you need to be aware of during pregnancy.

When you buy in larger quantities, you might be able to reduce your prices. We buy baking soda in twelve pound (yes, pound) bags from a warehouse or club store. This reduces our cost to a penny per ounce. We also buy our vinegar packaged as two one gallon bottles per box from the same store. This gives us additional savings.

Washing soda (sodium carbonate) can be found in most major grocery stores. If your regular store does not carry the Arm and Hammer Washing Soda, it is very likely they can order it for you. It may also be purchased in the lawn and garden section for pool pH under the brand pH Up™. This usually results in additional savings.

When purchasing lemon, you can use fresh or the bottled real lemon juice. We use both.

Citric Acid is a common canning ingredient and often found in canning supplies. Kool-Aid® lemonade flavoring can be used to replace citric acid.

To help with recycling we use our old brand name bottles for our green cleaners. As a precaution do not reuse any containers or spray bottles that once contained toxic chemicals such as bleach. There might be accidental dangerous chemical reactions involved.

What we do is use our window cleaning spray bottles for our window cleaners. Any cleaning recipe that uses vinegar can be stored in a vinegar bottle. Since we have an abundance of gallon vinegar bottles we make our recipes and store in the gallon bottles. This helps save time, save money and we always have what we need on hand. Make sure and label your cleaners.

If you continue to use up what products you already have, remember to read the labels very carefully in search of bleach or ammonia. Never mix bleach and ammonia.

CAUTION

Please read the cautions for using ammonia both on the ammonia bottle and with the recipes.

When using ammonia use a well ventilated area and never use with bleach. Do not use with any products containing bleach.

CAUTION:

NEVER USE AMMONIA WITH BLEACH OR PRODUCTS CONTAINING BLEACH. A DEADLY CHLORINE GAS IS PRODUCED.

If you add any chlorine bleach dry or liquid add a caution to avoid using with ammonia or vinegar.

Chlorine Bleach is a hazardous chemical and should be handled with care.

CAUTION: Essential oils to avoid during pregnancy include anise, angelica, basil, cedarwood (all sorts), cinnamon, clary sage, clove, fennel, hyssop, juniper, lovage, myrrh, nutmeg, rosemary, rose and peppermint and thyme (white variety).

See **Chapter Seven A Little Drop Will Do Ya'** for additional information. Please check with your health care professional before using essential oils with any medical concerns.

For more information see **Chapter Eight, Cleef's Notes.**

When making your own laundry products, remember to always label your containers with a list of ingredients.

"You never know what you can do until you try."

Old English Proverb

Chapter Two

Extreme Savings In the Laundry Room

Do you know how much are you spending on each load?

The three most commonly used laundry products:

Laundry Detergent 100 loads
MSRP $18.00 vs. Make It Yourself $3.00
A $15.00 or 500% Savings

Fabric Softener 32 loads
MSRP $4.00 vs. Make It Yourself $.37 cents
A $3.63 or 981% Savings

Stain Remover 32 oz.
MSRP $5.00 vs. Make It Yourself $.27
A $4.73 or 1752% Savings

If you use the three examples here you could have a savings of $23.36 with a single purchase.

By using these recipes you can obviously see a significant savings.

Our recipes usually make more than the packaged products. For ease of comparisons, all illustrations are ounce per ounce cost comparisons. We realize this is an approximate cost and savings cost based upon your purchase price and quantities.

Making your own laundry products you could be spending as little as **$7.22.**

Buying retail for laundry products, you could be spending as much as **$86.53.**

Buying eco-friendly products you could be spending up to **$116.09.**

Using the recipes in this chapter, you could be saving up to **$79.31 or 1,098%.**

Using eco-friendly products, you could be saving up to **$108.87or 1,508%,** with these recipes.

These figures are based on a onetime purchase of the many laundry products to meet all your needs.

Bleaches

"If every family in America simply replaced one 64 oz. bottle of bleach it would keep11.6 million pounds of chlorine from entering the waterways."

Seventh Generation Chlorine Free Bleach 2008

This is a very eco-friendly alternative to chlorine bleach. Safe to use without the risk of over bleaching or turning delicate fabrics yellow. It's safe for all colors, no more accidental bleaching from splashing or spilling.

Green and Chlorine Free Bleach

EASY! Yields: 32 oz. or 16 loads
Approximate cost: $.96 or less than $.06 per load
MSRP: $5.37 or $.34 per load
Savings: $4.41 or 459% back in your pocket
Prep Time 1 minute

1/4 cup 3% Hydrogen Peroxide

Add hydrogen peroxide to each wash load. For very full or dirty loads add 1/2 cup. Use instead of bleach. This can also be used as a soak.

Notes

You know the feeling when your delicates need some deep cleaning? It is so difficult to know what to do and how to clean them and not damage the fabric. This does the trick every time.

Delicate Fabric Bleach

EASY! Yields: 25 loads
Approximate cost: $3.25 or $.13 per load
MSRP: $6.99 or $.28 per load
Savings: $3.74 or 115% back in your pocket
Prep Time 2 minutes

1/2 cup hydrogen peroxide
4 cups cool water

Combine and soak delicates in the solution for up to 30 minutes to brighten and remove any discoloration. Rinse in clean water and dry the item as instructed.

Notes

Ammonia is fantastic, as it cleans many areas in your home, but did you know it is great for your laundry as well? It removes many stains and it brightens your clothes. Be cautious when using ammonia, do not breathe the fumes. Use in a well ventilated area. When used in the washing machine, pour the ammonia into the tub while the washer is filling with water. Ammonia should not be used with clothes containing spandex.

The vinegar works with the ammonia and the detergent to remove the harsh minerals that cling to clothes which dull the colors and harm the fibers.

Boost and Brighten

EASY! Yields: 32 oz. or 8 loads
Approximate cost: $1.12 or less than $.04 per load
MSRP: $5.37 or $.23 per load
Savings: $4.25 or 379% back in your pocket
Prep Time 1 minute

2 cups ammonia
2 cups white vinegar

Add ammonia and vinegar to the water as it fills the tub. Wash on any water temperature. The ammonia is a color booster and stain fighter and the vinegar is an anti static, fabric softener and removes soap residue.

NEVER USE AMMONIA WITH BLEACH OR PRODUCTS CONTAINING BLEACH. A DEADLY GAS IS PRODUCED!

Notes

Dena became acquainted with oxygen bleach as a mother with infants and loved it to clean stained clothes, bibs, etc. This works as well as or better than the commercial version.

The recipe is for a one load amount, we do this to keep the hydrogen peroxide from diluting its bleaching power. If you want to make the recipe for a larger quantity keep in a dark container away from direct light.

We keep all the ingredients on our laundry supply shelf and make it for each load. It is really so quick to do.

O_2 Clean

EASY! Yields: 8 oz. or 1 load
Approximate cost: $3.84 for 48 loads or $.08 per load
MSRP: $9.00 for 48 loads or $.19 per load
Savings: $5.16 or 134% back in your pocket
Prep Time 2 minutes

1/2 cup hot water
1/4 cup baking soda
1/4 cup hydrogen peroxide

Mix ingredients. Soak the clothing for a minimum of 20 minutes or as long as overnight. Wash as usual.

Notes

Hydrogen peroxide must be kept in a dark container. When it is exposed to sunlight for a period of time, the hydrogen peroxide which is two parts hydrogen, two parts oxygen, will turn into water. Pour what you will need in a spray bottle and return whatever is left into the dark bottle when you are finished. I found a sprayer that perfectly fits my hydrogen peroxide bottle. I mix my ingredients; attach the sprayer, problem solved.

Clean and Whiten

EASY! Yields: 36 oz.
Approximate cost: $1.04
MSRP: $5.99 for 48 loads or $.19 per load
Savings: $5.16 or 134% back in your pocket
Prep Time 2 minutes

32 oz. bottle of hydrogen peroxide
2 tablespoons baking soda
1 tablespoon laundry detergent
4 tablespoons white vinegar

Mix ingredients into a bowl or large measuring cup. Pour mixture back into the hydrogen peroxide bottle. Label and keep out of direct light.

Notes

A chemist friend of ours told us that it is safe to use ammonia in laundry to "bleach whites" without any damage to clothes. Chlorine bleach will "eat" the fibers of cotton and yellow the delicates. Ammonia will dissolve latex, use with caution.

I could not believe how white I got some old yellowed delicate whites.

Clean and Brighten

EASY! Yields: 64 oz. 32 loads
Approximate cost: $1.12 or less than $.02 per load
MSRP: $6.38 or $.10 per load
Savings: $5.26 or 470% back in your pocket
Prep Time 2 minutes

1/ 4 cup ammonia

Pour ammonia into the washer as water is filling. Add the detergent, fabric softener, white clothes, and wash as usual.

NEVER USE AMMONIA WITH BLEACH OR PRODUCTS CONTAINING BLEACH. A DEADLY GAS IS PRODUCED!

Notes

Caution: If you intend on using your soap making utensils with food products, wash and rinse very well. We advise using different pans and utensils for liquid soap making.

Detergent Liquid

"The sweet smell of fresh laundry may contain a sour note. Widely used fragranced products including those that claim to be "green" give off many chemicals that are not listed on the label; including some that are classified as toxic...More than a third of the products emitted at least one chemical classified as a probable carcinogen by the U.S. Environmental Protection Agency, and for which the EPA sets no safe exposure level."

(Science Daily, 2010)

Soap 101

Since my family has allergies, we experimented with the different types of soap available. A personal favorite is the ZOTE™ bar–white. (ZOTE™ is available in most Latin American grocery stores or it can be purchased online.) It has a nice fragrance (and having a sweet smelling laundry after years of having to go scent and dye free is a real plus for me). It is gentle on my clothes and skin, yet tough on every speck of dirt that my kids dish out. You can use Fels Naptha™, Ivory™, Sunlight™ bar soap or Kirk's Hardwater Castile™ soap. Don't use soap bars that have a heavy perfume or oils which may transfer stains to your clothes. This might also cause a chemical reaction with the other ingredients in your detergent.

Soaps that contain sodium palmate, sodium cocoate or sodium tallowate are safe soaps to use. Be sure your soap selection is a real soap and not a detergent beauty bar with added free oils, such as Dove.™ Also stay away from beauty bars, shower gels and body washes. Oil based soaps can leave spots on your clothes.

We air dry our soap for a day or two before we begin our powder detergent recipes. Make sure to cut your soap bar into pieces when moist, then place on a cookie sheet to air dry. When the soap bars are moist, the cutting is easier but the grating process isn't as fine as when air dried. Be cautious if your soap bar is really dry, your processor might pulverize the soap, (the finer the better) but your room might be filled with fine soap dust, been there done that, don't recommend it!

One of the most popular laundry recipes, Extra Plus H.E. Laundry Detergent is what we personally use and have eliminated our use of, oxygen laundry booster and additional adding of baking soda or Borax™ which we had used in all our loads before we made our own. When asked by a skeptical woman at one of our workshops if it really works, all we could was to point to our clothes and ask, “Do we look dirty to you?” The response was unanimous, “No!

The powdered detergent recipes are so easy to make and store, which is a bonus over the liquids. Do not misunderstand, the liquids work very well, they take more time to make, need more storage space and require a designated set of equipment. It is best to use dedicated cookware for making your liquid detergent than what you use for food preparation.

We suggest you decrease the recipe in half to try it out. Adjust as you go. If your clothes become dingy, your problem is probably the hard water. Try using our recipe for homemade water softener. Also try adding more soap to your recipe. The soap is the binding agent which removes the dirt and the minerals from the fabric.

How much a bar of soap equals

1 4.7 oz. soap bar yields 1 cup grated soap

2 4.7oz.soap bars yields: 2 cups grated soap

4 (4.7oz. bars) yields 4 cups

1 14.7 oz. bar yields 4 cups

Many families prefer liquid detergent. If your family does, here are a few tips to keep in mind. We suggest that you have the equipment (bowls, spoons pans, etc.) dedicated to the purpose of making laundry detergent.

Use caution with this recipe and having children helping as it uses boiling water. Some grocery store bakery departments throw out large containers which once contained cake frostings. You will need to wash the container; it is free and works great.

Clean and Bright H.E. Laundry Detergent

EASY! Yields: 2 gallons or 128 loads
Approximate cost: $3.50 or less than $.03 per load
MSRP: $17.25 or $.14 per load
Savings: $13.75 or 393% back in your pocket
Prep Time 20 minutes

1 quart water (boiling)
2 cups soap bar (grated)
2 cups Borax™
2 cups washing soda

Add finely grated bar soap to the boiling water. Stir on low heat until soap is melted. Pour the soap water into a large, clean pail and add the Borax™ and washing soda. Stir well until dissolved.

Add 2 gallons of tepid water, stir until well mixed. Cover pail and use 1/4 cup for each load of laundry. Stir the soap each time you use it (this will gel).

Notes

When making laundry soaps with bar soap, unwrap the soap and cut into small pieces. Let the pieces dry before grating. This will give you faster results when trying to grate your soap. The wetter the soap the easier it is to cut but harder to grate. When soap is dry it is harder to cut but easier to grate.

Green and Clean Laundry Detergent

EASY! Yields: 10 gallons or 160 loads
Approximate cost: $2.80 or less than $.03 per load
MSRP: $21.44 or $.14 per load
Savings: $38.92 or 434% back in your pocket
Prep Time 20 minutes

4 cups hot water
1 14.7 oz ZOTE™ soap bar or 4 4.7 oz soap bars
1 1/2 cup Borax™
1 1/2 cup washing soda
1 1/2 cup baking soda

Grate the bar soap and add to a large saucepan with 4 cups hot water. Stir over medium-low heat until soap is melted.

Fill a 10 gallon pail with 5 gallons of hot water. Add the melted soap, Borax™ and washing soda. Stir well until all powder is dissolved. Add 4 and 3/4 gallons of hot water to fill the 10 gallon pail. Use 1 cup per load, stirring soap before each use (This will gel). Yields: 10 gallons

Notes

Store with a secure lid to keep little fingers out and prevent an accidental finger painting or a child from falling into the bucket.

H. E. Extreme Laundry Detergent

EASY! Yields: 2 gallons or 64 loads
Approximate cost: $.67 or less than $.02 per load
MSRP: $9.00 or $.14 per load
Savings: $8.33 or 124% back in your pocket
Prep Time 20 minutes

6 cups hot water
1/3 soap bar (grated)
1/2 cup washing soda
1/2 cup Borax™

Pour 6 cups of water in a large pot and heat. Add the grated bar soap and stir until melted. Add the washing soda and Borax™. Stirring until the powder is dissolved, remove from heat.

In a 2 gallon clean pail, pour 4 cups of hot water and add the heated melted soap mixture. Stir the mixture before adding the additional water. Add 1and 1/4 gallons cold water to fill the pail and stir well.

Use 1/2 cup per load, stir soap before each use. This will be a gel like mixture.

Notes

If you like Ivory™ Soap, you will love washing your clothes in the same soap you use to bathe. As we all know Ivory™ Soap is 99 3/4% pure. You can substitute Ivory™ for any of the soaps in any recipe.

Allergy Friendly Laundry Detergent

EASY! Yields: 2 1/2 gallons or 80 loads
Approximate cost: $1.40 or $.02 per load
MSRP: $10.72 or $.14 per load
Savings: $9.32 or 665% back in your pocket
Prep Time 20 minutes

4 cups hot water
1 4.5 oz. Ivory™ soap bar grated
1 cup washing soda
1 cup baking soda

In a large saucepan add hot water and grated soap. Heat over medium-low heat and stir until soap is melted.

Fill a large pail with 2 1/4 gallons of hot water. Add hot soap mixture. Stir until well mixed. Add the washing soda, again stirring until well mixed. Set aside to cool.

Use 1/2 cup per full load, stir well before each use (this will gel).

Notes

We have added glycerin to this recipe because it is an excellent cleaning agent as well as a great degreaser. Glycerin is also an effective surfactant (making water wetter), which allows the oil and water to mix so the oily dirt and stains can be removed during rinsing. The glycerin is also used as a water softener.

This recipe is quite similar to a leading green detergent on the market. The biggest difference this is truly green.

Green and Easy Laundry Detergent

EASY! Yields: 2 1/2 gallons or 80 loads
Approximate cost: $2.28 or less than $.03 per load
MSRP: $12.80 or $.16 per load
Savings: $10.52 or 464% back in your pocket
Prep Time 20 minutes

4 cups hot water
1 soap bar grated
3/4 cup washing soda
3/4 cup Borax™
3/4 cup baking soda
2 tablespoons glycerin

Pour water and grated soap in pan. Melt soap over medium-low heat. Stir until soap is melted.

In a large pail, pour 2 and 1/4 gallons of hot water, add melted soap mixture, washing soda, Borax™ and glycerin. Mix well. Use 1/2 cup per full load.

Notes

A yardstick or paint stirrer is a wonderful tool to have handy to stir the liquid detergents. You can also use it to "poke" your clothes down in the machine as well.

Strong and Simple Laundry Detergent

EASY! Yields: 2 1/2 gallons or 40 loads
Approximate cost: $2.78 or less than $.07 per load
MSRP: $6.00 or $.15 per load
Savings: $3.22 or 116% back in your pocket
Prep Time 20 minutes

2 cups soap bar (grated)
2 to 2 1/2 gallons hot water
2 cups washing soda
1 cup baking soda

Melt grated soap in saucepan with water to cover. Heat over medium-low heat and stir until soap is dissolved.

Pour hot water in large pail. Add hot soap and washing soda. Stir very well. Use 1 cup per full load.

Notes

This recipe is well suited for soft water, but not really suited for hard water. As you will notice it is only soap and soda. The baking soda and soap work well together to release the soil and deodorize your laundry.

Soft Water H. E. Laundry Detergent

EASY! Yields: 2 gallons or 64 loads
Approximate cost: $2.14 or less than $.04 per load
MSRP: $8.96 or $.14 per load
Savings: $6.82 or 319% back in your pocket
Prep Time 20 minutes

2 gallons hot water
1 soap bar grated
2 cups baking soda

Melt grated soap over medium-low heat in a saucepan with 4 cups hot water. Stirring frequently until soap is melted.

In a large pail, pour in 1 and 1/4 gallons of hot water, add melted soap, and stir well. Add the baking soda, stirring well. Use 1/2 cup per full load, 1 cup per very soiled load.

Notes

Detergent Powdered

"A do-it-yourself mentality is one of the most reliable ways to save money."

(Freedman, 2010) MSN Money

In our workshops we make the **H**igh **E**fficiency Powder Laundry Detergent recipe. We found that this works great for about 95% of those using this recipe. What we discovered is that the hard water factor varies from water sources and water treatment in individual homes. Cut soap into pieces, unwrap, and dry soap for a day or two; depending on the humidity in your part of the country before beginning this recipe. The air drying of the soap will bring about a finer grating.

Extra Plus H.-E. Laundry Detergent

EASY! Yields: 100 loads
Approximate cost: $2.80 or less than $.03 per load
MSRP: $17.67 or $.18 per load
Savings: $14.87 or 531% back in your pocket
Prep Time 10 minutes

1/2 cup baking soda
5 cups finely grated soap
(1 14.1 oz. ZOTE™ soap bar, cut into pieces and 1 4.7 oz. ZOTE™ soap bar) is 5 cups of soap or
5 (4.7oz. bars) Fels Naptha™, Ivory™, or pure soap bar
Grate either by hand grated or food processor grated = 5 cups
1 1/2 cups washing soda
1 1/2 cups Borax™

Food Processor Method: use the cutting blade. Pour in baking soda and soap pieces. Process until mixture is a fine powder. Mix washing soda and Borax™ in bowl, add soap mixture. Store the detergent in an airtight container or a gallon bag.

Hand grate method: Unwrap soap and cut into pieces, leave to dry, for a day or more. Use a kitchen cheese grater to grate soap.

Mix washing soda and Borax™ in bowl, add soap mixture. Store the detergent in an airtight container or a gallon bag.

Use 1 tablespoon per load, 2 tablespoons very heavily soiled load.

Notes

This is a great recipe to use for starting out in the laundry soap making process. We used this recipe first. It has a great ratio of soap to laundry boosters. This recipe will clean, deodorize, disinfect and soften water. As an added bonus, it is a flame retardant. This is wonderful to use in your laundry.

Bonus Laundry Detergent

EASY! Yields: 32 loads
Approximate cost: $2.50 or less than $.08 per load
MSRP $5.78 or $.14 per load
Savings: $3.28 or 131% back in your pocket
Prep Time 10 minutes

2 cups Fels Naptha™ soap bar or other soap bar of your choice (grated finely)
2 4.7oz.soap bars Yields: 2 cups grated soap
1 cup washing soda
1 cup Borax™

Mix well and store in an airtight plastic container.
Use 2 tablespoons per full load.

Notes

When making this recipe, you need to have a large container or tub ready. It is ideal for the family that wants a large reserve. A plastic five quart ice cream bucket works great. (And you get to eat the ice cream to have a container!) We really like to recycle our old containers to store our recipes, this adds to the savings.

Super Strong Laundry Detergent

EASY! Yields: 266 loads
Approximate cost: $8.96 or less than $.04 per load
MSRP $47.88 or $.18 per load
Savings: $38.92 or 434% back in your pocket
Prep Time 10 minutes

12 cups Borax™
8 cups baking soda
8 cups washing soda
8 cups bar soap grated
8 cups grated soap equals 4 4.7oz.soap bars or
2 14.7oz.soap bars

Mix all ingredients well and store in a sealed tub.
Use 2 tablespoons of powder per full load.

Notes

Fabric Softeners

"According to the Allergy and Environmental Health Association, both liquid and dryer sheet fabric softeners are 'the most toxic product produced for daily household use."

Natural Alternatives to Toxic Fabric Softeners
Michelle Schoffro Cook, 2010

When making this recipe, add the vinegar slowly. Make sure that your container has adequate room to allow the baking soda and vinegar to react. The reaction is mild, if you follow the instructions. No baking soda volcano unless you have poured it all quickly.

Just the Way You Like It Fabric Softener

EASY! Yields: 112 oz. or 56 loads
Approximate cost: $.70 or less than $.02 per load
MSRP: $5.63 or $.12 per load
Savings: $4.93 or 704% back in your pocket
Prep Time 5 minutes

8 cups water
1 cup baking soda
6 cups distilled white vinegar
10-15 drops essential oils (optional)

In a gallon container, add 3 cups water. Add baking soda. Slowly add small amounts of vinegar. There will be a mild reaction. Add remaining water and swish around. Add essential oil. Add to final rinse. Use a fabric softener ball or 1/4 cup per load.

Notes

The inexpensive hair conditioner is the key here. This recipe has a texture similar to what most of us are accustomed to in a fabric softener.

Fresh and Sweet Fabric Softener

EASY! Yields: 88 oz. or 44 loads
Approximate cost: $.78 or less than $.02 per load
MSRP: $$5.36 or $.12 per load
Savings: $4.58 or 587% back in your pocket
Prep Time 20 minutes

6 cups water
3 cups vinegar
2 cups hair conditioner (inexpensive store brand works very well)

Combine in a gallon container. For a perfect container, wash a gallon milk jug. Use 1/4 cup per load or a softener ball.

Notes

Oh, the many uses of vinegar! We have a confession to make. We went through about a small quart of vinegar per year before we received Grandmother Ada's ingredient list. Now we buy it by the gallon! Try warehouse club stores, we have found 2 packaged, 1 gallon bottles, to save even more.

We keep a gallon of vinegar on our laundry shelf. We pour our vinegar into our laundry ball, toss into the machine, quick and easy. If you really need a helping hand to soften those rough towels add 2 cups to remove hard water deposits. You will have fluffy and soft towels.

Vinegar is a multi-tasking, hard working ingredient. Sounds like a "Mom" doesn't it?

Simple Fabric Softener

SUPER EASY! Yields: 128 oz. or 32 loads
Approximate cost: $2.13 or less than $.06 per load
MSRP: $5.36 or $.12 per load
Savings: $3.23 151% back in your pocket
Prep Time less than1 minute

1/2 cup white vinegar

Pour vinegar straight into the final rinse water or into the washing machine liquid dispenser.

Notes

Please remember to have a large container and mix ingredients slowly to avoid a strong reaction. The water will dilute the vinegar and does minimize the fizzing. For an additional green tip, recycle the gallon vinegar bottle to make and store this recipe.

This is the recipe that we use the most.

Oh So Simple Fabric Softener

SUPER EASY! Yields: 64 oz. or 32 loads
Approximate cost: $.37 or less than $.02 per load
MSRP: $5.36 or $.12 per load
Savings: $4.99 or 135% back in your pocket
Prep Time 2 minutes

2 cups white vinegar
2 cups baking soda
4 cups water

In a large container, slowly add vinegar, baking soda and water. Use 1/4 cup in the final rinse or/fabric softener ball.

Notes

Miscellaneous Laundry Needs

"We analyzed best-selling products, and about half of them made some claim about being green, organic or natural. Surprisingly, the green products' emissions of hazardous chemicals were not significantly different from the other products."

(Steinemann, 2010)

Depending on the time of the year, your water can change in quality and you can have hard water problems. If your clothes look dingy or you are not getting the results you desire, make a batch of this and add it to your wash.

H_2O Softener

EASY! Yields: 1 gallon or 16 loads
Approximate cost: $1.50 or $.09 per load
MSRP: $17.07 or $1.07 per load
Savings: $15.57 or 1038% back in your pocket
Prep Time 10 minutes

1 cup Borax™
2 cups washing soda
1 gallon water

Using a funnel, pour Borax™ and washing soda in a gallon container. (You can use a washed plastic milk container, it works great.) Fill the container with water. Mix well until the powder mixture completely dissolves. Add 1 cup to final rinse.

For really hard water you may need to use 2 cups per load. Reduce the amount of laundry detergent you use by half to begin with, too much detergent will negate the effects of your water softener.

Notes

Are you seeing the possibilities of vinegar yet? That "Mom" ingredient really can do a lot! Now you see why we buy vinegar by the gallon to have around the house.

Static Gone Spray

SUPER EASY! Yields: 12 oz.
Approximate cost: $.08 or less than $.01 per oz.
MSRP: $6.24 or $.52 per oz.
Savings: $6.16 or 7,700% back in your pocket
Prep Time seconds

3/4 cup white vinegar
3/4 cup water

Pour in spray bottle. Spray to prevent static cling on clothes, carpets, or just about anything. The vinegar fragrance will dissipate when dry.

Notes

Whether you are in an emergency out of spray starch or as a full replacement, this works beautifully! I scent mine with lavender essential oil, ironing isn't so bad when you enjoy the scent and my husband has never complained about the fragrance. Oh, your closets will have a nice fragrance as well!

This does not keep very well due to the lack of preservatives; the cornstarch (which is a food product) will sour if kept too long. I make only what I think I will need for each ironing session. This is so easy to adjust the amounts for a smaller amount.

Crisp and Fresh Spray Starch

EASY! Yields: 16 oz.
Approximate cost: $.06 or less than $.004 per oz.
MSRP: $1.10 or $.09 per oz.
Savings: $1.04 or 1,733% back in your pocket
Prep Time 2 minutes

2 tablespoons cornstarch
2 cups cold water

Combine ingredients and pour into spray bottle. Shake well before each use. Spray on clothes as needed when ironing. This is a heavy starch. For a lighter starch decrease the cornstarch or add additional water until you get the best results for your personal preferences.

Notes

Stain Removers

"Manufacturers are not required to disclose any ingredients in cleaning supplies."

(Science Daily, 2010)

My husband spilled some cherry juice on his best and most pricey white golf shirt. My first thought, "what do I have that will get this out in record time; I'm tired and want to go to bed." Quickly thinking, I poured hydrogen peroxide on the spill, it lightened it but it didn't come out completely. I dabbed a little ammonia on the stain and presto, the stain was out. I rinsed out the ammonia and put it in the laundry and went to bed.

There are many stain removing products available from the grocery store laundry aisle. Many of these products can be expensive, especially when you get the same results as low cost alternatives. It is also an added benefit when you discover you don't need to run to the store to buy the latest product.

Additionally, when you really need the product, you don't have time to go buy it. I keep a bottle of ammonia on my laundry shelf above my washing machine. I just love having everything that I need right at my finger tips.

Stain Away

EASY! Yields: 64 oz.
Approximate cost: $1.15 or less than $.06 per load
MSRP: $5.37 or $.23 per load
Savings: $4.22 or 366% back in your pocket
Prep Time1 minute

1/2 cup ammonia

Pour ammonia into washing machine tub as the water is being filled. Use in a well ventilated area. For stains, apply a small amount directly on the stain and wash as usual.

Notes

You will love the low cost of this one; it is so easy to make, and to use. Try mixing up a batch and putting a small spray bottle in your clothes hamper. Before putting a stained article of clothing in the hamper, spray with the stain buster. Now nothing will go into the wash untreated. You can even use ammonia on silk.

Stain Buster Spray

SUPER EASY! Yields: 80 oz.
Approximate cost: $.27 or less than $.01 per oz.
MSRP: $7.98 or $.10 per oz.
Savings: $7.71 or 2,855% back in your pocket
Prep Time 5 minutes

2 1/2 cups ammonia
1/2 cup homemade laundry detergent
2 1/2 cups vinegar
5 cups water

Pour in a spray bottle and shake before use. Spray on stains before washing.

NEVER USE AMMONIA WITH BLEACH OR PRODUCTS CONTAINING BLEACH. A DEADLY GAS IS PRODUCED!

Notes

This is another great recipe for stain remover. As you can see, there are many recipes to choose from. Each one can be changed to meet your needs. You can add more of something or less of another ingredient. You get to decide exactly what you want. Experiment, be bold, create your own personal solutions, and it is fun!

Super Power Stain Remover

SUPER EASY! Yields: 83 oz.
Approximate cost: $.21 or less than $.01 per oz.
MSRP: $7.98 or $.10 per oz.
Savings: $7.77 or 3,700% back in your pocket
Prep Time 5 minutes

1/4 cup baking soda
2 quarts water
1/2 cup ammonia
2 tablespoons laundry detergent
1/2 cup white vinegar

Dissolve the baking soda into water, and slowly add the remaining ingredients. Add the vinegar last. The vinegar and baking soda might react so mix slowly and with caution. Use a large container to allow space for the reaction. Shake well to mix. Pour into a spray bottle. Spray the solution on the stain and let it soak for a few minutes before washing. Shake the solution before each use.

NEVER USE AMMONIA WITH BLEACH OR PRODUCTS CONTAINING BLEACH. A DEADLY GAS IS PRODUCED!

Notes

We keep these ingredients right on our laundry shelf and make this up in no time. Works great and is super fast.

Color Safe Stain Remover

EASY! Yields: 32 oz.
Approximate cost: $.64 or less than $.02 per oz.
MSRP: $4.74 or $.15 per oz.
Savings: $4.10 or 640% back in your pocket
Prep Time 2 minutes or less

1 1/2 cups Borax™
1 1/2 cups white vinegar
1 1/2 cups lemon juice

Mix and pour on stain. Wait a few minutes then wash as usual. Removes ink as well as most stains.

Notes

You know what it looks like, that dirty yellow stain that makes clothes look so gross. I threw away (shh) shirts that were beyond help. Enter baking soda and water. Look for the best prices by buying in larger quantities.

Summer Stain Remover

EASY! Yields: 16 oz.
Approximate cost: $.08 or less than $.02 per oz.
MSRP: $2.88 or $.18 per oz.
Savings: $2.80 or 3,500% back in your pocket
Prep Time 2 minutes

1 cup baking soda
1 cup warm water

Make a paste and rub into the stain. For really bad stains, let the paste dry for about two hours before washing.

Notes

Perhaps this is going to age me, but I remember the old commercials in the 70's about "ring around the collar." (Check on YouTube™ if you don't know what I am talking about.) The problem is the same even if the hairstyles are different.

Dirty Ring Stain Remover

EASY! Yields: 64 oz.
Approximate cost: $1.12 or less than $.02 per oz
MSRP: $4.74 or $.15 per oz.
Savings: $3.62 or 323% back in your pocket
Prep Time 1 minute

1/4 cup ammonia

Dip the soiled collar in the wash water to complete saturate with water. Pour a small amount of ammonia on the collar, rub ammonia into the stain. Launder as usual.

Notes

Rust stains on clothes can be expensive and a real problem, but actually it is rather simple. Spending money on expensive cleaners or solutions with harmful chemicals is a thing of the past. There are several homemade solutions to remove rust and they are right in your kitchen. Here are a few different ways to remove rust on clothing and but just about anything else.

Cream of tartar is another wonderful multi-tasking ingredient from the kitchen that we used infrequently (homemade play dough), before we began our journey into homemade laundry needs.

It is simple to make up in the event you have rust stains on your clothes. We had to make a stain to test it out and it really works.

Rust Buster Stain Remover

EASY! Yields: 10 oz.
Approximate cost: $1.12 or less than $.12 per use
MSRP: $5.47 or $.34 per oz.
Savings: $4.35 or 388% back in your pocket
Prep Time 2 minutes

1 teaspoon cream of tartar
Water (drops)

Make a paste of cream of tartar to clean the rust from washable fabrics by mixing a small amount of water with some cream of tartar until you get the desired consistency. Apply paste to the rust stains and gently rub. Let the paste set for about 10 minutes and wash as usual.

Notes

I just don't think that there is anything more inconvenient than not having a solution to a laundry problem when I am doing the wash. I really like this recipe, I have everything I need at the time I discover the stain. A quick trip to the kitchen, not a trip to the store is all I need to tackle the stain. Now, that is convenient to me.

Citrus Rust Remover

EASY! Yields: 16 oz.
Approximate cost: $.19 or $.02 per oz.
MSRP: $5.47 or $.34 per oz.
Savings: $5.28 or 2878% back in your pocket
Prep Time 2 minutes

1 cup salt
1/2 tablespoon lemon juice

Add lemon juice in small amounts at a time to make the consistency of paste, use more lemon juice if needed.

Gently rub the salt paste onto the rust stain, allow paste to remain on the stain for 10 minutes. If the stain remains add more of the paste and let sit for an additional 10 minutes. If the stain is still present, place in the sun for 5 minutes. Be cautious for sun can fade colors. Wash after the stain is removed.

Notes

This is another easy way to remove the rust stain from clothes. The acid from the lemon juice works really well to remove rust on just about anything. This is a really inexpensive and an effective remedy to remove rust.

A Touch of Sun Rust Remover

EASY! Yields: 6.66 oz.
Approximate cost: $.14 or less than $.14 per use
MSRP: $2.65 or $.34 per oz.
Savings: $2.51 or 1,792% back in your pocket
Prep Time 2 minutes

1/2 cup of vinegar
1/3 a cup of lemon juice

Mix vinegar and lemon juice together. Soak the stain with the mixture and gently rub the rust stain clean. You can also place in the sun to remove the stain. Wash as usual when the stain is gone.

Notes

Who would've thought that the science experiment of vinegar and baking soda would yield so many uses? Can you see the possibilities yet?

Spot and Stain Lifter

EASY! Yields: 32 oz.
Approximate cost: $.23 or less than $.007 an oz.
MSRP: $4.74 or $.15 per oz.
Savings: $4.51 or 1,960% back in your pocket
Prep Time 5 minutes

1 1/2 cups baking soda
1 1/2 cups water
1 cup white vinegar

Mix slowly in a large container to allow for the reaction of baking soda and vinegar. Spray on stain before washing.

Notes

Washing soda can be a bit harsh on the skin. It is best to use a pair of gloves to rub this into the stains. You can also “downsize” the recipe for smaller spots.

E Z Pre-Treat

EASY! Yields: 32 oz. or 4 loads
Approximate cost: $.29 or less than $.08 per load
MSRP: $4.97 or $.15 per load
Savings: $4.68 or 1,613% back in your pocket
Prep Time 2 minutes

1 cup washing soda
4 cups warm water

Make a paste. Use rubber gloves and gently rub paste into dampened stain. Wash as usual.

Notes

This will brighten your colors and whiten your whites as well as remove stains. For an all-over pre-soak, use this recipe.

Simple Soak

EASY! Yields: 128 oz.
Approximate cost: $.07 per gallon
MSRP: $7.98 or $.10 per oz.
Savings: $7.91 or 11,300% back in your pocket
Prep Time 2 minutes

2 tablespoons washing soda
1 gallon of warm water

Use cool water for non-colorfast items as well as for blood and egg stains.

Pre-soak in a small tub, soak for 30 minutes.

Notes

This recipe works very well to whiten whites or for cleaning summer play clothes. When we need a laundry booster, we use this. We fill my washing machine with water, stop the cycle and let sit. Simply restart the washer after a good soak.

Super Simple Soak

EASY! Yields: 12 oz.
Approximate cost: $.14 or $.14 per load
MSRP: $5.99 or $.24 per oz.
Savings: $5.85 or 4178% back in your pocket
Prep Time 2 minutes

1/4 cup washing soda
1 cup ammonia
1 tablespoon detergent

Add washing soda, ammonia and detergent in washing machine. Fill with water, add clothes, and let sit for 30 minutes before washing through a regular wash cycle.

Notes

This is great to have on hand when you are doing your laundry sorting. You can even recruit your children to spray it on their stained clothes when they remove them before bed. To really engage your children's help, personalize a label to match your child's interest to be a super stain blaster, much like a computer game. Let them blast their stains away and give mom a much deserved hand. For each new bottle or batch, raise their level of mastery. Caution: Make sure they don't hear your amusement as mom rules once more.

Stain Blaster

EASY! Yields: 32 oz.
Approximate cost: $.035 or less than $.001
MSRP: $5.37 or $.17 per oz.
Savings: $5.34 or 15,243% back in your pocket
Prep Time 5 minutes

2 teaspoons cream of tartar
2 teaspoons Borax™
3 squirts liquid hand dish washing soap
1 quart water

Combine all ingredients in a spray bottle. Spray the solution to lift the stubborn stain from the fabric and let stand for a few minutes before washing. Just like the commercial stain removers, check your stained item before putting the garment into the dryer to ensure the stain is gone. If it's not, repeat and rinse.

Notes

A very dear neighbor taught Dena to embroider, and her first project was on a shirt that became her very favorite. She accidently got crude oil from the oil wells on this shirt which left her very unhappy.

While doing the laundry I continued to pre treat but to no avail the stains were not going away. I learned this recipe or trick from my sweet grandmother many years ago.

Granddad used to get so many dirty oil stains on his clothes when he worked on his farm equipment. She explained this was how she got out the really dirty oil stains in his clothes.

Dirty Oil and Grease Stain Blaster

EASY! Yields: 24 oz.
Approximate cost: $.14
MSRP: $5.99 or $.24 per oz.
Savings: $5.85 or 4178% back in your pocket
Prep Time 2 minutes

1/4 cup washing soda
1 cup ammonia
3 squirts liquid dish soap or hand soap
1 1/2 cup water

Combine ingredients in a spray bottle. Spray on the stain, and let stand for a few minutes before washing. Just like the commercial stain removers, check your stained items before putting the garment into the dryer to ensure the stain is gone. If stain is still present repeat and rinse.

To Treat the Dirty Oil Stain: First rub the crude oil or dirty used car or engine oil with clean vegetable shortening. Let sit overnight, wash in the hottest water possible for the fabric and color. Remove the garment and do not dry for this might set the stain. (As strange as this may sound, the clean vegetable shortening seems to act as an emulsifier to lift out the soil from the oil. When washed all you have left is the oil stain, now treat as an oil stain to completely remove the stain.

Next, rub in liquid dish washing soap into the now plain oil or grease stain. After applying the liquid soap, let sit overnight.

Before rewashing the garment, treat with this stain remover. Before drying, check to see that the stain is completely gone. If any oil stain remains repeat the process with liquid soap, stain remover and rewash.

Notes

Laundry Hints

21st Century convenience at a 19th Century price

TO TREAT YOUR DINGY LAUNDRY FROM THE EFFECTS OF HARD WATER:

Add 20 Mule Team Borax™ to your laundry as a water conditioner if you have hard water. Add 1/2 cup of 20 Mule Team Borax™ along with regular detergent to get your laundry cleaner and smelling fresh.

To reverse the damage to your clothing due to washing in hard water, fill the washer with the hottest water that is safe for the fabric you are washing. Add four times the normal amount of detergent recommended and one cup of water conditioner (such as 20 Mule Team Borax™). Run the washer just enough to get the clothes wet, then stop the machine and let them soak for about twelve hours. Continue the wash cycle. After the cycle is complete, wash the clothes in the normal way and continue this process until the yellowing has disappeared.

Problems Associated with Hard Water

Hard water requires the need to use twice as much soap and shampoo, etc. for washing clothes, dishes and yourself. Hard water reduces soap's ability to lather and does not rinse well.

"Soap scum" builds up on bathtubs, sinks, dishes and your skin and hair.

Water hardness or lime scale builds up on faucets, inside pipes and water heaters, reducing their efficiency and operating life and in extreme cases even blocking them completely.

Minerals associated with hard water build up on clothing fibers, weakening them and dulling colors.

Lime scale builds up on dishes causing unsightly white coating or spots.

Minerals build up on hair and skin, causing dryness and sometimes irritation.

Don't use bleach, which can cause further yellowing of clothes when used in hard water.

Any perspiration stains and/or "rings around the collar" that cause yellowing or graying should be treated as soon as possible with a laundry pre-treatment.

Never use any of our cleaning methods on clothing or fabric that is dry clean only.

Adding a single, plain aspirin to each load of laundry will keep the whites from getting dingy.

Always check the tags on all clothing before undertaking any of these cleaning methods to make sure your clothes can tolerate the water temperatures, wash cycles and cleaning treatments recommended.

Ammonia Stain Remover

To brighten your whites and colors or to fight stains, use 1 cup ammonia in your laundry. You might need to reduce the amount of detergent by half.

Ring Around the Collar

A quick and inexpensive way to remove the ugly stain around collars is to dab on a little ammonia and wash as usual. Be sure to use in a well ventilated area.

Blanket Freshener

Give your cotton and wool blankets a fresher, fluffier, softer feel, and free of soap residue by adding 2 cups of white distilled vinegar to the rinse cycle of the wash.

Deodorant Stains

Lightly rub deodorant, and antiperspirant stains with white distilled vinegar, and launder as usual to remove the stains from your clothing.

Dingy Be Gone White Again

This method takes time and effort, but will help to turn even the dingiest whites white again.

Check the tags on your clothes to make sure they will tolerate hot water. If not, adjust the water temperature to suit your clothes.

Fill sink or container with hot water and add about 2 tablespoons of dish soap. Add clothes and soak for 15 minutes. Drain water and rinse clothes with warm water.

Refill sink or container with hot water and add 2 tablespoons clear ammonia. Add clothes and soak for 15 minutes. Drain water and rinse with warm water.

Refill sink or container with hot water and add about 2 tablespoons of white vinegar. Add clothes and soak for 15 minutes. Drain water and rinse in warm water.

Set the water temperature on your washer to hot (again, check the tags on your clothes to make sure hot is okay to use) and set to the appropriate wash cycle for your clothes.

Add laundry detergent to the empty wash tub and allow washer to fill. When washer is about 1/2 full, add the laundry booster if desired. When washer has filled, add clothes and wash as usual. Add vinegar to final rinse to remove all soap residues from clothes and as a fabric softener.

Try hanging your clothes to air dry in the sun instead of drying your clothes in the dryer. Hanging in the sun will aid in the whitening process.

PLEASE NOTE: The above cleaning method should be safe for most clothing, but there is always a risk of damage or discoloration when treating extremely delicate fabrics or garments.

Keep White Clothes White

Drop a non coated plain white generic aspirin tablet into a load of white laundry to help prevent them from yellowing with time, age and exposure.

Remove Blood, Perspiration and Urine Stains

Remove bloodstains from clothing by blotting stain with 3% hydrogen peroxide, rinse promptly with cold water to avoid bleaching the fabric. Rub out perspiration, blood and urine stains on clothing by dabbing the area with a half-strength solution of ammonia and water before laundering.

Freshening Up Baby Clothes

To freshen up baby clothes, add 1 cup of white distilled vinegar during the rinse cycle. The vinegar will naturally break down uric acid and the soapy residue leaving them soft and fresh.

Hems and Seams Needle Hole Removal

When you remove a hem or seam, the needle holes can be visible and left in the fabric. This can easily be removed by moistening a cloth with white distilled vinegar and placing the cloth under the fabric and ironing.

Keeping Colors Colorfast

Soak color fabrics that tend to run in white distilled vinegar prior to washing. Just a few minutes will do the trick.

Refresh Black Clothing

If you want or need to refresh your black garments here is a safe, easy, and inexpensive way. Add 2 cups strong coffee or tea to the final rinse. This should return them to their original dark black hue when new. To prevent future fading, wash in cold water and rinse with vinegar. Dry on low heat setting.

The Magic in the Final Rinsing

Your clothes will rinse better if you add 1 cup of white distilled vinegar to the last rinse water. The acid in vinegar is too mild to harm fabrics, but strong enough to dissolve the alkaline in soaps and detergents.

Wine Stains

Fast action is the key to wine stain removal. Stains on all cotton, cotton/polyester, and permanent press fabrics can be removed if treated in 24 hours or less. Sponge white distilled vinegar directly on the stain and rub to release the stain from the fabric. Clean by the approved care tag.

Scorch Marks

To remove a scorch mark from fabric, gently rub the scorch mark with white distilled vinegar. Wipe with a clean cloth. Wash as usual.

To Clean a Scorched Iron Surface

Heat equal parts white distilled vinegar and salt in a small pan. Rub solution on the cooled iron surface to remove dark or burned stains.

Unclog Steam Iron

Pour equal amounts of white distilled vinegar and water into the iron's water chamber. Turn iron on to steam and leave on for 5 minutes in an upright position. Unplug and allow iron to cool. The loose mineral deposits should come out when you empty the water chamber.

To Set Colors

When color dyeing, add 1 cupful of white distilled vinegar to the final rinse water to help set the color.

Shower curtains

Add 1 cup of white distilled vinegar to the rinse water when you launder your shower curtain. Do not spin dry or wring out. Hang immediately to dry.

Cleaning Vintage Lace

Soak the lace in cold water, rinsing it several times. Hand wash lace gently with a mild detergent. If rust spots are a problem, try removing them with a mixture of white vinegar and hot water.

Removing Coffee Stains

To remove coffee stains from fabric, simply dab the stain with glycerin. Lightly rub into the stain; follow by rinsing in cold water. Wash.

Dry Cleaning Alternatives

Clean Wool:

This includes wool, angora, and cashmere; gently hand wash in mild soap and warm water not more than 100 degrees Fahrenheit. As you rinse add 1/2 cup white distilled vinegar to the rinse water. Lay flat to dry and gently reshape garment. Do not dry wool in the sun.

Clean Silk:

Gently wash in warm water (see above) and a mild soap that has a neutral pH. Do not rub or scrub, handle the garment gently and swish in the soapy water. Do not dry in the sun. Iron on a low setting or steam garment with a steamer or hand in your steamy bathroom.

Clean Rayon:

Hand wash in cool water with a mild soap. Do not wring the garment when rinsing. Use your hands to press water out of the garment and hand to drip dry. Press to remove any wrinkles.

Chapter Three

Super Simple Quick General Cleaning

Every surface, we've got you covered.

"The University of California-Berkeley and Lawrence Berkeley National Laboratory analyzed 21 household cleaners and air fresheners and found that many -- especially those with pine, lemon or orange scents -- emit excessive levels of toxic pollutants. This is the first study to measure household cleaner emissions during typical indoor use, as well as the potential related health risks."

(Greensfelder, Liese. 2006, UNC Berkeley News)

The three most commonly used general household cleaning products:

Window Cleaner
32 oz.
MSRP $2.50 vs. Make It Yourself $.10
Savings $2.40 or 2,400%

Furniture Polish
32 oz.
MSRP $3.50 vs. Make It Yourself $.31
Savings $3.19 or 1,029%

Air Freshener
10 oz.
MSRP $2.82 vs. Make It Yourself $.03
Savings $2.79 or 9,300%

If you use the three examples here you could have a savings of $8.38 with a single purchase.

By using these recipes you can obviously see a significant savings.

Our recipes usually make more than the packaged products. For ease of comparisons, all illustrations are ounce per ounce cost comparisons. We realize this is an approximate cost and savings cost based upon your purchase price and quantities.

Making your own general cleaning products you could be spending as little as **$10.63.**

Buying retail for general cleaning, you could be spending as much as **$74.92.**

Buying eco-friendly products you could be spending up to **$185.56.**

Using the recipes in this chapter, you could be saving up to **$64.29 or 605%.**

Using eco-friendly products, you could be saving up to **$174.93 or 1,646%,** with these recipes.

These figures are based on a one time purchase of the many general cleaning products to meet all your needs.

What the manufacturers don't tell you is, you don't need all of their products for each different surface. Most cleaners will do many different jobs. This will result in more savings for you!

Household Chemical Information

Household cleaning products contain different classes of chemicals: solvents, for dirt removal or chemical delivery; surfactants, chemicals that remove dirt away from the surface; dyes, fragrances, brighteners, preservatives and an assortment of other inert ingredients.

Currently there is no regulatory requirement for companies to disclose the full ingredients of their cleaning products. Most companies opt to meet the most minimum disclosure requirements. The listing of one or two "active" ingredients leaves a great gap in public disclosure and makes the consumer unaware of the harsh chemicals they are bringing into their environment.

When you make your own cleaning agents, you know exactly what you are bringing into your home and what you are exposing to your family.

The ingredients we use are much safer for your family as well as the environment. The harshest chemical we use is ammonia. Ammonia needs to be used with care and caution. It is a naturally produced chemical which our environment needs.

U.S. Department of Health and Human Services, Public Health Service Agency for Toxic Substances and Disease Registry; "Ammonia is very important to plant, animal and human life. It is found in water, soil and air and is a source of much needed nitrogen for plants and animals. Most of the ammonia in the environment comes from the natural breakdown of manure, dead plants and animals.

Ammonia does not last very long in the environment. Because it is recycled naturally, nature has many ways of incorporating and transforming According to The Department of Health and Human Services, Agency ammonia. In soil or water, plants and microorganisms rapidly take up ammonia."(ATSDR 2011)

Air fresheners often provide pleasant smell associations, in order to disguise bad odors. Air fresheners are more than a spray in order to make our rooms smell pleasant. However, there are dangers in the use of air fresheners and tips for living without them.

When the chemicals emitted from the air-fresheners are combined with ozone, pollutants of serious health concern are produced. These include formaldehyde (a known human carcinogen and a respiratory irritant with a very low threshold for health effects) and ultrafine pollutant particles.

Cleaning today with all the products available and the numerous chemicals which they contain can produce a "toxic dump site" right in your own home!

You can replace these expensive products with cleaners you make right in your own home, for pennies. No more guessing about safety. There aren't any ingredients you don't know about. There isn't anything that you can't pronounce! Just good old cleaning practices passed down from the wisdom of women before us.

You will be amazed how quick, easy, and convenient this really is. You will be surprised just how much cleaner and fresher you home will be. Using these recipes is not only safer for your family they improve your indoor air quality and help protect the environment by the reduction of harsh and hidden toxic chemicals, one household at a time.

With ancestors from the Emerald Isle, our family is blessed with the "gift of gab" and the ability to think on our feet. When my children saw large amounts of vinegar and baking soda that now found residence in our home, they honestly thought that they had died and gone to science fair heaven! They had heard us talking and formulating the recipes, tweaking them to fit our needs and they began to get in on the act. I have personally cleaned up after hundreds of these child made volcanoes in nearly every room of the house. The only thing is it leaves the area cleaner and disinfected. I wish that the children would do these in areas that I designate as science experiment friendly though, i.e. the ones that need to be cleaned!

One experiment of theirs did not turn out so well, however. I have a guilty self indulgence; I buy myself expensive shampoos. I love how they make my hair soft and shiny. One night, after a particularly long day of mixing (and might I add a long disappearance of my little chemist children), I stepped into the shower and poured my nearly new bottle of shampoo into my hand. The faint scent of my cosmetic depilatory cream wafted upwards. I examined my shampoo and realized it had changed color, texture and scent. Quickly, I rinsed my hands, jumped out of the shower, dried off and examined the counter of my bathroom basin. Sure enough, there my bottle of depilatory cream was in the trash. My dear, young children had been experimenting! Thank goodness that I'd caught the scent of aloe and cucumber before it reached my head! Moral of the story: your children might catch the bug. Always make sure that your hair remover is nowhere near your expensive shampoo! The next day my little chemists-in-training took their piggy banks and replaced my shampoo!

Yes, you can save money by making your own recipes. When making your own general cleaning products, remember to always label your containers with the ingredients. If you add any chlorine bleach, dry or liquid, add a caution to avoid using with ammonia or vinegar.

CAUTION: NEVER USE AMMONIA WITH BLEACH OR PRODUCTS CONTAINING BLEACH AS IT CREATES A DEADLY CHLORINE GAS.

Air and Fabric Fresheners

"The National Resources Defense Council conducted a study "Clearing the Air: Hidden Hazards of Air Fresheners" and found several types of phthalates, chemicals that have been linked to reproductive Harm in many leading name brand Air fresheners."

National Resources Defense Council 2007

For a soothing and relaxing environment for sleep, make an air freshener with a little bit of lavender. (We personally use lemon–my family's favorite.) Spray it in your children's room after you tuck them in, making it "Sweet Dreams Spray" or "Monster Repellant." It is very calming. If your kids have a cold–put a few drops of eucalyptus and lemon or peppermint essential oils in 6-8 ounces of water and spray in their room. This will help them breathe at night. Experiment–you can do this!

Sunshine Fresh Air and Fabric Spray

EASY! Yields: 64 oz.
Approximate cost: $.63 or less than $.01 per oz.
MSRP: $16.50 or $.26 per oz.
Savings: $15.87 or 2,519% back in your pocket
Prep Time 2 minutes

2 cups fabric softener (can use homemade see Laundry section or really inexpensive brand)
2 cups baking soda
4 cups warm water
10–15 drops of essential oil optional

Pour in spray bottle and shake to mix and occasionally during use.

Notes

The baking soda will leave tiny white spots on wood furniture if you spray over or above the furniture as the mist dissipates in the air. I use this on the spots where my poodles like to lounge on my carpet. I like the alcohol in this mixture. It is my replacement for the pricey fabric freshener. I add lavender and vanilla to my mixture.

Fresh Breeze Spray

EASY! Yields: 40 oz.
Approximate cost: $.84 or $.02 per oz.
MSRP: $10.00 or $.25 per oz.
Savings: $9.16 or 1,090% back in your pocket
Prep Time 5 minutes

1 cup fabric softener
1 cup isopropyl alcohol
1 cup baking soda
2 cups water
10–15 drops of essential oil optional

Combine ingredients and pour into a spray bottle. Test on a hidden area before using. Shake often as you spray.

Notes

All-Purpose Cleaners

If we can't pronounce an ingredient listed on a cleaning product label, it doesn't belong in our home.

This is a great cleaner for every room of your house. It will clean walls quickly and easily. It's just a great overall cleaner.

A 1 All-Purpose Cleanser

EASY! Yields: 17 oz.
Approximate cost: $.02 or less than $.002 per oz.
MSRP: $3.98 or $.23 per oz.
Savings: $3.96 or 19,800% back in your pocket
Prep Time 5 minutes

1/2 teaspoon washing soda
2 teaspoons Borax™
1/2 teaspoon liquid soap or detergent
2 cups hot water

Add ingredients into a spray bottle. Add hot water last; this will dissolve the minerals. Shake to completely blend and dissolve.

Spray surface once or twice, wiping off the cleanser with a cloth. For tough dirt, leave the cleanser on for a few minutes before wiping off.

Shake the bottle each time before using. Label and store in a spray bottle.

Notes

This is also another great inexpensive cleaner. You can even use this to remove stains on your carpet or upholstery. Be sure to check for colorfastness in an inconspicuous place first.

Amazing All-Purpose Cleaner

EASY! Yields: 32 oz.
Approximate cost: $.06 or less than $.002 per oz.
MSRP: $2.37 or $.08 per oz.
Savings: $2.31 or 3,850% back in your pocket
Prep Time 2 minutes

2 teaspoons washing soda
4 cups hot water

Combine and pour in a spray bottle. Spray and wipe using as you would any commercial all-purpose cleaner.

Notes

There are many uses for this. This is one is one of our favorite recipes. We find that this covers most of our cleaning needs.

Mighty Clean

EXTREMELY EASY! Yields: 32 oz.
Approximate cost: $.04 or less than $.002 per oz.
MSRP: $4.32 $.14 per oz.
Savings: $4.28 or 10,700% back in your pocket
Prep Time 5 minutes

2 tablespoons clear, non-sudsy ammonia
2 tablespoons laundry detergent
4 cups water

Mix in spray bottle.

CAUTION: NEVER USE AMMONIA WITH BLEACH OR PRODUCTS CONTAINING BLEACH. A DEADLY GAS IS PRODUCED.

Notes

Chlorine bleach and its fumes bring about an instant headache for all the female members of our family. It has been a real challenge for us. Cleaning and disinfecting products presented problems, which meant that the man in the family had the task of any chore which involved chlorine bleach. These cleaning chores seemed to get put off until they were screaming for attention.

My husband took it upon himself to rid the girls of their suffering. He set out and bought about everything he could find without bleach to rid our homes of chlorine. Much money was spent, we ate less! Of course he had to open each and every product to test and try, meaning that not one could be returned for a refund. To my utter dismay, I looked at the labels and found that the ingredients which they all had in common were water and hydrogen peroxide. I was transported back in my memory to my grandmother and her widespread uses of hydrogen peroxide. Could it be that simple? Of course, the good news is no more headaches from chlorine fumes, the cleaning is more regular and we are saving money. The bad news: we lost the delegation of those tasks!

Completely Green Non Chlorine Bleach Cleaner

EASY! Yields: 132 oz.
Approximate cost: $.12 or $.03 per oz.
MSRP: $11.99 or $.09 per oz.
Savings: $11.01 or 9,992% back in your pocket
Prep Time 2 minutes

1/2 cup hydrogen peroxide
1 gallon water

Add to one gallon of water. Store and label well.

This mixture isn't considered a disinfectant cleaner, but it does clean great. Add essentials oils for disinfecting properties. Store the container away from any direct light.

Notes

This works very well to clean many surfaces in your kitchen. I even use this to clean and shine my counter tops. I love this one.

Glass, Chrome, and Ceramic Tile Cleanser

EASY! Yields: 16.5 oz.
Approximate cost: $.45 or less than $.03 per oz
MSRP: $3.58 or $.22 per oz.
Savings: $3.13 or 695% back in your pocket
Prep Time 2 minutes

1 cup rubbing isopropyl alcohol
1 cup water
1 tablespoon ammonia

Mix in a spray bottle. Use on windows, mirrors, chrome fixtures, shiny finish and hard-surface ceramic tiles.

Caution: NEVER USE AMMONIA WITH BLEACH OR PRODUCTS CONTAINING BLEACH. A DEADLY GAS IS PRODUCED.

Notes

Disinfectants

"There is a myth that a clean home is automatically a healthy home. Cleanliness in itself isn't bad, but the chemicals used in those cleaners can be deadly. The decision to stop using synthetic chemical cleaners is one of the most important ones you'll ever make for the health of your family and the safety of your home."

(Hollender, *Naturally Clean, 2006)*

This is so inexpensive and very easy to make. Use caution if you are using around cooking surfaces. Areas must be rinsed well whenever using Borax™.

Spray and Swipe Disinfectant

EASY! Yields: 128 oz. (1 gallon)
Approximate cost: $.16 or less than $.002 per oz.
MSRP: $9.48 or $.08 per oz.
Savings: $9.32 or 5,825% back in your pocket
Prep Time 2 minutes

1/2 cup Borax™
1 gallon water

Combine and pour in spray bottle.

Notes

This is the basically the same disinfectant cleaner as the Spray and Swipe recipe. By adding Essential Oils with disinfecting properties, you have added a safe fragrance to your disinfectant cleaner.

Disinfectant Spray

EASY! Yields: 32 oz.
Approximate cost: $.03 or less than $.001 per oz
MSRP: $2.16 or $.07 per oz.
Savings: $2.13 or 7,100% back in your pocket
Prep Time 5 minutes

4 teaspoons Borax™
4 cups very hot water
Essentials Oils Optional 10-15 drops

Pour in a spray bottle. Shake to blend.

Notes

This is one of our favorites. It does a great job cleaning almost everything you can think of. I even use this to spot clean my tile floor. Just spray on and wipe; no rinsing necessary. Use this cleaner to wash down your counters, especially if you have a stain. The ammonia removes stains beautifully.

Xtra Strength Multi-Purpose Disinfectant

EASY! Yields: 142 oz.
Approximate cost: $.24 or less than $.002 per oz.
MSRP: $26.95 or $.19 per oz.
Savings: $26.73 or 11,138% back in your pocket
Prep Time 5 minutes

1/4 cup baking soda
3/4 cup household ammonia
1/2 cup white vinegar
1 gallon water

Mix all ingredients. Pour in spray bottle.

Notes

This is so inexpensive and easy to use in your cleaning. I use this to clean the areas where my dogs eat, as well as all my kitchen surfaces.

Rapid Disinfectant Cleaner

EASY! Yields: 32 oz.
Approximate cost: $.59 or less than $.02 per oz
MSRP: $2.37 or $.08 per oz.
Savings: $1.78 or 302% back in your pocket
Prep Time 5 minutes

1 cup ammonia
1 cup isopropyl alcohol
2 cups water

Mix in spray bottle and shake. Spray on surfaces to disinfect. Wipe dry with a soft cloth or paper towel.

Notes

This is by far my favorite all around cleaner. If I had to use just one cleaner in my home, this would be the one I would make and use. Always remember to use a very large container and add the vinegar and baking soda first. There will be foaming when mixed. Add the additional ingredients after the mixture of vinegar and soda settle.

Speedy Disinfecting Cleaner

SUPER EASY! Yields: 148 oz.
Approximate cost: $.49 or $.003 per oz.
MSRP: $10.96 or $.08 per oz.
Savings: $10.47 or 2,136% back in your pocket
Prep Time 10 minutes

1/2 cup Borax™
1/2 cup white vinegar
1/2 cup ammonia
1 cup baking soda
1 gallon hot water

Mix the ingredients. Label and store, pour in spray bottle for convenience in cleaning.

CAUTION: NEVER USE AMMONIA WITH BLEACH OR PRODUCTS CONTAINING BLEACH AS IT CREATES A DEADLY CHLORINE GAS.

Notes

This is quick and inexpensive cleaning at its very best. Who would have ever thought this could be done so quick and easy with virtually no cost at all? Use on all phones, switch plates, household fixtures, and doorknobs. Help stop the spreading of all the germs, viruses and bacteria which threaten your family.

Mom's Best Friend Anti-Viral Disinfectant

EASY! Yields: 32 oz.
Approximate cost: $1.78 or $.06 per oz.
MSRP: $9.97 or $.32 per oz.
Savings: $8.19 or 694% back in your pocket
Prep Time 1 minute

32 oz. bottle of isopropyl alcohol

Pour into a spray bottle or find a sprayer that will fit on your alcohol bottle. Spray isopropyl alcohol on cloth and wipe down dirty phones, light switch plates, household fixtures and doorknobs.

The alcohol will not only kill the germs and remove the grime but will also leave a shiny surface.

Notes

Glass and Window Cleaners

There are products on the market today to clean every surface of your home. This adds up to an enormous expense. This only benefits the manufacturers.

We have heard from some of our clients that they just don't think that window cleaner will clean a window if it isn't the color blue. To that we can only say, use a few drops of blue food coloring.

As you will find, we have a few different window cleaning recipes. Make a small amount to begin with to determine which you like the best.

Crystal Clear Glass Cleaner

EASY! Yields: 16.5 oz.
Approximate cost: $.45 or less than $.03 per oz.
MSRP: $2.50 or $.15 per oz.
Savings: $2.05 or 455% back in your pocket
Prep Time 2 minutes

1 cup isopropyl alcohol
1 cup water
1 tablespoon white vinegar

Pour in spray bottle. Spray and wipe clean. Use on chrome fixtures and for a shiny finish on hard-surface ceramic tiles.

Notes

You might think this was printed a few pages back. The ingredients are the same, but the amounts are different. If you want less of a disinfectant scent this is the one you might want to use.

Brilliant Window Cleaner

EASY! Yields: 34 oz.
Approximate cost: $.17 or $.005 per oz.
MSRP: $2.50 or $.07 per oz.
Savings: $2.33 or 1,370% back in your pocket
Prep Time 2 minutes

3 cups water
1/2 cup vinegar
1/4 cup isopropyl alcohol

Pour in spray bottle. Spray and wipe clean. Use on chrome fixtures and for a shiny finish on hard-surface ceramic tiles.

Notes

This is a great cleaner for glass and ceramic tile. I will be honest, sometimes when I am in a hurry and want to quickly clean my tile floor, I spray this on the floor and do a very quick once over with a paper towel or the wet mop. I love this one.

Sparkle and Shine Window Cleaner

EASY! Yields: 140 oz.
Approximate cost: $.45 or less than $.003 per oz.
MSRP: $2.50 or $.07 per oz.
Savings: $2.05 or 455% back in your pocket
Prep Time 5 minutes

1/2 cup ammonia
1 cup white distilled vinegar
2 tablespoons cornstarch
1 gallon water

Mix together well and pour the solution into a spray bottle. Spray on the windows, then wipe with a warm water rinse. Now rub with a dry paper towel or lint-free cloth. Don't let the milky solution fool you. This will leave an incredible shine.

Caution: NEVER USE AMMONIA WITH BLEACH OR PRODUCTS CONTAINING BLEACH. A DEADLY GAS IS PRODUCED.

Notes

Be cautious with this around a gas stove. The alcohol is flammable. This recipe will leave a clean and shiny finish. To really get a great shine on your windows and to recycle, use an old newspaper to wipe clean, dry, and shine.

While traveling my husband and I stopped at a McDonald's early one morning, to our surprise they were shining their windows with yes, you guessed it, old newspaper.

Shiny Streak-Free Glass Cleaner

EASY! Yields: 16 oz.
Approximate cost: $.08 or $.005 per oz.
MSRP: $2.50 or $.07 per oz.
Savings: $2.42 or 3,025% back in your pocket
Prep Time 2 minutes

1 cup water
1 cup rubbing alcohol

Mix together in spray bottle. Spray on windows and mirrors for a streak-free shine.

Rubbing alcohol makes a fabulous inexpensive cleaner but it is considered extremely flammable.

Caution: DO NOT USE PRODUCTS CONTAINING ALCOHOL NEAR AN OPEN FLAME. LABEL AND STORE IN A COOL, DRY PLACE AWAY FROM ANYTHING THAT EMITS HEAT OR SPARKS. DO NOT TAKE INTERNALLY.

Notes

Cleaning windows the clear and streak free way is so simple. This window cleaner will clean just about any type of surface dirt on windows or glass.

Superb Streak-Free Window Cleaner

EASY! Yields: 48 oz.
Approximate cost: $.56 or $0.012 per oz.
MSRP: $3.36 or $.07 per oz.
Savings: $2.80 or 500% back in your pocket
Prep Time 1 minute

2 cups water
4 cups clear ammonia

Pour the ammonia and water into a bottle. Mix together and pour into a spray bottle. Spray and wipe clean with a clean soft cloth, paper towels, or newspaper.

Notes

Leather and Vinyl Cleaners

"Levels of air pollution inside the home can be two to five times higher (and occasionally 100 times higher) than outdoor levels."

Environmental Protection Agency, 2011

The cleaning of leather can be tricky since the cleaning methods or solutions may change the appearance or color of your leather. First, test your cleaning solution on a small unseen area before proceeding.

We asked a reputable leather furniture dealer about the best ways to clean and condition fine leather furniture. The most important advice we received, "Place leather furniture away from windows, exposure to direct sunlight is very harmful for leather." Next, leather should be cleaned and vacuumed weekly to keep their pores clean. Avoid using shoe polish, waxes and mink oil when cleaning leather garments or furniture.

Luxury Leather Cleaner

EASY! Yields: 34oz.
Approximate cost: $.07 or less than $.002 per oz.
MSRP: $11.99 or $.35 per oz.
Savings: $11.92 or 17,028% back in your pocket
Prep Time 2 minutes

1 quart warm to tepid water
1 tablespoon very mild, natural baby soap
1 or 2 drops of vinegar

Mix ingredients together and apply to a large cloth. Wring out cloth and apply evenly to surface of leather. Allow to air dry.

Notes

Remember to simply keep your leather items out of direct sunlight and wiping them down regularly with a damp cloth is a great way to avoid needing to use expensive products later on. To keep your leather products in top condition, they should be conditioned about every three months. Water soluble conditioners seem to be the best for finished leather, as the natural oils in leather do not usually dry out and adding oil to leather may cause damage over time. Leather is absorbent, which means that your leather furniture will absorb body oils or any spills that occur.

To keep your leather furniture in good condition and clean is easier than you might think. With regular cleaning and conditioning with little time and effort your leather needs can be met.

Do not use harsh soap or baby wipes for your leather furniture needs. These are too harsh and the salts may strip your leather of its natural finish and could damage it. This would bring about very costly repairs. Saddle soap is also too harsh for home use leather. Be cautious of the leather wipes available, they also can be harsh and are not good for everyday use.

Kid Glove Leather Conditioner

EASY! Yields: 18 oz.
Approximate cost: $2.60 $.14 per oz.
MSRP: $14.40 or $.80 per oz.
Savings: $11.80 or 453% back in your pocket
Prep Time 2 minutes

1 1/2 cups olive oil or vegetable oil
3/4 cup vinegar
Few drops of lemon oil optional

Mix ingredients. Saturate cloth and apply. Use a soft cloth to regularly wipe and buff your leather furniture. Store it in a bottle and shake well before use. Spray this mixture on the leather and wipe it with a soft cotton cloth to buff.

Notes

Vinyl upholstery and plastic will absorb most stains and dye from fabrics that bleed (such as blue jeans on white vinyl or bright prints) that may bleed.

Act at once to remove stains from vinyl. Use a soft white cloth or paper towel to remove as much of the stain as possible. If you use solvents, keep these away from wood or metal parts. When solvents other than water are used to remove a stain, wash the area with detergent and water, rinse and dry.

You can use a soft bristle brush for stubborn soil and stains. Rinse and dry. Be cautious, some household cleaners and solvents remove plasticizers from vinyl, making them brittle. Abrasive cleaners can scratch the smooth surface.

Sometimes letting the solution stand on surface and "soak" a few minutes can help to loosen the soil and stains.

Vivid Vinyl Cleaner

EASY! Yields: 32oz.
Approximate cost: $.21 or less than $.007 per oz.
MSRP: $17.99 or $.56 per oz.
Savings: $17.78 or 8,466% back in your pocket
Prep Time 2 minutes

2 cups water
2 cups white vinegar

Mix water and vinegar together, spray it on any vinyl, or plastic surfaces that need cleaning. Allow it to soak in. Then wipe dry with a clean cloth.

Notes

Vinyl conditioners will clean, shine, condition, and protect vinyl, rubber and plastic surfaces. They also deep clean dirt and grime to enhance appearance. The lemon scent will leave your room refreshed.

Vibrant Vinyl Conditioner

EASY! Yields: 36oz.
Approximate cost: $5.76 or less than $.16 per oz.
MSRP: $20.16 or $.56 per oz.
Savings: $14.40 or 2,500% back in your pocket
Prep Time 2 minutes

3 cups olive oil
1 1/2 cups lemon juice

Combine ingredients in a spray bottle. Use a clean soft cloth to wipe a small amount on any plastic or vinyl surfaces. Wipe off the excess with another cleaning cloth to buff to a shine.

Notes

Miscellaneous Household Needs

"Only a few hundred of the more than 80,000 chemicals in use in the United States have been tested for safety."

Nicholas D. Kristof, 2010

You can also try a solution of half rubbing alcohol and half water in place of the vinegar solution. I use both; I have learned that either one works really well.

I move all my silks to the porch and spray away. The porch looks like a beautiful garden, the alcohol keeps the insects away as I spray.

Silk Flower and Plant Cleaner

EASY! Yields: 32 oz.
Approximate cost: $.08 or $.025 per oz.
MSRP: $22.35 or $.70 per oz.
Savings: $22.27 or 10,542% back in your pocket
Prep Time 1 minute

2 cups rubbing alcohol
2 cups water
10 or 15 drops essential oils of your choice

Pour the ingredients into a spray bottle. Spray the silk plants or flowers until the mixture drips from the plant or flowers. The alcohol smell will evaporate as the plant dries. The alcohol aroma can be dissipated with a spray of essentials oil of your choice if it bothers you. Colorfastness is not usually a problem with the alcohol.

Notes

I just love flowers and my house is filled with many silk creations. My family teases me that the bees should take up residence. My one problem was cleaning the dust from the beautiful blooms and greenery.

My husband was so kind and purchased an aerosol cleaner from our craft store. I was alarmed at the price; even more than that, I was appalled when I read the label. The caution (stated that the ingredients listed known carcinogenic chemicals) was enough to send me to the craft store for a full refund! My flowers would just have to stay dusty if this was my only alternative. I began to think creatively and came up with the idea that alcohol would evaporate, so I gave this a try. To my great delight, none of my silks fell apart or lost their vibrant colors.

When I found out that vinegar might brighten my colors I tried vinegar, alcohol and water. I just love the results and the money I am saving, not to mention that we are not exposed to carcinogens in the interest of keeping my silks clean.

Fresh Scent Silk Flower and Plant Cleaner

EASY! Yields: 32 oz.
Approximate cost: $.21 or $.006 per oz.
MSRP: $22.35 or $.70 per oz.
Savings: $22.14 or 10,542% back in your pocket
Prep Time 1 minute

2 cups white vinegar
2 cups water

Pour the ingredients into a spray bottle. Spray the silk plants or flowers until the mixture drips. The vinegar smell will evaporate as the plant dries. Colorfastness is not usually a problem with vinegar. In fact, vinegar is sometimes used to set dyes in fabric.

Notes

My husband is a great fan of the anti-static spray. He has used so many cans of the stuff and it does work but it gives me such a headache. This has been a tremendous help for my headaches. I put in the lavender and vanilla scents. He prefers not to have this scent on his dress slacks, so we compromise. He has his bottle, and I have mine. The vinegar scent vanishes when it dries.

Cling No More Anti-Static Spray

EASY! Yields: 32 oz.
Approximate cost: $.06 or less than $.002 per oz.
MSRP: $18.50 or $.58 per oz.
Savings: $18.44 or 30,733% back in your pocket
Prep Time 2 minutes

2 cups white vinegar
2 cups warm water

This is a one to one ratio. Pour into spray bottle. Spray anywhere there is static. This can be spray directly on fabric, carpets, and clothes.

Do Not Use on Electronics.

Notes

My husband has a home office and is most diligent at writing on his dry erase board. The walls around his board were looking terrible with black dry erase dust everywhere. When you try to wipe it clean, it leaves a gray-black trail. This was one task that I thought, "If I just close the door, I don't have to look at it." Now all I use is the isopropyl alcohol in a spray bottle and use a clean cloth or paper towel to wipe clean.

Dry Erase Board Cleaner

EASY! Yields: 32 oz.
Approximate cost: $1.78 or $.06 per oz.
MSRP: $9.28 or $.30 per oz.
Savings: $7.50 or 421% back in your pocket
Prep Time 1 minute

Spray isopropyl alcohol on dry erase board. Wipe clean with paper towel or cloth.

Notes

Oh boy, do I like this! I really decorate my brick fireplace for the holidays. My bricks look so much better and it just sets off my lights and decorations. Try it, you will be amazed! You might not even know you have soot on your fireplace.

We have also used this to clean the bricks outside on our house. What a difference this made! This is a must for spring cleaning inside and out.

Brighter Bricks Soot Cleaner

EASY! Yields: 16 oz.
Approximate cost: $.07 or less than $.01 per oz.
MSRP: $7.00 or $.44 per oz.
Savings: $6.93 or 9,900% back in your pocket
Prep Time 2 minutes

2 tablespoons washing soda
2 cups hot water

Mix washing soda and water. Wash sooty areas with a sponge or cloth. Let dry and then rinse.

Notes

Wood Furniture Care

Furniture polish can contain petroleum distillates, known to be highly flammable. Petroleum distillates are also known to cause lung and skin cancer. Why would I want to even think of using something this hazardous, how about you?

This is a must have! No more hard scrubbing on my knees to clean my baseboards. I just spray, wipe, and crawl around the room. It is so quick and easy. I even get my granddaughters to help me and we race to the corner.

E Z Woodwork Cleaner

EASY! Yields: 142oz.
Approximate cost: $.24 or less than $.002 per oz
MSRP: $9.59 or $.07 per oz.
Savings: $9.35 or 3,896% back in your pocket
Prep Time 5 minutes

1 cup ammonia
1/2 cup white or cider vinegar
1/4 cup baking soda
1 gallon warm water

Ease the job of washing painted walls, woodwork, and blinds by using this mixture. Wipe this solution over walls or blinds with a sponge or cloth and rinse with clear water.

Dirt and grime comes off easily and the solution will not dull the painted finish or leave streaks.

Notes

This is another of my favorites. I have some cherished antiques and this is all I use. I have tried many commercial brands, but this beats them all for me.

Citrus Furniture Polish

EASY! Yields: 12 oz.
Approximate cost: $.31 or less than $.03 per oz.
MSRP: $3.50 or $.29 per oz.
Savings: $3.19 or 1,029% back in your pocket
Prep Time 2 minutes

1 cup olive oil
1/2 cup lemon juice

Mix vegetable or olive oil and lemon juice. Pour in spray bottle. Shake well and apply a small amount to a flannel or soft cleaning cloth.

Spread evenly over furniture surface. Use clean cloth to polish.

Notes

This is easy and inexpensive and will save you a ton of money. I have used the most expensive products made and I have had very good results with this. I no longer buy anything else to use.

Wood Furniture Water Mark Eraser

EASY! Yields: 22 oz.
Approximate cost: $.16 or less than $.01 per use
MSRP: $4.89 or $.23 per oz.
Savings: $4.73 or 2,956% back in your pocket
Prep Time 1 minute

2 cups salt
1/2 cup water

Or for a one-time use
1 tablespoon salt
Few drops water

Mix to form a paste. Gently rub the paste onto the ring with a soft cloth or sponge and work it over the spot until it's gone.

After the watermark is removed, restore the luster of your wood with the **Citrus Furniture Polish** recipe.

Notes

I personally have tried everything to restore some of my antiques. Since some of the water rings have been on some pieces for many years, it just takes time and patience to remove them. I wait a day and try something else until I get the deep stain removed. I think the vinegar works the best. It goes through all the layers of polish and wax buildup.

Mediterranean Water Mark Remover

EASY! Yield 22 oz.
Approximate cost: $2.39 or $.10 per oz.
MSRP: $4.89 for 22 oz. or $.23 or oz.
Savings: $2.50 or 105% back in your pocket
Prep Time 2 minutes

1 1/2 cups vinegar
1 1/2 cups olive oil

Use equal amounts of vinegar and olive oil. Rub with the grain and polish with a soft clean cloth.

Notes

This is so easy. I love to do this just before a special dinner or family meal. It is great for a glossy shine on your table but it also disinfects your tabletop. This also gives a clean scent, and no you will not think you are in the hospital. You can add a drop of essential oil to complement your dinner fragrances.

Shiny Bright Tabletops

EASY! Yields: 32 oz.
Approximate cost: $1.78 or $.06 per oz.
MSRP: $9.97 or $.32 per oz.
Savings: $8.19 or 694% back in your pocket
Prep Time 1 minute

For dust and dirt that collect on your tabletop, pour or spray isopropyl alcohol on a cloth and wipe area clean.

Not only will it clean your tabletop, it will also leave a great shine.

Caution: TEST INCONSPICUOUS SPOT FIRST, ALCOHOL MAY NOT BE SUITED FOR ALL TABLETOP FINISHES.

Notes

General Household Cleaning Hints

When was the last time your children asked to clean?

The recipes in this chapter can be used throughout your house. We do not believe that you need different cleaning products for each different room or cleaning task. Find what you like and use it, tweak it, and make it with your own personal preferences.

As strange as this might sound, the same cleaning paste to clean carpet, strip paint and remove wax is just this simple. Washing soda is used for these tasks, truly just amazing!

We had a small repair job on our house, the repair man got paint on our bricks. This was so easy to fix we simply made a mixture of our paste paint stripper and smeared over the paint splatters. My husband used a brush to remove the paint splatters, the only problem which remained was that the bricks involved looked cleaner and brighter than the rest of the house so, yep, he needed to clean the remaining bricks.

Paint Stripper

Make a thick paste of washing soda and water. Smear it on the problem area; let dry and then rinse.

Note that washing soda can peel wax off a floor and is often used as a paint stripper, so make sure the place being cleaned is inert.

Wax Remover

Make a thick paste of washing soda and water. Smear it on the problem area; let dry and then rinse.

Note that washing soda can peel wax off a floor and is often used as a paint stripper, so make sure the place being cleaned is inert.

Remove the Roughness on Wood

To restore wood furniture that has become dry and rough, simply crumple a brown paper bag and rub over the surface with lemon and olive oil furniture polish. This will sand the area to a smooth finish once again. You will get amazing results on ash, bamboo, cedar, cherry, mahogany, oak, painted wood, pine, teak, and veneers.

"Dry" Cleaning Silk Flowers and Plants

For plants that are not colorfast, you can try a "dry" cleaning method. Use a dryer fabric softener sheet to gently wipe your plants. The textured surface of the wipe helps to remove the dirt and leaves the plant with a fresh aroma. Or, fill a large grocery bag (I like to use the brown paper bags) with table salt. Place the plant inside the bag with the salt and shake firmly. The salt will dislodge any dust or dirt. Turn the plant upside down and gently shake any salt back into the bag. The salt can be reused for cleaning. I have never had any luck vacuuming the dust from my plants; I have ruined a few before I used my homemade mixtures.

Cleaning Leather

Use very sparingly. Start with a damp cloth and only a small amount of the solution. You do not want to saturate the leather with water and the soap can leave a residue. Place vinegar into the soap solution to prevent residue when dry. Make the amount of soap based upon the size of the stain. Start with a lesser amount of soap to determine the strength required to remove the soiled area.

Dampen a clean cloth with cleaning solution (never apply soap directly on the leather surface) using a small amount and wipe on stain. Blot to avoid saturating the leather. Use another clean dry cloth to remove the excess. Dampen the cloth with small amounts of water to remove the soap residue. Remembering to keep as much moisture or water off the leather. Leather does not absorb water, it only repels water.

Dry off the excess film residue and water from the leather as quickly as possible. Allow to air dry when all excess moisture has been removed with clean dry cloths.

Condition the leather after the cleaning. This ensures the replacement of the oils that were removed during the cleaning process. Use only natural oils to condition your leather. Use a clean soft cloth to apply small amounts of oil back into the leather using a circular motion. Be cautious not to over-oil, if the surface appears shinier that normal, there is oil standing on the surface and it will attract dirt and grime. If the leather has a darker appearance this is another indication of too much oil on the surface.

Simply wipe off the excess with a clean cloth.

Mildew Stain Remover

Mix one cup rubbing alcohol with one cup water. Dampen cloth with the mixture and wipe the affected stain. Allow to air dry, follow with leather conditioner.

Leather Ink Stain Remover

Spray hair spray on the ink stain. Use a soft clean cloth to wipe off the stain. Let air dry. Consult a professional if these methods do not remove the stain.

Grease Stain Remover

Blot grease stains with a clean soft cloth. Sprinkle cornstarch on the area. Allow the cornstarch to absorb the grease six hours before removing. Wipe with a clean cloth.

Gum Remover

To remove gum from leather, simply remove with a bag of ice cubes. Rub the ice cubes over the stuck-on gum. The gum will harden and can easily be peeled off. For any remaining residue, follow up with a blow dryer to warm the gum and remove with a clean cloth.

Salt Stain Remover

To remove a salt stain that appears on leather, make a solution of 3 parts white distilled vinegar to 1 part water. Apply a dampened clean soft cloth to the affected area and allow to air dry.

Olive oil or Vegetable Oil for Furniture Polish

This is safe for use on wood. Most commercial polishes and sprays contain silicone oil. Silicone oil can penetrate tiny cracks in furniture finish and enter the wood, causing problems in the event refinishing is needed. Lemon juice dissolves dirt and smudges, (see lemon section) while olive oil shines and protects the wood.

Chapter Four

I Can't Believe it's So Easy Floors and Carpets

Simple to make, safe to use, and savings you'll love!

"VOCs (*Volatile Organic Compounds*) are ground-water contaminants of concern because of very large environmental releases, human toxicity, and a tendency for some compounds to persist in and migrate with ground-water to drinking-water supply wells...Some VOCs may occur naturally in the environment, other compounds occur only as a result of manmade activities, and some compounds have both origins."

Zogorski and others, 2006 U.S. Geological Survey

"Many floor-maintenance products contain high levels of VOCs (Volatile Organic Compounds) that contribute to indoor air pollution. These greatly affect human health since most people spend up to 90% of their time indoors. VOCs can cause nose and lung irritation, rashes, headaches, nausea, and asthma."

Green Seals' 2004

The three most common carpet and
Floor care products:

Carpet Cleaner
192 oz.
MSRP $4.62 vs. Make It Yourself $.02
Savings: $12.27 or 4,231%

Floor Mop and Shine
32 oz.
MSRP $4.62 vs. Make It Yourself $.02
Savings $4.60 or 2,300%

Carpet Freshener
10 oz.
MSRP $1.92 vs. Make It Yourself $.36
Savings $1.56 or 433%

If you use the three examples here you could have a savings of $18.46 with a single purchase.

By using these recipes you can obviously see a significant savings.

Our recipes usually make more than the packaged products. For ease of comparisons, all illustrations are ounce per ounce cost comparisons. We realize this is an approximate cost and savings cost based upon your purchase price and quantities.

Making your own carpet and floor care products, you could be spending as little as **$11.17.**

Buying retail for carpet and floor care, you could be spending as much as **$69.05.**

Buying eco-friendly products you could be spending up to **$167.73.**

Using these recipes in this chapter, you could be saving up to **$57.88 or 518%.**

Using eco-friendly products you could be saving up to **$156.56 or 1402%,** with these recipes.

These figures are based on a one time purchase of the many carpet and floor care products to meet all your needs.

When making your own carpet and floor products remember to always label your containers with the ingredients. If you add any chlorine bleach, dry or liquid, add a caution to avoid using with ammonia or vinegar.

Carpet Cleaners and Fresheners

With the amount of time our loved ones spend on the carpet and furniture, it is so important to know the chemicals to which they are being exposed.

Having two poodles, my husband and I really liked to use the baking soda carpet freshener to keep our carpets fresh smelling. This became a bigger expense than we thought, but I really liked the lavender and vanilla scent. I needed to compromise, or so I thought. So we made our own. This works great and we aren't running to the store when we need it.

We kept the containers from our purchased brand so that we could easily apply our own. If you don't have a shaker container, you can use a glass jar or a plastic jar with a screw on lid. Take a nail and hammer to make holes in the lid.

If you are using a plastic lid, you might want to try to poke holes in the lid by using a small screw or nail from the back of the lid. File the rough plastic with an emery board or sandpaper to prevent injury from the plastic particles. Jelly jars also work very well!

Freshen Up Carpets

EASY! Yields: 56 oz.
Approximate cost: $.92 or less than $.02 per oz.
MSRP: $3.36 or $.06 per oz.
Savings: $2.44 or 265%
Prep Time 5 minutes

6 cups baking soda
1 cup cornstarch
10 to 15 drops essential oil of choice

Mix well place in an airtight container. Sprinkle generously on carpet. Leave for one hour before vacuuming.

Notes

I really like to use this recipe when my dogs have gotten into the mud outside. The salt helps absorb the earthy aroma as well. My favorite scent is the lavender vanilla.

Sweet Smelling Carpet Cleaner

EASY! Yields: 32 oz.
Approximate cost: $.36 or less than $.02 per oz.
MSRP: $1.92 or $.06 per oz.
Savings: $1.56 or 433%
Prep Time 5 minutes

3 1/2 cups baking soda
1/2 cup salt
10 to 15 drops essential oil of choice, optional

Sprinkle over carpets, (overnight works best). Vacuum up.

Salt absorbs the moisture; it is an abrasive and increases the effectiveness of lifting dirt during vacuuming.

Notes

This probably sounds too cheap to be true, but let me tell you of my experiment. A friend of Dena's dropped by for a visit and brought along her small child. A short time after the visit a trail of black crusty little spots on began appearing on the carpet (the baby bottle milk spots). Shampooing was the last thing she wanted to do.

The research and development kicked in. Wanting to know just how good vinegar would work, this seemed like the best way to find out. I used a small cloth, moistened with a small amount of vinegar and rubbed it into the spot. I was shocked. The entire black spot disappeared. I crawled around the floor taking the same trail as the darling little girl did and removed all the unsightly spots.

When Dena came home, she was mortified to find me crawling around on her carpet. But I'm no dummy. My granddaughters helped me clean with our experiment. Work is easier when it is an experiment and children love to experiment. So, yes, this works. And, no, your carpet will not smell like a salad when it dries. The vinegar smell dissipates as it dries.

The next amazing discovery, the spots did not reappear! Hurray!

Green and Clean for Steam Machines

EASY! Yields: 1 gallon
Approximate cost: $2.13 or less than $.02 per oz.
MSRP: $51.18 or $.40 per oz.
Savings: $49.05 or 2,302%
Prep Time 2 minutes

2 cups vinegar per 1 gallon water

Fill tank of carpet cleaner with very hot water. Add vinegar in the cleaning solution tank or in water tank.

You can also add 1/2 cup of Borax™ or washing soda to boost the cleaning process.

Notes

We like this recipe for a really deep cleaning. A word of caution: do not use more baking soda. It could clog your machine and make it very difficult to remove. Also if you use a baking soda carpet freshener, make sure you vacuum thoroughly before cleaning. Boy, will you be sorry if you don't!

Power Plus Steam Carpet Cleaner

EASY! Yields: 192 oz.
Approximate cost: $.29 or less than $.01 per oz.
MSRP: $76.80 or $.40 per oz.
Savings: $76.51 or 26,382%
Prep Time 20minutes

1/2 cup Borax™
1/2 cup white vinegar
1/2 cup ammonia
1 cup baking soda
1 gallon hot water

Before you trying this recipe, mix a very small amount of the ingredients together to test for color fading. Blot on in an inconspicuous area. Some dyes and fibers are not set as well as others and you could experience discoloration of the fabric, making the end result worse than the soiled area.

Mix all ingredients. Label with ingredients and store. Use as directed by any steam cleaner. This is a non-foaming formula.

Caution: NEVER USE AMMONIA WITH BLEACH OR PRODUCTS CONTAINING BLEACH. A DEADLY CHLORINE GAS IS PRODUCED.

Notes

As we previously mentioned, vinegar works really well for removing stains in carpet and upholstery. This works great if you want to have a stain remover on hand. Label, the bottle and you are ready to go.

All Natural Carpet Stain Lifter

EASY! Yields: 32 oz.
Approximate cost: $.21 or less than $.01 per oz.
MSRP: $9.99 or $.32 per oz.
Savings: $9.78 or 4,657%
Prep Time 2 minutes

2 cup white vinegar
2 cup water

Mix in a spray bottle. Spray directly on stain. Allow the mixture to sit on the stain for several minutes before cleaning the area with a brush or sponge. Use warm water. If you feel the absolute need to use soap, always rinse with a vinegar water solution to remove any soap residues. Label and store in a container.

Notes

This is a paste that is really easy and quick to use. The salt helps to release the dirt and works as an abrasive to lift the dirt out. I really like this when I have smeared in mud or deep stains from the pets.

Ultra Strong Carpet Cleaner

EASY! Yields: 6 oz.
Approximate cost: $.15 or less than $.03 per oz.
MSRP: $1.19 or $.20 per oz.
Savings: $1.04 or 693%
Prep Time 2 minutes

1/4 cup salt
1/4 cup Borax™
1/4 cup vinegar

Mix paste. Rub into carpet and leave for a few hours. Let dry completely. Vacuum carpet, this will refresh your carpet for a quick fresh cleaning.

Notes

Floor Care

"Annually, Americans spend over $1 billion on floor-care products."

Green Seals' Choose Green Report 2004

Now this is an easy and really inexpensive floor cleaner and the finish is really pleasing. I mix this in an empty gallon vinegar bottle. I then pour a small amount into a spray bottle labeled “floor cleaner” and spray on my floor as I mop. This makes a quick and easy cleaner without the need to mix in a bucket and mop. You can use the bucket and mop method for really big jobs or really heavy traffic areas if you are so inclined. The choice is yours; just know that this works really well.

Squeaky Clean Floors

EASY! Yields: 132 oz.
Approximate cost: $.06 or less than $.01 per oz.
MSRP: $23.60 or $.18 per oz.
Savings: $23. 54 or 39,233%
Prep Time 2 minutes

1/2 cup white vinegar
1 gallon water

Dip sponge mop in floor cleaning solution. Squeeze several times until mop is almost dry. Rinse mop frequently.

No need to rinse floors, but you may want to take a clean cloth or towel and dry the damp areas.

Notes

I used this on some old stains and it worked really well. My husband is amazed we don't need all the cleaning products advertized. We now skip the cleaning aisle at the store.

Super Strong and Simple Floor Cleaner

EASY! Yields: 128 oz.
Approximate cost: $2.13 or less than $.02 per use
MSRP: $22.88 or $.18 per oz.
Savings: $20.75 or 1074%

Apply full strength white vinegar directly to tough linoleum stains. Leave for 15 minutes.

For stubborn stains, sprinkle baking soda over vinegar, scrub with brush. Rinse clean with water.

Caution: DO NOT USE THIS SOLUTION ON YOUR WOOD FLOORS.

Notes

Notice that this recipe calls for one full cup of vinegar. This works great for all your non-wood floors such as non wax, vinyl and linoleum.

Again I use this as a spray cleaner for a quick mop job.

Clean and Shiny Finish

EASY! Yields: 128 oz.
Approximate cost: $.10 or less than $.01 per oz.
MSRP: $20.87 or $.16 per oz.
Savings: $20.77 or 20,770%
Prep Time 2 minutes

1 cup white vinegar
1 gallon water

Use one cup vinegar in a gallon of water. Mop as usual; no need to rinse. For a quick mop job add vinegar and water into a spray bottle for a quick mop and shine job.

Caution: DO NOT USE THIS SOLUTION ON YOUR WOOD FLOORS.

Notes

This is a simple, quick and easy way to clean your floor. It is pennies to use and you will be pleased with the results. I like this mixture with the disinfecting of the alcohol. I use this in the area where I feed and water the dogs as well as in my bathroom. I also use this after I have spilled food on the floor.

Disinfecting Floor Cleaner

EASY! Yields: 24 oz.
Approximate cost: $.45 or less than $.02 per oz.
MSRP: $4.27 or $.18 per oz.
Savings: $3.82 or 849%
Prep Time 2 minutes

1 cup vinegar
1 cup alcohol
1 cup water
3 drops liquid dish soap

Mix in spray bottle. Spray sparingly and mop.

Notes

Manufacturers of hardwood floors recommend the use of a neutral pH hardwood floor cleaner made especially for wood floors. Many times they recommend a specific brand cleaner, which can be very pricey considering what they contain. We did some research and found that the term neutral pH cleaner is nothing more than what we already were using. Once again we blindly believe what we are told for the profit of others at our own expense. A little scare here and a caution there and we are hooked by the cleaning industry.

This is so easy to make and the same results as the very pricey neutral pH cleaners. This cleaner will leave your floors clean and free of the residues that build up with harsh cleaners. Now you can effectively clean floors as recommended for just a few cents per cleaning.

Perfect Neutral pH Hardwood Floor Cleaner

EASY! Yields: 32 oz.
Approximate cost: $.18 or less than $.01 per oz.
MSRP: $5.12 or $.16 per oz.
Savings: $4.94 or 2,744%
Prep Time 2 minutes

2 cups hot water
1 cup baking soda
1 cup baby shampoo (neutral pH soap)

In a bowl add water, stir in the baby shampoo. Stir in the baking soda, to combine all ingredients. The baking soda will assist in both cleaning and deodorizing the floor, which is perfect for kitchen areas as well as homes that have pets.

Dip a mop in the solution, then remove from the bucket and wring out any excess water. Many floors can become water damaged from too much of a water application, so wringing out the mop is important.

Mop the floors as you normally would and go over the floors several times if there is a film coating from the use of previous cleaning products.

Let floors air dry, or go back over the floors with a dry mop to collect any excess water. This solution will clean, deodorize and leave a shine free of streaks or film, making for the perfect everyday floor cleaner.

You can also pour this cleaner into a spray bottle to use as a quick spray floor cleaner. This solution can also be used to clean countertops, cabinets and other household areas that should be cleaned with a mild cleanser.

Notes

Upholstery Cleaners

Don't go shopping for new furniture or slip covers just yet!

My beautiful poodles do not get on my furniture unless my husband allows them. I find he does that more than he wants to admit. When I walk into the room he then tells them to get down. The damage is already done! Cleaning the couch is no longer a time-intensive task. I just use this recipe to clean my upholstery.

One of our poodles loves to pose at the back of our couch. He looks very regal, but he does get it a little dingy looking. Now it is not a difficult time or a consuming task. I just spray on a little of this cleaner and wipe off with a clean cloth. He is in good graces once again.

Couch and Chair Saver

EASY! Yields: 28 oz.
Approximate cost: $.29 or less than $.02 per oz.
MSRP: $9.99 or $.36 per oz.
Savings: $9.70 or 3,345%
Prep Time 5 minutes

1/2 cup white vinegar
1/2 cup salt
1/2 cup Borax™
2 cups warm water

Use clean cloth. Wring out excess liquid. Press firmly and work back and forth over upholstery surface. Use special attention to the soiled areas such as arms and headrest. Blot dry with clean cloth. Let dry.

Notes

One of our little darlings found a black ball point pen and proceeded to express their artistic talents. To my great dismay, my upholstered white on white stripped dining room chairs were so badly marked the only choice was to send them out to be reupholstered. To make matters worse, my fabric was not available, new fabric had to be selected which meant all eight chairs had to be recovered. Before going to this expense I decided to try and remove the ink stain myself.

This worked so well with very little effort. I just could not believe my results. I am so glad I tried this.

Irked by Ink

EASY! Yields: 12 oz.
Approximate cost: $.07 or less than $.005 per oz.
MSRP: $2.82 or $.23 per oz.
Savings: $2.75 or 3,929%
Prep Time 5 minutes

1/2 cup ammonia
1/2 cup warm water
1/4 cup baking soda
1/4 cup hydrogen peroxide

Before you trying this recipe, mix a very small amount of the ingredients together to test for color fading. Blot on in an inconspicuous area. Some dyes and fibers are not set as well as others and you could experience discoloration of the fabric, making the end result worse than the soiled area.

Blot ink stains and heavily soiled areas with straight ammonia. Lightly rub the area to remove the ink. Mix the ammonia, baking soda and hydrogen peroxide together making a paste. Be cautious not to overly wet your fabric. Apply paste on the areas and allow drying. Ink needs to be rinsed out. Use small amounts of water to rinse out the ink by blotting.

Use clean cloth. Wring out excess liquid. Press firmly and work back and forth over upholstery surface. Use special attention to the soiled areas such as arms and headrest. Blot dry with clean cloth. Let dry.

Notes

Carpet and Floor Care Hints

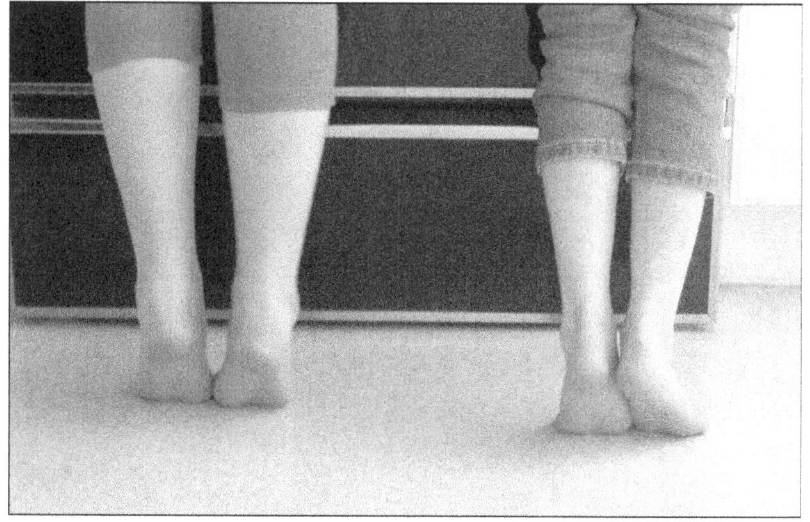

Clean and sweet down to your feet.

Carpets need to be vacuumed regularly. This will prevent the dirt falling down into the deep fibers making it harder to clean.

It is best not to use liquid carpet shampoo. It seems next to impossible to rinse out all the shampoo. Ever notice how quickly your carpets get really dirty shortly after shampooing? The soap residue stays in the carpet, attracting or pulling the dirt from shoes, all the under stains, dirt and soap seem to come to the top.

There is a cure for the older carpets with dried soap or shampoo residue. Use either a dry carpet cleaner or remove the soap residue with a few easy methods.

Rent a carpet shampoo machine which uses water. Mix 2 gallons of water and 1 cup white distilled vinegar. The vinegar will pull out the old left over soap and clean your carpets at the same time. It might take a few times of cleaning in this manner to remove the shampoo residue. Your carpets will be clean, soft and refreshed. The vinegar smell dissipates as it dries. Hot water activates soap. Always rinse with cold water and vinegar.

To remove stains in carpet, never rub the stain. Rubbing breaks down the fibers and will spread the stain, so blot, blot and blot! We have found that vinegar works very well in removing most stains. Pour a small amount on a soft cloth and blot the stain. Repeat as needed until the stain is lifted.

Heavy Duty Carpet Cleaner

Make a thick paste of washing soda and water. Smear it on the soiled area; let dry. Brush the dried paste to break up the residue into small pieces to for ease of vacuuming. This should do the trick. Use a clean cloth to remove any residue.

Note that washing soda can peel wax off a floor and is often used as a paint stripper, so make sure the place being cleaned is inert.

If you feel you must use a soap to remove a stain remember to always rinse with a vinegar and water solution to cut the soap residue. To remove red wine stains use club soda. This generally does the trick.

Red Dye Stain Remover

Removing red dye stains can be troublesome. Use a solution of 3 parts hydrogen peroxide to 7 parts water. Hydrogen peroxide is a bleach, test on an inconspicuous spot to test for color fastness. Blot on mixture and wait for 30 minutes. Blot up the moisture, rinse again with vinegar and water again by blotting method. If stain remains, increase the amount of hydrogen peroxide and allow the liquid to penetrate the stain longer, repeat as stated above.

Pet Stains and Odor Remover

To remove pet stains and odor, use a baking soda and hydrogen solution to remove the stains. Mix 3 parts peroxide to 7 parts water and add a teaspoon of baking soda. The baking soda will neutralize the odor and the peroxide will remove the stain. Blot up what you can with an old towel and rinse well with 1/2 cup vinegar per quart of water.

Remove Oily Spot Remover

To remove oily spots in your carpet try using rubbing alcohol. Blot on, blot off. Sometimes it just requires some massive action such as paint thinner. Again, blot on, blot off. This should remove the stain. Use a vinegar and water solution to rinse. Use caution with paint thinner, it is highly flammable. Use with well ventilation.

Ink Stain Remover

Before you try this tip, mix a very small amount of the ingredients together to test for color fading. Blot on in an inconspicuous area. Some dyes and fibers are not set as well as others and you could experience discoloration of the fabric, making the end result worse than the soiled area.

To remove ink in your carpet, try blotting with rubbing alcohol. You can also use the upholstery recipe by making a paste of baking soda, ammonia and peroxide. Leave on carpet until dry. Rinse with vinegar water. Blot up the moisture, if the stain is still present, repeat the process.

Remove Gum from Carpet

To remove gum, place ice cubes on gum and peel or chip off what you can with the bowl of a teaspoon. Try using a few drops of orange essential oils to remove the rest of the gum. Treat the oil stain as stated above.

Cleaning Hardwood Floors

Preventive Care: Dirt, Grit and Sand

The harshest thing for your hardwood floors is dirt, grit and sand. These act as sandpaper on the finish, causing scratches, dents and dulling. Whenever possible, place floor mats at entrances to trap dirt and prevent damage. Sweep floors regularly, but be certain your broom does not scratch your floors. Also, vacuum floors frequently to get the floors thoroughly clean. This will also assure cleaning the gaps between the planks where dust and dirt can be missed with broom sweeping. A vacuum cleaner with beater bars should not be used on hardwood floors it could potentially scratch and mar your floor.

Water and Liquid Spills

Always wipe up spills as they happen, standing liquid can damage the finish and can warp a poorly finished floor.

Hard Cleaners

It is best to avoid the use of oil soaps and hard cleaners. These soaps and cleaners can cause a buildup can be problematic when applying a maintenance coat on the floor.

They can build up and create problems when it's time to put a maintenance coat on the floor. Instead, use neutral pH soap cleaner. It is quite confusing to buy pH neutral soap when we don't even know what that really is. To put it really simply it is like a baby liquid soap, body wash or shampoo, a no tears product.

Ammonia

Do not use ammonia or ammonia products on your hardwood floors it will soften and whiten the surface.

Furniture

Always lift the furniture when moving, to avoid dragging anything on your floors. Felt contacts under the legs will help prevent scratches.

Damp Mopping

Some professionals recommend that you damp mop your hardwood floor and others cringe at the suggestion. Just remember, if your floor's finish is in good shape and mopping is done correctly, the water won't penetrate even the oil and wax finishes. You're cleaning the finish, not the wood, so don't use water if the finish is in poor shape.

Dents

Vacuum with a brush attachments, don't use vacuums with beater bars.

Dust Mop

Use a good dust mop, one that will pick up the dust and dirt not just spread it around.

Sun Damage

Avoid direct sun on your hardwood floors, they can discolor. Close curtains and blinds or add sheer drapes to protect from the sun's intense UV rays.

Sweep

Brooms with fine, exploded ends trap dust and grit effectively.

Vacuum

Canister vacuums with special bare floor attachments are the best way to get rid of all the dirt and dust.

Vinegar

Vinegar is often recommended to clean hardwood floors. Be cautious whenever using any liquid on hardwood floors. Too much liquid can cause your wood to warp.

Wax Buildup

We helped an elderly woman move and clean her home. The wax buildup on her kitchen floor was problematic. By making a thick paste and putting the paste in the corners of her linoleum floor the task was completed in no time and so little work involved.

Chapter Five

Quick and Convenient Make It Yourself

Safe enough to use around food, strong enough to kill nasty germs.

Kitchen Cleaners

The two challenges in the kitchen: toxic chemical cleaning products versus infectious bacteria. We think you should be able to meet all your cleaning needs without the added concern of hidden toxic chemicals.

The three most commonly used kitchen products:

Disinfectant Wipes
160 sheets
MSRP $10.72 vs. Make It Yourself $.97
Savings: $9.72 or 1,002%

Disinfectant Cleaner
32 oz.
MSRP $2.37 vs. Make It Yourself $.08
Savings $2.29 or 286%

Sanitizing Spray
23 oz.
MSRP $4.19 vs. Make It Yourself $.05
Savings $4.14 or 8,280%

If you use the three examples here you could have a savings of $16.15 with a single purchase.

By using these recipes you can obviously see a significant savings.

Our recipes usually make more than the packaged products. For ease of comparisons, all illustrations are ounce per ounce cost comparisons. We realize this is an approximate cost and savings cost based upon your purchase price and quantities.

Making your own kitchen cleaning products,
you could be spending as little as **$6.24.**

Buying retail for kitchen cleaning products, you could be spending as much as **$85.55.**

Buying eco-friendly products you could be spending up to **$217.07.**

Using the recipes in this chapter, you could be saving up to **$79.31 or 1,271%.**

Using eco-friendly products you could be saving up to **$210.83 or 3,378%,** with these recipes.

These figures are based on a one time purchase of the many kitchen cleaning products to meet all your needs.

"The EPA reported that the toxic chemicals found in every home are three times more likely to cause cancer than airborne pollutants outside."

Environmental Protection Agency 2010

When making your own kitchen cleaning products remember to always label your containers with all the ingredients. If you add any chlorine bleach, dry or liquid, add a caution to avoid using with ammonia or vinegar.

Air Fresheners

"Air fresheners interfere with a person's ability to smell the offensive odors by releasing a nerve-deadening agent or by coating the nasal passages with an undetectable film. Air fresheners are not regulated by the federal government and manufacturers are not required to list ingredients on the label. For these reasons, consumers should be wary of all air fresheners, even those that claim to be 'all-natural.'"

(Breyer, 2009, Healthy and Green Living)

Lemon, orange, lavender and vanilla essential oils make a great aroma for this air freshener. Experiment with your favorite fragrances. Shake often as you spray. This refreshes the air all over your house.

Sinus Safe Air Freshener

EASY! Yields: 34oz.
Approximate cost: $.09 or $.003 per oz.
MSRP: $8.46 or $.25 per oz.
Savings: $9.27 or 3,090% back in your pocket
Prep Time 2 minutes

2 teaspoons baking soda
2 tablespoons white vinegar
4 cups water
10/15 drops essential oil of choice

Combine in a spray bottle mix, after foaming stops put on the lid shake, before using.

Notes

Okay, it is honesty time! I began to smell something that was terribly wrong in my kitchen. Just certain that it had to be dog related, (after all the smell was coming from the area where they ate). I made my husband shampoo the poodles. He kept telling me it was not them, but my nose just knew it had to be. Clean dogs, still smelly kitchen.

My next guess (yikes!) did I have a dead mouse somewhere, no it couldn't be just one it had to be an entire army with the assaulting stench. The search was on. I would have waited for my husband, but I had a friend coming over. Great, I have rotting mice, my kitchen reeks, but my dogs are clean. No good, she will certainly notice the vile aroma. Well at least I might not need to worry about serving refreshments, no one could think of eating in my house with this smell.

Good news, it wasn't an army of mice, bad news it was a bag of potatoes gone terribly wrong. To my great dismay, I forgot that I had left a bag of potatoes in the cabinet. Now this wasn't one of those quick and easy cleanups this was the entire bag turned to liquid mush. We won't be eating any potatoes in the near future.

The smell seemed to be coming out of everywhere, once I opened this cabinet. At this point, I'm ready to just sell the house and move, or better yet start a fire in the kitchen someone else would have to clean this mess. Oh was the smell foul! Now I had to tackle the horrific odor. I sprayed on all my different homemade fresheners, there was a little change but nothing was totally removing the smell. I finally poured straight baking soda in the bottom of the cabinet. This neutralized the spot, but didn't remove the odor in the air.

During all this clean up mess, my granddaughters come over and saw the baking soda out. That is all it takes for them to get these very creative ideas about a vinegar and baking soda volcano experiment. I had more important things to do but the grandmother kicked in and I gave in to their wishes.

We made a high powered volcano! We had so much fun adding more vinegar and baking soda that we exploded all over the kitchen sink. We forgot just how much it stunk in the kitchen and kept up the heavy lava flowing. More vinegar, more baking soda, more overflowing, the girls were having such a good time as we made up all kinds of stories as the lava flowed. To our amazement the odor vanished. We decided to leave our volcano in the sink continuing to working in our favor!

Isn't it amazing how the simplest of things work really well? The dogs are clean, the cabinet has been sanitized, the air is fresh, the cleanup was easy, and I spent time with my granddaughters.

I used apple cider vinegar instead of white distilled vinegar for this adventure. I had an abundance of the apple cider and thought it was for fun not cleaning. I don't know if the apple cider vinegar made any difference or not. However as much fun as I have experimenting and tweaking our recipes, this stands without future testing. Research and development is finished on this one! If anyone has the unfortunate need to try this and uses white distilled vinegar let us know how it works!

Serious Odor Eliminator

EASY! Yields: 32oz.
Approximate cost: $.60 or $.02 per oz.
MSRP: $ $8.46 or $.26 per oz.
Savings: $7.86 or 1,311% back in your pocket

1 cup baking soda
32 oz. apple cider vinegar

Place jar or bowl in the sink and pour vinegar and baking soda slowly. Leave in sink to freshen the air. When finished and the air is clean pour down the drain to clean and freshen your pipes. Follow up by running a lot of water down the drain.

Notes

Dishes and Dishwasher Needs

Did you know that many cleaning product manufacturers do not disclose ingredients (some of which are highly toxic) on product labels?

Women's Voices, 2010.

We want the confidence that the products we purchase are completely safe for our family and homes. Upon research we have discovered that this may not always be the case. One such case is dishwasher detergent.

Dry chlorine is usually present in most dishwasher detergents which become activated when dissolved in water. Steam releases chlorine fumes into the air, from the dishwasher which may cause eye irritation and difficulty breathing. There is another chemical that may be contained in dishwasher detergents called quarternium 15. This is an eye and skin irritant and an allergen which can release carcinogenic formaldehyde. Also be aware of the artificial fragrances and dyes that are commonly used ingredients, which may also present health risks.

This has really bothered us because this is a source of potentially harmful chemicals we were not able to remove from our homes. We have been working on this recipe for many months now trying to get just the right mixture.

Super Simple Dishwasher Detergent

EASY! Yields: 16 oz. 32 loads
Approximate cost: $1.56 or less than $.05 per load
MSRP: $9.60 or $.30 per load
Savings: $8.04 or 515% back in your pocket

1/2 cup Borax™
1/2 cup washing soda
1/2 cup citric acid or 12 packages of lemon unsweetened Kool Aid.
1/2 cup kosher salt
*1/4 to 1/2 cup of baking soda

*For hard water, add 1/4 to 1/2 cup baking soda per batch.

Add all ingredients in an air tight container. (I use my old tub from former dishwashing detergent.) Secure the lid and shake to mix up all the ingredients. The citric acid will cause the mixture to be clumpy not a problem, just stir to mix.

Use 1 tablespoon per load.

Citric acid might be in the canning section of your grocery store or can be purchased online.

If you do not use the citric acid you may experience a cloudy residue on your dishes and glassware.

Use vinegar in the rinse cycle.

Notes

After much research and many different combinations we have the right mixture. You will love the savings not to mention removing the chemical exposures to your family and home.

This recipe uses table salt and baking soda. If you have hard water this could be the one for you.

Citrus Dishwasher Detergent

EASY! Yields: 20 oz. or 40 loads
Approximate cost: $.63 or less than $.02 per load
MSRP: $9.60 or $.30 per load
Savings: $8.97 or 1,423% back in your pocket

1 cup Borax™
1 cup baking soda
1/4 cup salt
1/4 cup citric acid*
30 drops a citrus essential oil

(You can use: lemon, grapefruit, orange, tangerine, or a combination mixture of your choosing.)

Mix in a plastic container with a firmly fitting lid, shake to mix.

Use vinegar in your rinse dispenser.

*You can substitute two packets of lemonade unsweetened flavored Kool-Aid, USE ONLY lemon, or you will dye your dishwasher

For cloudy glassware, use more citric acid or lemonade Kool Aid packets until the desired results.

Notes

This is a must for a rinsing agent in your dishwasher. This will remove of the cloudy residue left on your glasses. Glasses and dishes come out beautifully clean. Try this. It does work and is very inexpensive. No more high priced rinsing agent needed for spot free glassware. This does not replace dishwashing detergent.

Dazzling Dry Dishwasher Rinse Aid

EASY! Yields: 4 oz.
Approximate cost: $.05 per use
MSRP: $4.99 per use
Savings: $ 4.95 or 9,900% back in your pocket
Prep Time 1 minute

White distilled vinegar

Pour distilled white vinegar into the dishwasher rinsing agent dispenser.

Notes

Oh, the dreaded job of scouring those unsightly pans! Not a problem anymore, simple, so easy and no more scrubbing with steel wool, splinters and horrible fingernails. This is easy, I just love this trick!

Green Grime Grabber

EASY! Yields: 32 oz.
Approximate cost: $.68 or $.02 per oz.
MSRP: $2.78 or $.09 per oz.
Savings: $2.10 or 309% back in your pocket
Prep Time 2 minutes

1 cup washing soda
4 cups water

Fill a sink or pail with washing soda and hot water to cover the pans.

Soak the pans overnight. Rinse and dry.

Notes

Disinfecting and Sanitizing

"Nearly 100 volatile organic compounds were emitted from…six products, and none were listed on any product label. Plus, five of the six products emitted one or more carcinogenic 'hazardous air pollutants,' which are considered by the Environmental Protection Agency to have no safe exposure level."

(Steinemann, 2008)

We go through this stuff like crazy. This is great to use any time anywhere. I prefer the lavender and vanilla essential oils scent. To me, it is so much more pleasing than the tea tree oil. Lemon essential oil is also a disinfectant and has a great aroma.

Simple Sanitizing Spray

EASY! Yields: 23 oz.
Approximate cost: $.05
MSRP: $7.99 or $.35 per oz.
Savings: $7.04 or 2,269% back in your pocket
Prep Time 2 minutes

2 1/2 teaspoons hydrogen peroxide
8 drops of tea tree oil or other disinfectant essential oil

Pour 21 oz. water in 22 oz. spray bottle. Add hydrogen peroxide and essential oil. Mix. Spray in the air or on surfaces to sanitize.

Notes

Okay, we love to use the handy wipes to clean just about everything around our home, but the cost was outweighing the convenience. Not a worry any longer. We just make our own and it is so easy. Don't be intimidated to try this. You can do this and you will be really happy with your results. Baby-wipe containers work great to make and store your wipes. We use peroxide for making our home chlorine bleach free. This is the wipe we use in the kitchen and the bathroom.

Why Didn't I Know This Before Wipes

EASY! Yields: 162 sheets
Approximate cost: $1.05 or $.0065 per sheet
MSRP: $10.32 or $.06 per sheet
Savings: $9.27 or 883% back in your pocket
Prep Time 10 minutes

1/2 roll Bounty™ paper towels (different brands do not have the strength and will fall apart)
2 1/2 cups water
1/4 cup hydrogen peroxide

With serrated or electric knife, cut Bounty™ in half as if to resemble two rolls of toilet tissue. Place cut side down in airtight container. Boil water. Add bleach or peroxide. Pour over paper towels. Remove wet cardboard tube. Pull out wipes one at a time from center.

Notes

We make this with the other half of the paper towels when we make the above recipe. It is so quick and easy. A must have for quick clean ups. This is a **D**elightfully **D**iscounted **D**isinfectant wipes recipe at its best, so we named it accordingly.

3 D Wipes

EASY! Yields: 162 sheets
Approximate cost: $1.00 or $.0061 per sheet
MSRP: $10.32 or $.06 per sheet
Savings: $9.27 or 883% back in your pocket
Prep Time 10 minutes

1/2 cup disinfectant cleaner from General Cleaning Chapter
1 1/2 cups of water
1 roll Bounty™ paper towels

With serrated or electric knife, cut Bounty™ in half as if to resemble two rolls of toilet tissue. Place cut side down in airtight container. Boil water. Add bleach or peroxide. Pour over paper towels. Remove wet cardboard tube. Pull out wipes one at a time from center.

Use essential oils for fragrance, antibacterial, antiviral and antifungal properties. 10-15 drops of tea tree, lavender, lemon, orange, or grapefruit also work very well.

Notes

Metal Polishes

Protecting fine metals has never been easier without all the risks of hidden toxic chemicals.

I do not like to clean my metals. This has been a job that my husband would do for me. The chore assignment has changed now that I have found this recipe. He helps, but I don't mind doing it now. This is easy and I don't get the chemical headaches from this mixture.

Brass, Copper, and Pewter Cleaner

EASY! Yields: 16 oz.
Approximate cost: $.18 or less than $.02 per oz.
MSRP: $5.38 or $.34 per oz.
Savings: $5.20 or 2,888% back in your pocket
Prep Time 2 minutes

1 cup salt
1 cup vinegar

Make a paste. Use a small amount of cleaner on soft cloth. Rub the metal to clean, rinse and dry. Brass, copper pots and pewter will look new again.

Notes

Ugh, it was time to polish the silver for the holiday dinners. This once was a long and time consuming job with my nails and hands ending up looking such a mess. I do love the shiny silver pieces on the holiday table and this paste makes things much easier.

All Natural Silver Polish

EASY! Yields: 20 oz.
Approximate cost: $.16 or less than $.01 per oz.
MSRP: $9.48 or $.47 per oz.
Savings: $9.32 or 20,000% back in your pocket
Prep Time 2 minutes

2 cups baking soda

Add water to make a paste, rub on with soft cloth. Wash with soap, rinse with water and shine.

Notes

This isn't nearly the work of the silver polishes I have used in the past and the cost is certainly much less.

Citrus Silver Cleaning Paste and Polish

EASY! Yields: 16 oz.
Approximate cost: $.32 or $.02 per oz.
MSRP: $6.40 or $.40 per oz.
Savings: $6.08 or 1,900% back in your pocket
Prep Time 2 minutes

1 cup lemon juice
Salt to make paste

Add water to make a paste, rub on with soft cloth. Wash with soap, rinse with water and shine.

Notes

The aluminum foil trick is amazing. Try it. You will be pleased with your results. If you have really tarnished silver, it might take more time soaking and a little help with a rub here and there.

Too Good to Be True Silver Cleaner

SUPER EASY! Yields: 32 oz.
Approximate cost: $.12 or less than $.01 per oz.
MSRP: $12.80 or $.40 per oz.
Savings: $ 12.68 or 10,566% back in your pocket
Prep Time 2 minutes

1 quart water
1 tablespoon baking soda
1 tablespoon salt

Mix all ingredients together. Line a pan with aluminum foil. Place pieces in the aluminum foil covered pan. Soak 10–20 minutes. Wash with soap. Rinse with water and dry well.

Notes

Uniquely Kitchen

"Consumers have a right to know if they are spraying their child's high chairs with toxic chemicals. Without full ingredient disclosure from these companies, there's simply no way to be sure."

Erin Switalski, 2010

This is so quick and easy to make. You can add essential oils for disinfecting. No rinsing needed.

Spotless Surface Cleaner

EASY! Yields: 32 oz.
Approximate cost: $.11 less than $.003 per oz.
MSRP: $2.37 or $.08 per oz.
Savings: $2.26 or 2,054% back in your pocket
Prep Time 2 minutes

2 cups warm water
2 cups white vinegar or lemon juice
2 teaspoons salt

Pour all ingredients in a spray bottle, let the salt dissolve. Spray on your counter tops to clean.

Notes

We just have to love the cost of making this cleanser. Use this on your counter tops and sink. You can also use this to clean your tub, tile and shower. The best part is: no grit! Wiping up is quick and easy.

Sponge and Scour

EASY! Yields: 24 oz.
Approximate cost: $.02 or less than $.002 per oz
MSRP: $.96 or $.005 per oz.
Savings: $.94 or 4,700% back in your pocket
Prep Time 2 minutes

2 cups baking soda
1/2 cup liquid detergent
1/2 cup white distilled vinegar

Mix baking soda and detergent. Add just enough white distilled vinegar to make a thick but creamy texture.

Notes

This is easy and inexpensive. You will love the results and the money you save.

Automatic Coffee Maker Cleaner

EASY! Yields: 16 oz.
Approximate cost: $.44 or less than $.03 per oz.
MSRP: $3.29 or $.20 per oz.
Savings: $2.85 or 647% back in your pocket
Prep Time 2 minutes

White distilled vinegar

To dissolve mineral deposits from hard water that collect in automatic drip coffee makers, fill the reservoir with white distilled vinegar and run it through a brewing cycle. Rinse thoroughly with water, when the cycle is finished.

To clean the stains from the coffee pot simply make a paste or the soft scrub using baking soda and water to the desired consistency. Use a clean soft cloth or a clean sponge and clean the stains with the soft scrub. If the stains are burned on, allow the pot to soak overnight in a baking soda solution to remove the stains. If additional cleaning is needed, use Borax™ as a soft scrub to remove any residue.

Notes

My husband had a meal go terribly wrong in our microwave. He exploded food, which included eggs, all over the inside and the door. The caked on food disaster was beyond words. He wanted to throw out the microwave and go buy a new one, before I came home.

Knowing how cheap I am, he knew I would never go for the expenditure. He decided he had to tackle the crispy dried explosive food mess on his own. Bless his heart he was trying his best to clean up his mess, but he was having a terrible time. "Do you know how hard it is to clean the inside of a microwave," he asked, when I arrived home.

I showed him a trick that he uses most regularly now. This works well, my husband can attest to this one! (I also reminded him he still hasn't read our book.)

Easy Microwave Cleaner

EASY! Yields: 16 oz.
Approximate cost: $.06 or less than $.004 per oz.
MSRP: $8.00 or $.67 per oz.
Savings: $7.94 or 13,233% back in your pocket
Prep Time 2 minutes

1/4 cup of white distilled vinegar
11/2 cups of water

Boil a solution of vinegar and water in the microwave approximately 2–3 minutes. This will loosen splattered on food and deodorize. Simply wipe clean.

Notes

Of course we all know that orange and lemon rinds work great in the garbage disposal to freshen your sink, disposal and the air. I don't have lemon or orange rinds and I have a smelly drain. Not to worry. Vinegar is certainly your best friend here.

No More Stinky Sink

EASY! Yields: 8 oz.
Approximate cost: $.11 or less than $.02 per oz.
MSRP: $2.68 or $.34 per oz.
Savings $ 2.57 or 2,336% back in your pocket
Prep Time 2 minutes

1 cup white distilled vinegar

Pour down the drain once a week. Let stand 30 minutes and then flush with cold water.

Notes

This is so easy and quick. No need to rinse. I use a spray bottle for a quick cleaning job, just spray and wipe clean. I don't mind cleaning out the refrigerator!

Simple and Green Refrigerator Cleaner

EASY! Yields: 16 oz.
Approximate cost: $.11 or $.007 per oz.
MSRP: $6.99 or $.44 per oz.
Savings: $6.88 or 6,255% back in your pocket
Prep Time 2 minutes

1 cup white distilled vinegar
1 cup water

Wash with a solution of equal parts water and vinegar. Kills bacteria, molds and also disinfects. This will remove bacteria and odors from inside the refrigerator as well as outside the refrigerator.

Notes

Don't be fooled into thinking you need another product to clean your stainless steel appliances. This is so inexpensive you probably have everything you need right in your cabinet. Give it a try.

Soft Scrubbing Stainless Steel Cleaner

EASY! Yields: 18 oz.
Approximate cost: $.19 or less than $.02 per oz.
MSRP: $6.79 or $.38 per oz.
Savings: $6.60 or 3,474% back in your pocket
Prep Time 2 minutes

2 cups baking soda
Liquid dish soap

Add liquid soap to make a "frosting texture." Smear soft scrub on counters and appliances. Scrub clean.

Rinse well with water. For an added shine and a high polished finish, rub down the surface with white vinegar. Store in an air tight container, a frosting container works great.

Notes

We like to use our juicer yet we always stain our counters. This was once a great source of concern; and a reluctance to eat healthier food, but not any longer. Now it is so easy to remove the fruit stains. Ammonia also works really well. I sometimes just spray on my homemade window cleaner with ammonia and wipe clean. The stains disappear.

Natural Nonabrasive Cleaner

EASY! Yields: 21 oz.
Approximate cost: $.67 or $.03 per oz.
MSRP: $2.78 or $.13 per oz.
Savings: $2.11 or 314% back in your pocket
Prep Time 2 minutes

1/2 cup white distilled vinegar
1/2 teaspoon cream of tartar
1 1/2 cups baking soda
1/2 cup ammonia

Mix vinegar and cream of tartar in a small dish Apply with cleaning cloth or scrub brush and let it sit for 5-10 minutes. Scrub area with cleanser. Wash with hot soapy water. Rinse well.

Notes

I have built-in cutting boards under my counters. My husband is great about helping in the kitchen, but he forgets to clean the cutting boards. This is always around the time I bake bread and need the cutting boards. I pull them out and I am greeted with a strong onion aroma. This is no longer a problem. Vinegar comes to the rescue once again. I have learned to check the cutting boards before I begin my baking.

I keep a spray bottle filled with vinegar in my kitchen for many uses.

Cutting Board Cleaner and Sanitizer

EASY! Yields: 32 oz.
Approximate cost: $.22 or less than $.01 per oz
MSRP: $9.95 or $.31 per oz.
Savings: $9.73or 4,422% back in your pocket
Prep Time 1 minute

White distilled vinegar

Wipe with full strength vinegar. Let dry.

Notes

You may want to use gloves when cleaning with hydrogen peroxide. This not only kills the bacteria on your counters but also on your cutting board. This is so inexpensive and safe for all areas in your kitchen.

Antibacterial Cutting Board Cleaner

EASY! Yields: 32oz.
Approximate cost: $.48 or less than $.02 per oz.
MSRP: $9.95 or $.31 per oz.
Savings: $9.47 or 1,972% back in your pocket
Prep Time 2 minutes

3% hydrogen peroxide

Use full strength peroxide. Apply to clean cloth and wipe down counter tops and cutting boards to help kill salmonella and other bacteria. Use gloves to protect your skin.

Notes

This is a must have in your kitchen. With all the news about e-Coli on fresh produce, all fresh produce that comes into my kitchen gets a fresh spray as soon as it is removed from the bag.

Using hydrogen peroxide to decontaminate produce is a quick and easy way to protect foods that are or might be infected with strains of e-Coli or salmonella.

Simply Safe Fruit and Veggie Spray

EASY! Yields: 8 oz.
Approximate cost: $.12 or less than $.002 per oz
MSRP: $7.99 or $.99 per oz.
Savings: $7.87 or 6,559% back in your pocket
Prep Time 2 minutes

1/2 cup 3% hydrogen peroxide
1/2 cup water

Mix in a spray bottle. Spray and rinse well. Mist with mild vinegar water mixture.

Notes

I use the wash for fresh fruits and leafy vegetables. You will be amazed how well this works and how confident you will feel feeding fresh produce to your family without the high cost of a fruit and vegetable wash you purchase from the store.

A spray or wash with hydrogen peroxide and a mist of vinegar decontaminates all fruits that are or might be infected with strains of e-Coli and salmonella.

Fabulously Frugal Fruit Wash

EASY! Yields: 8 oz.
Approximate cost: $.24 or $.03 per oz.
MSRP: $7.99 or $.99 per oz.
Savings: $7.75 or 3,229% back in your pocket
Prep Time 2 minutes

1/4 cup 3% hydrogen peroxide

Use a peroxide wash to help kill bacteria such as e-Coli on fruits and vegetables. Fill sink with cold water, add peroxide and immerse produce. Rinse with cold water and drain. As an added benefit by removing bacteria, you will also help keep fruit and vegetables fresher longer.

Follow with a mist of a mild acetic acid (vinegar) and water mixture.

Notes

Kitchen Hints

Sparkling clean and green surfaces without hidden toxic chemicals.

Baking Soda in the Kitchen

Barbecues

Clean with a thick paste of vinegar and baking soda. Use with a scrub brush to loosen grease, dirt and grime on the interior and the exterior of your grill!

Bread Box

To remove the stale or moldy smell from your bread box, wipe inside with baking soda and water for a great fresh, clean scent.

Burnt Food on Pans

To easily remove burnt food from pans, simply sprinkle with baking soda and add hot water. Let soak an hour. The odor will disappear and the burnt on food will loosen.

Cast Iron Pans

To remove rust spots from the cast iron pans, make a thick paste of vinegar and baking soda. Scrub with dish cloth and then rinse with hot soapy water.

Dishwasher

To clean out your dishwasher and get rid of any sour smells, use a gallon of hot water, a cup of baking soda and a cup of vinegar. Run your dishwasher through a short wash cycle. This will break down all hard water stains and leave your dishwasher fresh smelling.

Food Processors and Blenders

For cleaning stains and foods from your blender or food processor use a cup of baking soda and a cup of hot water. Turn on the kitchen appliance. The baking soda cuts through grease in your processor. Simply rinsing with hot water will leave your appliance spot free.

Glassware Coffee Stain Remover

To remove the stains on glasses and coffee cups, make a thick paste of baking soda and water. Rub with a soft cloth and rinse clean.

Grease

To aid with the removal of greasy food on dishes and cookware, add a half-cup of baking soda to hot soapy water when you are washing dishes. The baking soda will break up the grease quickly and easily.

Greasy Stoves

Clean up a greasy stove or any greasy area by using one teaspoons of baking soda, one teaspoons of dish soap and 32 oz. of hot water. The cleanup will be quick and easy because the baking soda will break up the grease fast.

Microwave Cleaner

Wipe down the inside of your microwave with a water and baking soda paste. This will get stubborn stains out while deodorizing at the same time. For really heavy splattered food, you might want to try to place a bowl of hot water in your microwave. Bring to boil. Remove bowl and wipe down with the water and baking soda mixture.

Pans

To remove the stains from the pots and pans use a little sprinkling of baking soda on a wet cloth or sponge.

Caution: DO NOT USE THIS METHOD ON NON-STICK PANS OR YOU COULD HARM THE FINISH OF YOUR PANS.

Plastic Containers

To clean plastic containers, use a thick paste of baking soda and vinegar. This will help deodorize, while it takes out messy crusty foods.

Rubber Gloves

Sprinkle a little baking soda inside your rubber gloves each time you are finished using them. This will allow a smooth slide on with ease for the next use and it will keep them fresh smelling when your hands sweat.

Scuff Marks

For scuff marks on your tile, linoleum, or on your concrete floors, use a thin paste of baking soda and water. Rub with a soft cloth. Be cautious, the thicker the paste, the stronger and harder scrubbing power. For easily scratched floors use less baking soda in the paste.

Steel Wool Pads

To prevent the steel wool pads from rusting, simply store steel wool in a container with baking soda.

Stove Top

Lifting up the top of your stove, you will most likely find a cooked-on mess. Wet this area with a dish cloth and sprinkle baking soda over the entire area, making a paste. Let this sit about half an hour and then wipe up the mess quickly and easily. This also works for glass top stoves.

White Vinegar in the Kitchen

Clean Can Opener

To clean the food and grime from the wheel of a can opener use white distilled vinegar and scrub with a brush or use an old toothbrush.

Clean Exhaust Fan

To clean grease off the exhaust fan, wipe down the grids or blades with a sponge or soft cloth soaked in white distilled vinegar. You can also use this to wipe the grease from the inside of your oven, or anywhere grease collects.

Clean Sponges and Dish Cloths

Soak sponges and dish cloths in enough water to cover them, add 1/4 cup white distilled vinegar. Soak overnight to renew and refresh.

For Cloudy Glassware

Use full strength white distilled vinegar and soak either the paper towels or a cloth and wrap around the inside and outside of the glass. If you have a number of cloudy glasses, pour full strength white vinegar in your sink and place glassware in sink to soak. Rinse and dry.

Prevent Etching from Good Glassware

Wash glassware, spray with full-strength white distilled vinegar. Give the glasses a hot water rinse before letting them dry or drying them with a towel.

Removing Dark Stains in Aluminum Cookware

Use 1 cup white distilled vinegar and 1 cup hot water. Boil the mixture to remove the stains.

Notes

Chapter Six

Green and Clean in the Bathroom

Tough enough to clean this room, gentle enough for children.

The three most commonly used bathroom cleaning products:

Bathroom Cleanser
32 oz.
MSRP $3.74 vs. Make It Yourself $.04
Savings: $3.70 or 9,250%

Shower Tub and Tile Cleaner
32 oz.
MSRP $3.17 vs. Make It Yourself $.10
Savings $3.07 or 3,070%

Toilet Bowl Cleaner
32 oz.
MSRP $4.97 vs. Make It Yourself $.24
Savings $4.73 or 1,970%

If you use the three examples here you could have a savings of $11.50 with a single purchase.

By using these recipes you can obviously see a significant savings.

Our recipes usually make more than the packaged products. For ease of comparisons, all illustrations are ounce per ounce cost comparisons. We realize this is an approximate cost and savings cost based upon your purchase price and quantities.

Making your own bathroom cleaning products, you could be spending as little as **$7.16.**

Buying retail for bathroom cleaning products, you could be spending as much as **$90.24.**

Buying eco-friendly products you could be spending up to **$166.19.**

Using the recipes in this chapter, you can be saving up to **$83.08.**

Using eco-friendly products you could be saving up to **$159.03,** with these recipes.

These figures are based on a one time purchase of the many bathroom cleaning products to meet all your needs.

According to OSHA, "884 toxic substances were identified in a list of 2,983 chemicals used in the fragrance industry as capable of causing breathing difficulty, allergic reactions, multiple chemical sensitivities, and other serious maladies, including neurotoxicity."

The National Institute of Occupational Safety and Health

(OSHA) 2011

All-Purpose Bathroom Cleaners

When making your own bathroom cleaning products remember to always label your containers with the ingredients. If you add any chlorine bleach, dry or liquid, add a caution to avoid using any ammonia or vinegar.

This removes water deposit stains in the shower, on bathroom chrome fixtures, windows and bathroom mirrors. This cleans and shines bathrooms without the chemicals or harsh fumes. We love this cleaner.

Ceiling to Floor Bathroom Cleaner

EASY! Yields: 68 oz.
Approximate cost: $0.09 or less than $.002 per oz.
MSRP: $11.90 or $.18 per oz.
Savings: $11.81 or 13,122% back in your pocket
Prep Time 3 minutes

1/4 cup baking soda or 2 teaspoons Borax ™
64 oz. (half gallon) water
1/2 cup vinegar

Mix 4 cups water with baking soda. In a gallon container add the remaining 4 cups water and baking soda mixture. Slowly add the vinegar to the gallon container to reduce the amount of fizzing. Store and label with list of ingredients.

Notes

Use this as a disinfectant spray on the toilet seat and around the toilet. This is quick, easy and inexpensive to use.

Darn Good Disinfecting Bathroom Cleaner

EASY! Yields: 32 oz.
Approximate cost: $.24 or less than $.01 per oz.
MSRP: $4.99 or $.16 per oz.
Savings: $4.75 or 1,979% back in your pocket
Prep Time 2 minutes

16 oz. 3% hydrogen peroxide
16 oz. water

Pour in spray bottle. Use as a bathroom and toilet disinfectant and cleaner.

Notes

When we were first married, my husband took on the job of scouring out the bath tub for me. This was so kind and loving of him, but the grit was never completely rinsed out when I would take a hot relaxing bath. Yuck! I learned quickly I needed something else to give him to clean the tub. We started using laundry detergent as a scouring powder. It cost more but it rinsed much better than the grit of the scouring powder. Now we use baking soda, it is much cheaper, works great and the tub sparkles.

Honeymoon Promise

EASY! Yields: 28 oz.
Approximate cost: $.28 or $.01per oz.
MSRP: $2.78 or $.10 per oz.
Savings: $2.50 or 892% back in your pocket
Prep Time 1 minute

3 1/2 cups baking soda or Borax™

Sprinkle directly on a wet cloth or sponge. Wipe on, wipe off. Rinse well. This works great to clean tubs, showers, sinks and counters without the grit of scouring powder.

Notes

This recipe refreshes the air all over your house. Air fresheners interfere with a person's ability to smell offensive odors by releasing a nerve-deadening agent or by coating the nasal passages with an undetectable film. Air fresheners are not regulated by the federal government and manufacturers are not required to list ingredients on the label. For these reasons, consumers should be wary of all air fresheners, even those that claim to be "all-natural."

Purifying Bathroom Air Freshener

EASY! Yields: 34 oz.
Approximate cost: $0.04 or $.001
MSRP: $4.00 or $ .21 per oz.
Savings: $3.96 or 9,900% back in your pocket
Prep Time 2 minutes

4 teaspoons baking soda
4 tablespoons white distilled vinegar
4 cups water

Mix ingredients. Shake well before and during use, or spray into the air. Add a few drops of essential oil: lavender, lemon, orange, or vanilla if desired.

Notes

Bathtub, Shower, Tile, and Grout Cleaners

This is a great way to reduce the chemicals your family may be exposed to.

This is easy at its best! Children can even do this chore. After each bath, give your bathtub the vinegar and soda wipe down. This is so simple to do and you will never have a buildup of soap scum. Your bathtub will be sparkling clean all the time.

Bathtub Film Away

EASY! Yields: 16oz.
Approximate cost: $0.18 or $.01 per oz.
MSRP: $3.50 or $.18 per oz.
Savings: $3.32 or 1,844% back in your pocket
Prep Time 1 minute

1 cup white distilled vinegar
1 cup baking soda

To remove bathtub film, wipe tub with full strength vinegar then with baking soda. Rinse clean with water.

Notes

Save a bottled water bottle and fill with vinegar. Place in shower with a cleaning sponge. This works very well on maintaining the stubborn deposits of hard water on those glass shower doors. After your shower, squirt vinegar on the sponge and wipe down your shower door and walls. It is as easy as pie, and you have a clean and spot-free shower. Another chore completed and marked off the "to do list."

Shiny Shower

EASY! Yields: 32 oz.
Approximate cost: $0.42 or $.01 per oz.
MSRP: $3.17 or $.10 per oz.
Savings: $2.75 or 654% back in your pocket
Prep Time 1 minute

White distilled vinegar

Rub down shower doors with a sponge soaked in white vinegar to remove soap residue.

Notes

Another use for vinegar that is so quick and easy to use. I have a spray bottle just for this use in my bathroom. After each shower we spray down the tiles preventing the need for a heavy cleaning. Once again it is vinegar to the rescue to make these cleaning jobs effortless.

Cinderella's Dream Ceramic Tile Cleaner

EASY! Yields: 130oz.
Approximate cost: $0.04 for 130 oz.
MSRP: $22.75 for 130 oz. or $.18 per oz.
Savings: $22.71 or 56,775% back in your pocket
Prep Time 2 minutes

1/4 cup white vinegar
1 gallon water

Pour vinegar into a gallon bottle. Fill with water. Spray and wipe. This solution removes most dirt without scrubbing and doesn't leave a film. Increase amount of vinegar if needed for extra scummy tile.

Notes

This cleaner is just as effective as using chlorine bleach cleaners, and you won't have the harsh smell, or the dangers of bleach. Not to mention the safety features of removing chlorine bleach in our environment. I found a sprayer top that fits the bottle of the hydrogen peroxide bottle. I just spray down the shower after showering.

Grubby Grout Cleaner

EASY! Yields: 32 oz.
Approximate cost: $0.98 or less than $.03 per oz.
MSRP: $3.17 or $.10 per oz
Savings: $2.19 or 224% back in your pocket
Prep Time 1 minute

32 oz. bottle of hydrogen peroxide

Pour in spray bottle, spray and rinse. If stained, allow to dry about 1 hour, then rinse or pour on wet sponge or cloth (use gloves) wipe on grout lines, rinse.

Notes

Mineral Deposit and Drain Cleaners

This is so easy, simple and inexpensive, vinegar the miracle solvent.

My husband hates to do plumbing jobs, almost more than anything else! He claims even the most minor of jobs always ends up out in the street. When those unfortunate times become a necessity we all wish we were someplace else.

A bathroom sink faucet failed to release any water when it was turned on. Being cheap, I considered the options of calling a plumber or telling my husband. The cheap side won. I reluctantly told him that another plumbing problem needed his attention. After his two second appraisal, he informed me a plumber needed to be called. He didn't have the time or the inclination to do this project.

This brought a great dilemma; I didn't want to pay the high charges of a plumber. Since there wasn't a leak anywhere I felt that this could be resolved without a costly house call. I removed the screen from the end of the faucet and quickly saw the problem. The metal ring screen was filled with mineral deposits from the hard water. I used simple vinegar and within 24 hours, the problem was resolved.

My husband admitted he could have fixed the problem; he just didn't want to start a plumbing job that exposed his granddaughters to a whole new vocabulary.

Mineral Deposit Zapper

EASY! Yields: 28 oz.
Approximate cost: $.49 or less than $0.02 per oz.
MSRP: $4.96 or $.18 per oz.
Savings: $4.47 or 912% back in your pocket
Prep Time 2 minutes

White vinegar:

Soak a cloth or paper towel with vinegar. Wrap it around the faucet. You can leave it on overnight. A baggie can also be filled with vinegar and rubber banded to the faucet.

Rinse and polish.

Notes

This works so great and you don't have to use the costly mineral cleaner for calcium, lime and rust remover.

Shower Head Mineral Deposits Dissolver

EASY! Yields: 4 oz.
Approximate cost: $0.49 or less than $.02 per oz.
MSRP: $4.96 or less than $.18 per oz.
Savings: $4.47 or 912% back in your pocket
Prep Time 2 minutes

1/4 to 1/2 cup white vinegar

Pour vinegar in a plastic food storage bag. Secure the bag to the showerhead with a rubber band. Soak for 2 hours or overnight. Rinse and buff the fixture to a shiny finish.

Notes

The bubbling volcano of baking soda and vinegar does work in your drain without the damage to your clothes or skin if spilled. We really like this. I can do a little preventative plumbing and save my husband some plumbing frustrations. As an added benefit, the drains are freshened and smell so nice.

Volcanic Drain Cleaner

EASY! Yields: 16 oz.
Approximate cost: $0.18 or $.01 per oz.
MSRP: $5.79 or $.34 per oz.
Savings: $5.61 or 3,116% back in your pocket
Prep Time 3 minutes

1 cup baking soda
1 cup of vinegar

To unclog a drain, or just want to help keep the drains clear, pour baking soda down the drain followed by the vinegar. Wait 15 minutes before running water down the drain. Follow up by pouring hot water down the drain.

Notes

This solution has saved us a great deal of plumbing expense. We have an older home and the build up in the pipes causes us the need for regular plumbing repairs. Since we have been using this mixture, our plumbing needs have greatly been reduced.

Simply Salt Drain Cleaner

EASY! Yields: 48 oz.
Approximate cost: $0.06 or less than $.01
MSRP: $12.00 or $.25 per oz.
Savings: $11.94 or 19,900% back in your pocket
Prep Time 2 minutes

1/2 cup salt
48 oz. hot water

Mix salt and hot water. Pour the strong salt brine down the sink drain regularly to eliminate odors and keep grease from building up. No chemicals needed. This can be used at any time.

Notes

Mold and Mildew Eliminators

People who live or work in buildings that are exposed to moisture and not adequately ventilated are more at risk of illnesses caused by mold. Populations at particular risk include: infants and children, elderly persons, immune compromised patients and people with existing respiratory conditions, such as allergies and asthma.

To have a really clean and shiny bathroom, just make a trip to the kitchen. All you need is right at your fingertips without the high cost of specialty cleaners. This works great on mold, mildew, grout, stainless steel and chrome.

Mold and Mildew Terminator

EASY! Yields: 32 oz.
Approximate cost: $1.16 or less than $.04 per oz.
MSRP: $5.69 or $.18 per oz.
Savings: $4.53 or 391% back in your pocket
Prep Time 2 minutes

2 teaspoons cream of tartar
1 cup white vinegar
1 cup baking soda
1 cup salt
1 cup washing soda

To remove mold and mildew from tile grout, combine equal amounts of cream of tartar with vinegar for a tough, toxin-free cleaning solution. The amount needed varies as to the area that needs to cover the affected area.

For a milder solution, combine one part cream of tartar with half the amount of vinegar or water until you create a paste.

Rub the compound over the stain, scrub with a brush in a circular motion.

Also use the cream of tartar and vinegar solution on chrome or stainless steel without leaving those acid stains you see when using regular bleach.

Notes

Spray and rinse. It's as easy as that. If you have stubborn mold, let sit for a while to bleach clean.

No Scrubbing Mold Killer

EASY! Yields: 24 oz.
Approximate cost: $0.12 or $.005 per oz.
MSRP: $3.82 or $.12 per oz.
Savings: $3.70 or 3,083% back in your pocket
Prep Time 2 minutes

2 cups water
1 cup 3% hydrogen peroxide

Mix in a spray bottle. Spray on bathroom tile.

Be cautious with the application; as it will bleach painted items.

Notes

Hydrogen peroxide loses its effectiveness if it is exposed to sunlight so it is important to keep in a dark bottle. I found a sprayer lid that fits onto my hydrogen peroxide brown bottle. When you can reuse product bottles not only are you recycling, you are saving yourself more money.

Mold and Mildew Blaster

EASY! Yields: 16 oz.
Approximate cost: $0.35 or $.02 per oz.
MSRP: $3.82 or $.12 per oz.
Savings: $3.47 or 991% back in your pocket
Prep Time 3 minutes

1 cup hydrogen peroxide
1 cup white vinegar
2 tablespoons baking soda

Mix ingredients in a large container and store in a dark spray bottle. **Be careful when mixing, as this will foam up.** This can also be used on clothes to remove mold and mildew.

Notes

(Ahem) Toilet Cleaners

"One of the most dangerous activities you can do in your home is to clean your toilet bowl!"

Ken Duggan, 2010

A few years ago, I was cleaning my toilet bowl and I accidently splashed some of the cleanser in my eye. After the treatment for a bad eye infection, I started looking for a replacement. I found that my replacement to traditional toilet cleanser was in my kitchen. No more harsh chemicals to spill or splash. This is safe and easy to use.

Toilet Bowl Non-Chemical Cleaner

EASY! Yields: 32 oz.
Approximate cost: $.08 or less than $.03 per use
MSRP: $4.97 or $1.25 per use
Savings: $4.89 or 1,250% back in your pocket
Prep Time 1 minute

1 cup white vinegar

Pour in toilet undiluted. Let it stand for 5 minutes. Flush.

Notes

Your toilet will be clean, disinfected and shiny once again. This is just too easy to do. Try this little trick, before you leave the house, pour Borax™ in your toilet. Also if you are going away on vacation, pour Borax™ in your toilets. You come home to a fresh and clean bathroom.

Disinfecting Toilet Bowl Cleaner

EASY! Yields: 24 oz.
Approximate cost: $ .48 or $0.02 per 2 oz. use
MSRP: $2.97 or $.12 per oz
Savings: $2.49 or 519% back in your pocket
Prep Time 1 minute

1/4 cup Borax™

For regular toilet bowl cleaning, pour in Borax™. Scrub with bowl brush. Flush. This is a quick and easy cleaning job finished with ease.

Notes

Use this for a stubborn mineral ring around your in your toilet bowl. This recipe works really well and no harsh chemicals are needed.

Ring Around the Bowl Cleaner

EASY! Yields: 28 oz.
Approximate cost: $.39 or less than $0.02 per oz.
MSRP: $4.96 or $.18 per oz.
Savings: $4.57 or 1,172% back in your pocket
Prep Time 1 minute

1/2 cup baking soda
1/2 cup vinegar

To remove mineral ring, drain bowl. Scrub with baking soda and spray with vinegar. Another way is to scrub with a paste of Borax™ and lemon juice. Flush.

Notes

This is so easy! Pour, sleep, swish and flush. Clean toilet bowl around the clock.

Easiest Toilet Bowl Cleaner Ever

EASY! Yields: 24 oz.
Approximate cost: $.96 or $.04 per oz.
MSRP: $2.29 or $.10 per oz.
Savings: $1.33 or 139% back in your pocket
Prep Time 1 minute

1 cup Borax™

Pour Borax™ into toilet bowl before retiring for the night.

In the morning, clean bowl with a brush and flush. The job will be effortless. This will also remove a rust ring.

Notes

Bathroom Cleaning Hints

Cleaning the bathroom, without the use of hidden toxic chemicals.

Countertops of plastic laminate, cultured marble or ceramic tile get smeared with any and all substances from toothpaste to hair spray to shoe polish.

Tips to Clean Countertops:

Plastic Laminate

Plastic laminate is comprised of many layers of plastic on craft paper which is overlaid on plywood or particle board. Most plastic laminates color the top layer only and the surface finish is also overlaid.

To brighten and protect laminate surfaces, use a light application of olive oil and lemon, or furniture polish.

To clean: use a soft cloth or sponge with baking soda to clean, loosen and release the smears and build up. The soft abrasiveness of the baking soda will remove just about anything that you can imagine. Rinse clean with water and buff dry.

Cultured Marble

Cultured marble appears as real marble, but the care and cleaning is much easier. Only use a soft scrub such as baking soda. Anything harsher will permanently scratch or mar the surface.

Bathtubs

Bathtubs are made from acrylic, fiberglass, or porcelain; porcelain on cast iron or porcelain on steel. Newer tubs can be made of fiberglass and acrylic. These are lighter and much easier to install but need special care when cleaning. You must avoid scratching the surface with any harsh powders.

Remember to remove hair from the trap in the drain to prevent clogs.

To Clean Porcelain Tubs

Use a nonabrasive powder or liquid cleanser such as our homemade soft scrub using baking soda or the general all-purpose spray cleaner. Rinse well.

To Clean Fiberglass Tubs

Use only nonabrasive cleaners such as baking soda, homemade laundry detergent or liquid all purpose cleanser. Apply a small amount on a sponge or soft cloth to clean. Rinse well.

To Clean Bathtub Ring

You can use a nylon net ball to remove the ring with or without the use of cleansers. For heavy ring stains, make a paste of cream of tartar and hydrogen peroxide. Apply to tub and allow drying. Wipe off and rinse well.

To Clean Discolored Porcelain Fixtures

To clean discolored porcelain fixtures, make a paste of cream of tartar and hydrogen peroxide. Using a brush, scrub the lightly stained areas and rinse well.

An additional paste can be made using Borax™ and lemon juice. Use as above.

Remove Soapy Film

Remove soapy film on countertops with a solution of white distilled vinegar and water.

Clean Grout

Grout cleaner use full-strength white distilled vinegar and scrub with a scrub brush or an old toothbrush.

To make a stronger grout cleaner use equal amounts of salt, baking soda and vinegar. Mix together and apply to grout. Allow the mixture to remain on the grout 10 to 15 minutes before brushing the area with a scrub brush. Rinse with water.

A great and inexpensive grout cleaner is mixing lemon and salt and scrub with a brush, rinse with water. Old tooth brushes work really well.

Ammonia is another cleaner for grout. Use with baking soda and vinegar to make a paste, to dilute add water, apply to grout. Wear gloves and use in a well ventilated area.

Disinfectant Spray

To make a disinfectant spray that is great and inexpensive, use full strength white distilled vinegar. Pour vinegar in a spray bottle. Spray and wipe clean with a damp cloth.

Remove Grime, Mildew and Soap Scum

To remove grime, mildew and soap scum and add a great shine, wipe down the tub, tile, shower curtain or door with undiluted white distilled vinegar. Rinse with water.

Cleaning the Shower Stall

Cleaning the enclosed shower is a harder chore. These hints and tips might be of some help to you.

To prevent mildew from forming, regularly spray down the shower walls to inhibit the growth of mildew and to disinfect.

By leaving the shower door slightly open, this will help prevent the growth of mold and mildew and allow air circulation in the shower to deter the growth of molds and mildew.

Hard Water Spots

Wipe down your shower enclosures with a solution made of equal parts water and white vinegar. As the vinegar dries, the "salad dressing" smell disappears. If it really bothers you, add a few drops of essential oil to the solution.

Caution: NEVER USE AMMONIA WITH BLEACH OR PRODUCTS CONTAINING BLEACH. A DEADLY GAS IS PRODUCED

Cleaning the Shower Curtain and Mats

Shower curtains and mats need to be treated for molds and mildew as much as your shower. Here are some tips to make this chore easy.

Wash the curtain in the washing machine on a gentle cycle, using cold water. Using hot water may be conducive to melting the curtain.

To prevent the wrinkles, add 1/2 cup baking soda to your detergent and wash with two large bath towels. These towels are necessary as they act as scrubbers during the wash cycle. Add one cup vinegar to the final rinse cycle. Remove immediately and hang to air dry.

For continued softness of your shower curtain, wipe it down occasionally with a solution of warm water and mineral oil. To prevent mildew and soap scum from attacking a new or a newly washed shower curtain, spray with a disinfectant cleaner before using.

Washing Bath Mats

Washing your rubber or vinyl bath mat in the washing machine is quick and easy by washing it with bath towels. This works great because the terry cloth acts as a scrubber in the wash. Everything comes out clean and fresh.

Cleaning Toilets

Toilet bowls and tanks are made of nonporous china, which is easy to clean. Follow the recipe of your choice in the recipe section.

The use of a long handled brush makes light of a messy and unpleasant job.

Borax™ poured into the bowl to sit overnight makes for a quick and easy clean toilet.

Caution: DO NOT USE AMMONIA OR VINEGAR WITH BLEACH OR PRODUCTS CONTAINING BLEACH. A DEADLY GAS IS PRODUCED KNOWN AS CHLORINE GAS!

Chapter Seven

A Little Drop Will Do Ya' Essential Oils

This little drop packs a punch!

"The obsession for 'fresh' smelling air is skyrocketing. Americans are expected to spend 1.72 billion dollars on air fresheners this year—that's enough money to buy 82,100 brand new Toyota Prius cars."

Melissa Breyer, *senior editor of Healthy and Green Living, 2010*

About Essential Oils

Essential oils are concentrated liquids distilled from the flowers, leaves and stems of a plant. Because of the high concentration, a few drops are all that is needed. Additionally, essential oils have natural anti-bacterial properties which make these great for cleaning products.

You can find pure, organic essential oils by visiting your local health food store. Essential oils are also sold online. You might want to try making your own at some point. It is not that difficult a process and your children can even help. Making your own blends can be a fun family project as well as a great science lesson.

WARNINGS: Essential Oils are not to be OVERUSED!

Some persons can be highly sensitive to the aromas of essential oils. This could lead to asthma exacerbation, headaches, skin irritation or other health issues.

Please note: we only use drops of essential oils in the recipes. We do not recommend using essential oils in their concentrated form (without dilution)! All recipes with the option of adding essential oils are diluted in water or another substance.

We do not recommend using essential oils for any other use than for cleaning products. Do not ingest or use directly on skin.

Essential Oils to Avoid During Pregnancy

In our research we came across this list of essential oils to avoid during pregnancy:

Anise
Angelica
Basil
Cedarwood (all sorts)
Cinnamon
Clary sage
Clove
Fennel
Hyssop
Juniper
Myrrh
Nutmeg
Ovage
Peppermint
Rosemary
Rose
Thyme (white variety)

Please check with your health care professional before using essential oils if you have any medical concerns.

While essential oils are generally considered safe, some are considered dangerous for pregnant women. To be safe and simple, stick with eucalyptus, lemongrass, and tea tree oils for all recipes if you're pregnant or are planning to become pregnant.

Cleaning Properties

The following is a list of essential oils we suggest for cleaning, disinfecting, and for fragrance. You do not need to use all of them, pick the fragrances and properties that you need and want. This in no way is a complete list! These are the ones we like to use. There are many to choose from; check with your local health food and vitamin store for additional choices.

Cinnamon: Anti-bacterial, anti-fungal, anti-microbial, disinfectant
DO NOT USE IF PREGNANT

Clove: Anti-fungal, anti-microbial, anti-viral, disinfectant
DO NOT USE IF PREGNANT

Eucalyptus: Anti-bacterial, disinfectant

Grapefruit: Disinfectant, clean, fresh scent

Jasmine: Anti Septic: Anti-fungal, anti-viral, disinfectant

Lavender: Disinfectant, anti-fungal, great fragrance

Lemon: Disinfectant, degreaser, refreshing scent

Lemongrass: Anti-microbial, anti-fungal

Pine: Degreaser, anti-bacterial, disinfectant

Orange: Degreaser, natural solvent, stain remover, refreshing scent

Oregano: Anti-fungal, anti-bacterial, anti-viral, disinfectant

Sage: Anti-bacterial, anti-fungal, anti-microbial, disinfectant **DO NOT USE IF PREGNANT**

Tea Tree: Anti-bacterial, anti-viral and anti-fungal, disinfectant

Thyme: Anti-bacterial
DO NOT USE IF PREGNANT

Vanilla: Timeless classic scent

Notes

Holiday Cleaning

Now your entire house can keep the holiday fragrance even after cleaning.

We love the holidays, especially the wonderful aromas that fill our home. When we clean, the cleaning odors can diminish and remove the holiday aroma. Since we were unable to use the air fresheners or scented candles on the market, we were at the mercy of the aromas from our baking, which did not last much longer than the trays of cookies presented to our loved ones!

When we started making our own cleansers, it dawned on us we could now control our home fragrance safely without the chemicals. We realized just how great and refreshing it was having added aromas in our homes without the migraine headaches. We are delighted with our newly found favorite scents incorporated with our cleaning recipes.

With the use of different essential oils in our cleaning recipes, you can have the fragrance you desire. Add a few drops of your favorite aromas without using the costly air fragrances with the undesirable chemicals.

This is a great way to spice up your home without interfering with your favorite holiday aromas! Cleaning using my favorite aromas really gets me in the holiday spirit. I look forward to my cleaning, as crazy as that sounds. I use oils from the list below to accent my decorating. Whatever artificial items I use, I add complementing oils to make the fragrance of my decorations come alive.

For aromas associated with going into the forest to cut down your own Christmas tree, we find fir needle, spruce, pine and Scotch pine as favorites. If you want a minty aroma, you might like peppermint or spearmint. Frankincense and myrrh can be used to bring a memorable and historical scent. This blend brings a warm and musky scent of incense and spice. Add a hint of vanilla and orange for an aroma that can be most pleasing and very fragrant. You might find this aroma especially charming during the Christmas season.

For a woody aroma you might want to try cedarwood, spruce, pine, juniper, cardamom, cypress or sandalwood.

Lastly, if you want a spicy and warming aroma, we might suggest cinnamon, clove bud, nutmeg or ginger. Use sparingly as these are strong. Sweet orange is a milder essential oil and blends nicely with the stronger oils. Experiment with various oils to get your personalized aroma.

For refreshing springtime scents, try lavender or lilac, vanilla mix, pear and vanilla, sweet pea, rose, gardenia, orchid, and honeysuckle, cherry, almond. Vanilla mixes well with nearly all these aromas.

Summer brings to mind the aromas of watermelon, floral or floral mixtures, apples, pears, oranges, pineapple, lemon and lime. Essential oil of jasmine blends well with essential oils of bergamot, sandalwood, rose and citrus fruits such as orange, lemon, lime and grapefruit.

Autumn harvest brings rich scents of apple, cinnamon, sage, almond, maple, cloves.

Winter fragrances might include pine, spruce, juniper spearmint, peppermint, chocolate mint, or almond vanilla.

Experiment with your personal favorites.

We have included a list of essential oils you might find will add to the spirit of the season. We chose these oils for their specific fragrances that could bring different holiday scents into your home. We discovered how to enhance our holiday decorating by using specific oils with our cleaning either floral, spicy, warming or woody aroma into your home.

Scents for all Seasons

Allspice: sharp yet sweet with a spicy, clove-like aroma

Ambrette: musky intriguing hibiscus aroma used as a natural musk substitute

Amyris: dry, earthy, balsamic aroma

Anise: distinctive scent of licorice rich and sweet
DO NOT USE IF PREGNANT

Basil: holy strong, warming and spicy, cross between traditional basil and clove essential oils
DO NOT USE IF PREGNANT

Bay: medicinal, fruity, spicy, herbaceous aroma

Bay Laurel: an herbaceous, sage and spice aroma that will blend well with other oils such as eucalyptus, rosemary, and sage

Cardamon: spicy, woody, rich, sweet

Cassia: spicy, sweet, woodsy, earthy, resembling cinnamon oils in aroma

Cedarwood Virginian: fresh, woody, balsamic. It strongly resembles the aroma of cedar chests and closets
DO NOT USE IF PREGNANT

Chocolate Peppermint: soft and smooth peppermint aroma with a detectible chocolate note
DO NOT USE IF PREGNANT

Cinammon: much richer in aroma than ground cinnamon **DO NOT USE IF PREGNANT**

Clove Bud: spicy, warming yet slightly bitter, woody, reminiscent of true clove buds, but richer
DO NOT USE IF PREGNANT

Coffee: strong, rich aroma of fresh brewed coffee

Common Sage: fruity, fresh, camphoric

Cypress: fresh, herbaceous, slightly woody evergreen aroma

Dill: fresh, sweet, herbaceous, slightly earthy

Fennel: sweet, somewhat spicy, licorice-like (Anise) aroma **DO NOT USE IF PREGNANT**

Fir Needle: fresh, woody, earthy, sweet

Frankincense: fresh, woody, balsamic, slightly spicy and fruity

Galbanum: fresh, earthy, balsamic, woody, spicy

Ginger: warm, spicy, earthy, woody

Jasmine: strong but sweet, pleasing and romantic fragrance

Juniper Berry: crisp, woody, sweet, earthy, with almost a hidden fruity note
DO NOT USE IF PREGNANT

Marjoram: herbaceous, sweet, woody, with a camphoric, medicinal aroma

Myrrh: warm, earthy, woody, balsamic
DO NOT USE IF PREGNANT

Myrtle: aroma is thought to be elevating and euphoric; a clear, fresh, camphoric, sweet herbal scent somewhat similar to Eucalyptus

Nutmeg: rich, spicy, sweet, woody, similar to the cooking spice, but richer and more fragrant
DO NOT USE IF PREGNANT

Oakmoss: rich, earthy, woody

Olibanum: fresh, woody, balsamic, slightly spicy and fruity

Peppermint: minty, reminiscent of peppermint candies, but more concentrated and fragrant than spearmint
DO NOT USE IF PREGNANT

Rosemary: uplifting, bright, and sweet
DO NOT USE IF PREGNANT

Sage, Common: herbaceous, fruity, fresh, camphoric

Sage, Dalmation: herbaceous, fruity, fresh, camphoric

Sage, Spanish: herbaceous, camphoric, and reminiscent in aroma to rosemary
DO NOT USE IF PREGNANT

Sandalwood: rich, sweet, fragrant yet delicate, woody, floral

Scotch Pine: fresh, woody, earthy, balsamic

Spearmint: minty, slightly fruity aroma that is less bright than peppermint

Spikenard: earthy, woody, harsh, musty

Spruce: fresh, woody, earthy, sweet, with a hint of a fruity note

Sweet Orange: citrusy, sweet, reminiscent of orange peels, but more concentrated

Thyme: fresh, medicinal, herbaceous
DO NOT USE IF PREGNANT

Vanilla: rich, warm, sweet vanilla aroma

Wintergreen: intense sweet-woody aroma

Ylang Ylang: sweet, heavy, distinctive fragrance

Essential Oils Hints

Make Your Own Natural Essential Oils Air Freshener

Natural air freshener leaves the home smelling fresh without heavy perfumes. Make your own natural air freshener with natural essential oils. Natural air freshener made with natural essential oil is so subtle guests will wonder about your secret.

Natural Essential Oils Air Freshener Lavender Spray

Combine 10 drops natural essential oils with 2 cups water in a spray bottle. Shake before spraying. My favorites are lavender and vanilla or cherry and almond natural essential oils. It has a fresh spring scent. I use this spray to freshen the air and fabrics and eliminate stale odors. Lavender natural essential oils air freshener results in a calming effect.

Natural Essential Oils Air Freshener Lemon Cloths

Leaving fresh cut lemons in a dish in your kitchen will certainly refresh the air. You might want to try this when cutting onions and garlic. The smell of lemon natural essential oil is invigorating. Mix a few drops of lemon essential oil with the strained juice of one lemon and 1 cup water in a spray bottle. Spray on a clean dry cloth to leave out on your counter in the kitchen or bathroom. You can also spray the mixture into the air to freshen the room.

Natural Essential Oils Air Freshener Jasmine Bathroom Freshener

We have an idea to get the same effect as the spinning fragrance toilet tissue holders without the high cost! Use jasmine or any essential oil of your choice to create natural air freshener.

All you do is place a few drops of the natural essential oil to the inside of the toilet tissue cardboard. With each spin of the tissue the room will be scented with the lovely fragrance of the natural essential oil.

Pine Trash Can Freshener

Give your kitchen the just cleaned aroma by putting a few drops of pine essential oils on folded newspaper or paper towels and place in the bottom of your trash can. Each time you change the bag, the pine air freshener will waft out of the can and into the air.

Natural Essential Oils Air Freshener
Cedar Closet Air Freshener

If you like the scent of a cedar closet but don't have one, here is a quick and inexpensive hint. Use cedar essential oils in your closets. Simply place a few drops of cedar essential oil on a small piece of cloth. Place the cloth in an organza drawstring bag and hang the bag by the strings over a hanger. Now you have the scent of a cedar closet, the protection of a cedar closet from moth eaten clothing without the expensive of remodeling your closets.*

***DO NOT USE THIS HINT IF YOUR ARE PREGNANT OR PLAN TO BECOME PREGNANT.**

For a dollar stretcher in buying different oils, since they can be expensive by the bottle, share your bottle and costs with family and friends to reduce your cost outlay. Remember, you only use a few drops for each recipe.

DO NOT USE THE FOLLOWING ESSENTIAL OILS IF YOU ARE PREGNANT OR PLAN ON BECOMING PREGNANT:

Anise
Angelica
Basil
Cedarwood (all sorts)
Cinnamon
Clary sage
Clove
Fennel
Hyssop
Juniper
Lovage
Myrrh
Nutmeg
Rosemary
Rose
Peppermint
Thyme (white variety)

Chapter Eight

Cleef's Notes

This is truly all you need!

It is better to understand a little than to misunderstand a lot.

Anatole France
French novelist (1844 - 1924)

This chapter we call our "Cleef's Notes," much like the little yellow and black books we would read in high school and college when we were required to read something but we thought our time was much better spent dreaming, doodling and planning our social life. (By the way, we have no idea who Cleef is!)

Doodles, Dreams, and Dilemmas

High School doodles, dreams and dilemmas.

Did you ever get caught doodling, maybe your new hopeful "married name" over and over again in your notebook? Do you remember those dreamy eyes of either a high school cutie or a dashingly handsome science teacher? Were you starry eyed staring out the window thinking of that big date? Were you to busy making circles and hearts over your "i's" or passing notes? Did you think you won the lotto when you were able to dodge the science classes? Whatever the reasons (and they were most important at the time) some of us missed the basics of simple science.

The purpose of this chapter is to help you better understand the how's, why's, and what's about the simple chemistry of cleaning ingredients. The dilemmas are dispelled, the guess work is gone it is really not hard nor complicated.

We start off this chapter with a brief classification (three A's and a B) of the ingredients. This might seem a bit strange, but if you know the types of cleaners, it will be easier to determine what you will need and why it works. Personally, I had never thought that cleaning products were in categories; I just purchased the leading brands that were advertised to do the job at hand, or clean a specific room or surface. Having this basic understanding shed a brand new light on the subject.

Next, we explore the different ingredients and their properties and uses. There is a wealth of information in this chapter. Get acquainted with the chemical aspect of these ingredients to develop your own personalized cleaning recipes. We learned so much doing this chapter and yes, we weren't as attentive in our science classes as we should have been; you were not alone!

Was any of this ever covered in class? What about Home Economics? Nope, this information was never addressed. Of course Home Economics is now a thing of the past. This is not a class still offered in the mainstream school systems.

We are giving you the information that has been missing to allow you to take back control of what you really need. With this information, you will see the manufacturer's selling point to get you to buy their products. It is so simple, and it is so much cheaper.

Please do follow the cautions, they are very real!

Three A's and a B

The classifications of ingredients used in cleaners or cleaning products are:

Abrasives

Acids

Alkalis

Bleaches

All cleaning products either manufactured or homemade need one or more of these properties to create the optimum cleaning result. Just knowing a few basics in chemistry without needing a PhD will give you knowledge and confidence to embark on the fun and money saving adventure of making your own cleaning and laundry needs.

Abrasives are used to rub off undesired substances and deep cleaning when necessary. Regular use of harsh abrasives damage surfaces by scratching and dulling the surface.

Acids have pH numbers less than 7. Acids are used to remove hard water deposits as well as to remove discoloration from aluminum, brass, bronze, and copper. It also removes rust from sinks and counteracts with alkaline oven cleaners.

Alkalis are present in many cleaning substances we use in our homes today, especially in kitchen cleaners like oven spray, floor cleaners, and creams for sinks. Kitchen cleaners are alkaline because they contain ammonia or sodium hydroxide which attack grease. Alkalis also remove greasy, oily dirt without scrubbing.

Bleaches are used to whiten fabrics and remove stains. Chlorine bleach is a disinfectant. It also is a deadly ingredient in chlorine gas. Chlorine gas is produced when bleach is combined with ammonia or products containing ammonia. Chlorine gas can cause death, chemical pneumonia and respiratory complications. It is for this reason we recommend the use of non-chlorine bleach known as oxygen bleaches.

Oxygen bleaches release oxygen for cleaning and bleaching of stains and dirt upon addition to water. Many colorfast and delicate fabrics are safe with the use of oxygen bleach. Hydrogen peroxide is a type of oxygen bleach. This is the liquid form. Powered oxygen bleach is also available.

This quick reference may be used to determine what your needs might be and the areas where you can cut your costs. Just by knowing the properties of each of our Fantastically Frugal Fifteen gives you the know-how to tackle each job you encounter.

Ammonia: Alkaline

Cleans
Antibacterial
Disinfects
Degreaser
Use in well-ventilated area

NEVER USE AMMONIA WITH BLEACH OR BLEACH CONTAINING PRODUCTS. A DEADLY GAS IS PRODUCED.

Baking Soda (Sodium Bicarbonate): Abrasive and an Alkaline

Cleans
Deodorizes
Softens water
Scours
General cleaner

Borax™ (Sodium Borate): Abrasive and an Alkaline

Cleans
Deodorizes
Disinfects
Softens water
Cleans wallpaper, painted walls, floors, tile, tubs, and sinks

Citric Acid: Acid
- Anti viral
- Antioxidant
- Anti septic
- Biodegradable
- Versatile cleaner
- Disinfecting
- Industrial strength cleaner
- Natural preservative
- Degreaser

Cornstarch: Abrasive and an Acid
- Cleans windows
- Polishes furniture
- Shampoo carpets and rugs

Cream of Tartar: Abrasive, Bleach and an Acid
- Bleaching agent
- Remove tough stains

Glycerin: Acid
- Solvent
- Degreaser

Hydrogen Peroxide: Bleach
- Antibacterial
- Antifungal
- Disinfects
- Sanitizes
- Bleaches and whitens clothes
- Stain remover
- Produce wash for fruits and vegetables
- Washes carpets, floors, and windows
- Store in dark container and out of direct sunlight

USE GLOVES WITH DIRECT USE

Isopropyl Alcohol: Alcohol
- Cleans
- Disinfects

Lemon: Acid
Strong food acid
Effective against most household bacteria

Olive Oil: Acid

Salt (Sodium): Abrasive
Cleans
Deodorizing agent

Soap: Alkaline
Biodegradable
Cleans about anything
Use unscented

Washing Soda (Sodium Carbonate): Abrasive
Cuts grease
Removes stains
Softens water
Cleans walls, tiles, sinks, and tubs
Do not use on aluminum

White Vinegar: Acid
Antifungal
Effective for killing most mold, bacteria, germs,
Degreaser
Removes mildew, odors, some stains, and wax build-up.
DO NOT USE WITH BLEACH

CAUTION: NEVER USE CHLORINE BLEACH WITH AMMONIA, TOILET BOWL CLEANERS, DISHWASHING DETERGENT OR RUST REMOVERS BECAUSE A POISONOUS DEADLY GAS, CHLORINE GAS MAY BE PRODUCED.

Break Out the Smelling Salts

Ammonia

Smelling salts are made from ammonia and because of the very sharp odor were used widely in the Victorian Era when fashionably dressed women would fall faint due to the tightly-laced corsets. Oh, the challenges of vanity!

We have found it is so much more than smelling salts. Ammonia is a colorless liquid or gas found in many household and laundry cleaners.

Ammonia is a compound of nitrogen and hydrogen with the formula NH_3. It occurs naturally and is found in water, soil, and air and is a source of much needed nitrogen for plants, animals, and humans. It is produced by human activity such as the bacteria found in the intestines. Most of the ammonia in the environment comes from the natural breakdown of manure, dead plants, and animals.

Ammonia gas can be dissolved in water. This kind of ammonia is called liquid ammonia or aqueous ammonia. Once exposed to open air, liquid ammonia quickly turns into a gas.

Ammonia is always the topic of a spirited discussion. As a society, we have been warned so frequently about the dangers of ammonia, that ammonia has almost become a bad word. We are not saying that ammonia use is something that should be taken lightly. Every precaution should be taken.

New research has shown that chemical irritants can trigger asthma. These irritants are not allergens but things that irritate the tissue of the lungs. Ammonia is listed as a chemical that has fumes that can be irritating to breathe. Bleach and certain household cleaners are also listed.

Caution: Always use ammonia in a well ventilated area and never around children.

Ammonia can create a potentially fatal chemical reaction if mixed with bleach or bleach containing products.

We have confronted this danger head on and put many reminders for you in the book. Additionally, for protection from the possibility of this dangerous cleaning cocktail of chemicals, we have no bleach or bleach containing products in our recipes. Bleach has totally been removed from our homes.

What we are not really told is that ammonia is naturally occurring and biodegrades well. Ammonia does not last very long in the environment. It is rapidly taken up by plants, bacteria and animals.

Ammonia does not build up in the food chain and serves as a nutrient for plants and bacteria.

Whenever we have a workshop and during our Round Table discussion, we see everyone's blood pressure raise a few notches when we talk about the benefits of using ammonia as a cleaner. According to the EPA, "Ammonia is applied directly into soil on farm fields and is used to make fertilizers for farm crops, lawns and plants." (ATSDR 2011)

As we point out in our workshops, we know ammonia is a wonderful fertilizer for the lawn. Our proof, we have a street sign in our front lawn and the grass is more robust there than anyplace else in the lawn, even though we don't do anything different. Why do we have such a healthy stand of grass? You guessed it, the dogs are all helping us along – and depositing concentrations of nitrogen on the sign post in the unending quest for territorial marking dominance. Of course we have to water this area more frequently to avoid the high levels of nitrogen burning the lawn.

Many household and industrial cleaners contain ammonia. Once again, **we caution use ammonia with care.**

Solutions made of ammonia can be irritating to the eyes and mucous membranes (respiratory and digestive tracts) and to a lesser extent the skin.

NEVER mix ammonia with chlorine bleach or any product containing chlorine bleach. The resulting fumes ARE fatal. If you accidentally mix the two, leave the area immediately.

Try to open windows and doors to ventilate the area and remove pets from the area. If you inhale any fumes, call 911 immediately and explain the situation.

Ammonia can trigger asthma use in a well ventilated area.

Don't use ammonia on latex fabrics or latex blend fabrics. Latex will dissolve in ammonia, which is why it's great in removing latex paint from fabrics!

Caution: Ammonia is poisonous. Avoid inhaling its fumes. It will cause burns or irritation if it comes in contact with the skin or eyes. Observe all label precautions.

Uses of Ammonia

To clean your crystal, add several drops of ammonia in two cups water. Use a soft cloth to wipe crystal with the solution. Rinse well and use a clean and dry soft cloth to shine!

To remove unpleasant odors, place a small bowl in the room to absorb the odor.

Laundry

Ammonia is a trusted laundry aid. Despite the strong aroma, it leaves your laundry smelling fresh and clean. It is gentle enough for delicates and can also be used to clean silk when diluted properly. It is also safe for colored clothes.

Stain Remover

To remove stains, use plain household ammonia, no added scent or color. Ammonia can affect some dyes; always pretest in on a hidden area of the stained item. To restore a color changed by the use of ammonia, simply rinse with water and white vinegar. Follow by another rinse with clear water.

Do not use on wool or silk, ammonia damages these fibers.

Types of Ammonia

Ammonia comes in two types: sudsy, which contains a small amount of detergent and non-sudsy, or regular. Non-sudsy is usually used in the laundry. Sudsy can be used in the laundry as well, although you may need to reduce the amount of laundry detergent if you find you have too many suds in your washing machine.

Ammonia is also available in unscented, lemon and pine. The scent doesn't make much difference in the wash, but may smell a little better out of the bottle. Use only the non-sudsy varieties of household ammonia for all the cleaning recipes. Reducing the suds makes for an easier and cleaner rinsing. Non-sudsy ammonia creates a stronger window and all-purpose cleaning recipe than acidic vinegar.

Uses of Ammonia

Laundry freshener, stain remover, grease remover
Remove stains from clothing use solution of 1/2 ammonia 1/2 water
Clean fireplace doors
Clean blackened soot from doors
Clean tarnish from gold and silver
Remove grease and soap scum
Clean your white tennis shoes
Clean carpets and rugs
Clean upholstery
Clean windows
Strip floor wax
Clean bathroom tiles
Remove stains on sidewalk
Remove stains on driveway
Fight mildew
Cleans refrigerators
Cleans appliances
Sinks
Bathrooms
Dishes
Glassware
Pots and pans
Garbage pails
Mirrors
Linoleum
Ceramic Tile
Floors
Venetian blinds
Ovens and broilers

It Does More Than Freshen the Fridge

Baking Soda

We would be lost without the little orange box of baking soda. It is probably used more than anything else in our recipes.

Baking soda, (sodium bicarbonate), also known as bicarbonate of soda, is a chemical salt with diverse practical uses. Baking soda is a weak alkaline. It has a neutralizing action on acidic scent molecules, making this an effective deodorizer.

When added to laundry, it stabilizes making the water wetter to break down the dirt which clings to clothes.

It has a finely gritty texture making it an excellent yet gentle abrasive cleaner.

Baking soda is great as a fire extinguisher for electrical and grease fires. When baking soda is heated, it releases carbon dioxide and produces water. Since carbon dioxide is heavier than air and does not support combustion like oxygen does, it smothers the fire while the water that is formed cools the fire below the ignition temperature.

Of the many benefits of baking soda, it is inexpensive, environmentally friendly, fragrance-free, and safe for nearly all surfaces, all of which make it ideal for household use. Baking soda has many natural deodorizing properties which make it a powerful replacement for harsh commercial scouring powders.

We have found that we can save more money by buying baking soda in the 12 pound pouches, available at a membership warehouse. Whether you use the little orange box or use a store brand, baking soda is baking soda and it is wonderful!

Uses of Baking Soda

Just For Baby's Needs:

Clean Baby Toys

To clean and deodorize baby toys safely and effectively, dissolve 1/4 cup of baking soda in one quart of warm water. Wash toys with a clean damp sponge or cloth, rinse and dry.

Cleaning Baby Equipment

For safe cleaning of baby's needs, i.e. car seat changing table, crib, high chair, play pen and stroller, sprinkle baking soda on a clean damp sponge and rub the item clean. Rinse thoroughly and allow to dry. This leaves baby's equipment sparkling clean without harsh cleaners to worry about!

Clean Baby Spills on Carpet

To clean and deodorize baby spills or accidents on carpets soak up by blotting as much of the spill as possible. Avoid rubbing and scrubbing, this will damage the fibers in the carpet. Clean the stain according to the carpet manufacturer's directions and allow drying. In **Chapter 4 I Can't Believe It's So Easy Floors and Carpets,** there are many recipes to choose from which will clean and deodorize at the same time. Or deodorize the area when it is completely dry by sprinkling the area liberally with baking soda and let sit for 15 minutes before vacuuming it up. Always check for color-fastness first before applying baking soda.

Deodorize and Freshen Diaper Pail

To freshen up baby's diaper pail, sprinkle baking soda liberally over dirty disposable diapers in the diaper pail.

Baby Laundry

To boost your baby laundry needs, baking soda is gentle enough for the tiniest baby clothes, yet effective enough for big baby stains and odors. For tough stains add 1/2 cup of baking soda with your liquid laundry detergent or a 1/2 cup in the rinse cycle for deodorization!

Clean Baby Comb

To clean baby combs and brushes, soak in a solution of one teaspoon baking soda to a jar of warm water. Rinse and allow drying.

Deodorizing Baby Bottles

For easy, safe cleaning and deodorizing of baby bottles fill sink with warm water and add 1/4 tablespoons baking soda. Allow bottles to soak overnight, rinse and dry. For a quick deodorizing sprinkle baking soda in the bottom of the bottle and add warm water. Swirl the liquid and clean as usual.

Clean and Freshen Favorite Stuffed Toys

To keep baby's favorite stuffed toys fresh, sprinkle baking soda on the toys and allow to sit or 20 minutes. Brush thoroughly to remove the residue.

Bathroom

Shower Grime

To cut through the toughest dirt and soap scum use a baking soda soft scrub. It is so easy to make and simple to use. Pour some baking soda on a cloth or sponge and add water to make the desired paste consistency.

Deodorizing Wastebasket

For fresh smelling bathrooms, sprinkle baking soda in the bottom of the wastebaskets. To wash wastebaskets, use one cup of baking soda and one gallon of water. It cleans and deodorizes all at the same time.

Deodorizing Drains

To keep lingering odors from resurfacing, pour a 1/2 cup of baking soda down the drain while running warm tap water. Baking soda will neutralize odors for a fresh drain. If you use baking soda in the fridge or freezer, when you replace the old box, pour the old baking soda down the drain.

Surface-Safe Cleaning

For safe a and effective easy way to clean bathroom tubs, tile, sinks, shiny fiberglass, and glossy tiles, sprinkle baking soda on a clean damp sponge and scrub as usual. Rinse thoroughly and wipe dry. Afterwards, you can take a nice relaxing bath without the worry of harsh chemicals being left behind.

Shower Curtains

If you wish to clean your shower curtain while hanging up instead of in the washer, sprinkle baking soda on a clean damp sponge or brush and scrub the curtain. Rinse and allow drying.

Septic Care

With regular use of baking soda in your drains will assist in keeping your septic tank system flowing freely. For added maintenance and for the proper pH in your septic tank add one cup of baking soda each week.

Cleaning Bathroom Floors

Baking soda helps remove the dirt and grime from bathroom tiles or no-wax floors quickly and easily. Mix 1/2 cup baking soda in a bucket of warm water, mop, and rinse clean for a sparkling floor.

Carpets & Floors:

Carpet Odors

Carpet odors can get trapped deep in the fibers of your carpet, baking soda to the rescue. Sprinkle baking soda on your dry carpet and allow 30 minutes before vacuuming. For heavy carpet deodorizing allow to sit overnight before vacuuming.

Cleaning Floors

To remove dirt and grime and without the unwanted scratch marks on no-wax and tile floors, use 1/2 cup baking soda in a bucket of warm water. Mop and rinse clean for a sparkling floor. For unsightly scuff marks, use baking soda on a clean damp sponge by making a no grit soft scrub, then rinse.

General Household:

Clean Furniture

To clean and remove marks from walls and painted furniture use a soft scrub by pouring baking soda on a damp sponge and rubbing lightly. Marks easy are wiped away, even crayon. Wipe off with a clean, dry cloth.

Freshen Sheets

To get sheets and towels with the freshness of outdoor drying by adding 1/2 cup of ARM & HAMMER® Baking Soda to the rinse cycle.

Deodorize Gym Bags

Place a box of baking soda in your gym bag and in the bottom of your locker. You can also take a clean tube sock and fill with baking soda and knot the end to place in your gym bag.

Upholstery Spills

To clean and deodorize upholstery spills or accidents by blotting soak up as much of the spill as possible. Avoid rubbing and scrubbing, this will damage the fibers in the upholstery. Clean the stain according to the manufacturer's directions and allow drying. In **Chapter 4 I Can't Believe It's So Easy Floors and Carpets,** there are many recipes to choose from which will clean and deodorize at the same time. You can deodorize the area when it is completely dry by sprinkling the area liberally with baking soda and let sit for 15 minutes before vacuuming. Always check for color-fastness first before applying baking soda.

Freshen Ashtrays

Sprinkle baking soda in the bottom of ashtrays to eliminate stale tobacco odors. Replace the baking soda when each time you empty the ashtray. The baking soda helps extinguish cigarettes and cigars!

Deodorize Garbage Can

A simple solution to keep unpleasant odors at bay is to shake baking soda in the garbage cans. Sprinkle regularly as the trash accumulates. Wash out the garbage cans with baking soda and water.

Clean and Freshen Sports Gear

Baking soda will take care of all your cleaning needs. Use a solution of one quart warm water to 1/4 cup baking soda to clean sports equipment, fishing, and camping gear, golf bags, gym bags, and golf clubs. Baking soda paste or soft scrub of 1 part water to 3 parts water works wonders on golf clubs without scratching.

Recyclables

Sprinkle the recycle bins with baking soda to keep smelling fresh. Clean those bins with a solution of baking soda and water.

Freshen Closets

Use baking soda in your closets just like your fridge. Place a box next to your shoe rack; you will be amazed!

Kitchen Uses:

Baking Soda for Extinguishing Fires

Baking soda is useful in extinguishing small grease or electrical fires. When heated, baking soda undergoes a chemical reaction that releases carbon dioxide and produces water. Baking soda is great as a fire extinguisher for electrical and grease fires. When baking soda is heated it releases carbon dioxide and produces water.

It is a great idea to have a tub of baking soda in the, garage, the workshop, the trunk of your car, or anywhere that you could be at risk of fire.

Fridge

Using baking soda in the refrigerator is common knowledge these days, but did you know that by changing the box every 30 days will stop the flavor transfer to other foods and keep foods tasting fresher longer.

Greasy Dishes

For the simple cleanup of those greasy dishes, add 1/4 cup to the dishwater along with the dish detergent. Let soak for 15 minutes then clean. The baking soda is an effective and gentle cleaner and deodorizer.

Dirty Microwave

Microwaves retain the odor of everything we place in them. For an instant cleaning and deodorizing wipe inside down with a damp cloth or sponge sprinkled with baking soda. Rinse well. You can also place a box of baking in the microwave when not in use.

Coffee Maker

To make your coffee maker pot sparkle and shine, add 1/4 cup of baking soda to one quart of warm water and allow sitting overnight if possible. For a quick clean up make a soft scrub using baking soda and water and wipe down coffee maker pot and mugs. Rinse well. Ever burn the coffee and want to remove the smell? Soak the pot in a baking soda solution. Use 1/2 cup of baking soda and a small amount of water. Next place baking soda in a spray bottle and add water, shake to mix and spray in the air.

Stinky Sink

When the foul aroma in your kitchen is emitting from your drain, pour baking soda down your drain while running warm water. This is a perfect time to replace the box in the fridge by using the old box for the drain.

Clean & Deodorize Lunch Boxes

The forgotten scraps of lunch can cause a real challenge in lunch boxes, no problem; baking soda will remove those offending odors and leave you with a fresh aroma. Simply sprinkle baking soda into the box and allow to sit overnight. Wipe clean and it will be ready for the next day's feast.

Pots & Pans

A simple and inexpensive burden eliminated with the use of baking soda. Sprinkle a generous amount of baking soda on those baked on, burned on, dried on food in your pots and pan. Add dish detergent and hot water and let sit for 15 minutes. The baking soda penetrates and lifts stuck-on food off. Wash as usual.

Surface Cleaning

Keep your food preparation area food safe by using baking soda instead of harsh cleaners. Sprinkle counter tops stainless steel sinks, cutting boards, back splashes, stove tops, and more with baking soda and wipe with a damp sponge or soft cloth. Rinse well.

Fruit & Vegetable Scrub

Baking soda is a safe inexpensive fruit and vegetable wash. Sprinkle a small amount on a veggie brush or a clean damp sponge to scrub and then rinse.

Silver Polish

Baking soda will add a sparkling shine to all you silver pieces with ease. Make a baking soda paste using three parts baking soda to one part water. Using a soft clean cloth or clean sponge, rub the baking soda paste onto the sterling and silver plated pieces. Rinse and dry thoroughly.

Plastic Containers

To keep plastic containers smelling fresh, wash in a sink of baking soda and warm water. Use 1/4 to 1/2 cup baking soda to a sink of warm water. Let soak to remove any leftover food odors. Rinse well.

Dishwashers

To keep your dishwashing smelling clean and fresh, sprinkle baking soda on the bottom of your dishwasher before running your next load of dishes.

Deodorizing Fridges and Freezers

Placing a box of baking soda in your freezer, helps eliminate freezer odors that can be absorbed by even the ice cubes. A box of baking soda in the fridge is a must for eliminating odors.

Sponges

No more smelly slimy sponges! Soak those soiled or smelling sponges in a baking soda solution. Use a solution of 1/4 1/2 cup baking soda to 1 quart of warm water.

Garbage Disposals

No need to purchase a garbage disposal cleaner, baking soda will neutralize acids, food odor, and more. Pour baking soda down the disposal and run warm water down the drain.

Tea Pots

Remove unsightly tea stains and eliminate the bitter tastes by washing mugs and tea pots in a solution of 1/4 cup baking soda in 1 quart of warm water. For really heavy stains soak overnight or use a soft scrub baking soda paste.

Laundry Uses:

A task that never goes away is laundry. Stains and mishaps are just a part of life. For tough laundry problems use baking soda, and some stained clothes may be saved from the rag pile. Baking soda in your laundry will also leave your wash brighter and softer.

Lemon Bleach

A natural way to bleach your laundry is by adding one cup of baking soda and one cup of lemon juice. Hang your laundry to dry in the sun to bleach them whiter.

White Clean

If you are unable to hang your clothes outside but want to bleach them, add a cup of baking soda and a cup of hydrogen peroxide to your wash load for a great clean that is nice and white!

Brighter Wash

For brighter laundry both colors and white add a half cup of baking soda per wash load to brighten up colors and whites.

Hamper Odor

To keep your laundry hampers fresh smelling, just sprinkle some baking soda at the bottom of the hamper each time it is empty. For humid areas, sprinkle baking soda every other day between clothes to keep it fresh smelling.

Cleaning Clothes and Rags

To keep the cleaning rags fresh smelling, try dipping them in baking soda before you hang them up to dry.

Grandmother's Secret

Borax™

We have an emotional connection to Borax™; this was one of Grandmother's secrets she left to us in her long forgotten trunk. Buried deep inside and through the years, what other family members thought of as junk, we discovered a treasure trove of valuable recipes with all natural ingredients. This was our starting point in this long journey to rid our own homes and yours of the many chemicals in today's commercial cleaners.

Borax™, or sodium borate, is a naturally occurring alkaline mineral. It is usually a white powder consisting of soft colorless crystals that dissolve easily in water.

It is found in large quantities in the Western United States as well as in the Tibet area of China.

Borax™ has a wide variety of uses. It is a component of many detergents, cosmetics and enamel glazes. It is also used to make buffer solutions in biochemistry, as a fire retardant, as an anti-fungal compound for fiberglass, and as an insecticide.

Borax™ is best known as a laundry booster; it helps soften hard water to leave your clothes cleaner and brighter. Borax™ is usually found in the cleaning aisle of your grocery store next to the powdered laundry soaps. It cleans, deodorizes, disinfects, softens water, and as an added bonus is a flame retardant. It's wonderful to use in your laundry.

At one of our workshops one of the women shared with us that she had previously worked for the hotel/casino/ restaurant industry in Las Vegas, Nevada. To comply with the fire safety codes, all linens were required to be washed in Borax™ due to the flame retardant qualities.

Borax™ has non toxic fumes and is safe for the environment.

Caution: BORAX™ CAN IRRITATE THE SKIN.

Borax™ Uses

You might have seen a box of 20 Mule Team Borax™ in the laundry detergent aisle and you might even use it to boost the effectiveness of your washing machine. Did you know that Borax™ has many other household uses? If you pick up a box of Borax™ you can test it on your laundry and try one of these handy tips, using Borax™ as a great tool for cleaning around the home.

Make a paste of Borax™, water and a squirt of dish soap. Use paste to scrub the shower, stove, or kitchen sink. This Borax™ paste works really great and leaves a clean, fresh smell.

Borax™, a natural mineral compound has a wide range of uses in the home.

Borax™ has a pH of 9, which is higher than baking soda (which is 8.1; 7 is neutral). It is a good deodorizer and mold inhibitor.

General Cleaning Uses:

Remove Urine Smell from Furniture and Mattresses

Borax™ can remove the smell of urine from furniture and mattresses. Just wet the areas of the mattress or furniture that are affected and shake on some Borax™. Wait for the entire area to dry completely, and then vacuum it away.

Mold Inhibitor

Make a thick paste of Borax™ and water. Spread the paste on the moldy area. Allow to dry overnight or longer. Sweep up the powder, then rinse off the rest. This method of inhibiting mold growth is very good to use on areas where mold and mildew is growing.

DO NOT USE THIS METHOD IF YOU ARE CONCERNED OF PAINT DAMAGE. WEAR A PROTECTIVE MASK WHEN DEALING WITH MOLDS.

Carpet Stain Remover

If you're looking for a way to keep your carpets clean and smelling fresh, Borax™ can do the job. It can remove stains from carpet if you mix it into a paste and rub into the stain. Let the paste dry and vacuum it away. If you have a liquid stain on the floor you can mix a half a cup of Borax™ into a cup and a half of water and pour onto the stain. Blot up the liquid and repeat until the stain is gone. To make the carpet smell fresh spray it with a fine mist of water and sprinkle on Borax™. When it is dry, simply vacuum it up.

All-Purpose Cleaner

To make an all purpose cleaner mix two tablespoons Borax™ and two cups hot water in a spray bottle. Use as you would any all purpose cleaner.

Floor and Wall Cleaner

Make your own floor and wall cleaner by mixing 1/3 cup Borax™, one tablespoon ammonia, and one teaspoon dish detergent into one gallon of water.

Laundry Uses:

Hard Water Softener

To help soften your laundry water, add 1/4 cup Borax™ to each load of laundry.

Laundry Detergent

If you use store purchased laundry detergent, use Borax™ as a laundry detergent booster.

Remove Rust

Mix a tablespoon of lemon juice with one cup of Borax™ and two 2 cups of warm water. Apply the paste directly to the stain. Allow 30 minutes before laundering as usual.

Bathroom Uses:

Bath Water Softener

If you have hard water, add a bit of Borax™ to your bath to soften it. Hard water makes soaps and shampoos less effective.

Toilet Bowl Cleaner

To make your toilet bowl clean and fresh, shake a 1/2 cup of Borax™ into the toilet and let it sit for an hour or so. Scrub the bowl with a toilet brush and it will be sparkling and odor free.

Drain Opener

Borax™ is a safe drain opener and a great alternative to those expensive store-bought drain cleaners. Just mix 1 cup of Borax™ with some boiling water and empty it down the drain. Any grease stuck in your drain will melt away.

Stain Remover

To remove stains from stainless steel, make a paste of 1 cup Borax™ with 1/4 cup lemon juice. Use a soft cloth to rub the paste on the stain. Rinse well with warm water. This paste will also remove stains from porcelain sinks.

Kitchen Uses:

Shine China

To restore the beautiful shine your china had when it was new, you can wash it in a sink of warm water (increase the water temperature as needed) with a 1/2 cup of Borax™. Wash as usual and dry to a brilliant shine. To cut down on water spots in the dishwasher just add 1 tablespoon of Borax™ to your detergent cup. Mix some Borax™ with water to clean your aluminum pots and pans.

Pots and Pans Scrubber

Since Borax™ is non-abrasive, it works great to scrub pots and pans clean. Use as a scrub cleanser and rinse well.

Garbage Disposal Cleaner Sanitizer

To clean and deodorize your garbage disposal, pour 3 tablespoons of Borax™ down your drain, the side with the disposal. Let sit for an hour and flush with warm water. This does the job of cleaning as well as sanitizing your disposal from any bacteria.

Unclog Drains

To unclog any drain use 1/2 cup of Borax™ followed by 2 cups of boiling water. Allow to it sit for 15 minutes, run water for a few minutes to flush out the clog.

Clean, Deodorize and Sanitize the Fridge

To clean and deodorize your fridge make a solution of Borax™ and water using 1/4 cup Borax™ to 1 gallon warm water.

Deodorize Garbage Pail

Mix Borax™ with water and let soak in the bottom of the garbage pail. Rinse out and sprinkle Borax™ in the bottom of the pail to detract bugs and absorb any offending odor.

Pot of Gold

Citric Acid

We think we have uncovered nature's pot o' gold in the form of citric acid, naturally found in: lemon, lime, orange, tangerine, grapefruit, pineapple, strawberry and many other acidic fruits. The benefits are numerous; citric acid is much more than a fruity fresh fragrance.

The list of the diverse properties for citric acid: anti-viral, antioxidant, anti-septic, it is biodegradable, versatile cleaner, disinfecting, industrial strength cleaner, natural preservative, and a degreaser. It is also being used to clean up polluted toxic waste from both soil and steel.

Possibly the best benefit of citric acid in all its applications is that it is natural, poses little to no risk to the environment ,and very few people are allergic to citric acid.

It is usually available in powder form and mixes well with liquids, making it a valuable acid. The highest concentrations are contained in lemons and limes, giving their bitter flavor. Oranges, tangerines and grapefruit are also rich in citric acid, but less bitter than other citrus fruits. Amazingly enough, raspberries and blackberries also contain citric acid.

We all are aware that citric acid is used for flavoring in many food products, such as flavored drinks, soft drinks, sour candies as well as being a source of vitamin C.

Interestingly, citric acid bonds easily to minerals and metals, called chelation. Look in your vitamin supplements; it can help to take certain minerals with citric acid, since the body will more easily digest chelated minerals. Calcium supplements can come in the form of calcium citrate and are better absorbed by the body. It can also be used as a treatment to prevent kidney stones.

While citric acid has the ability to bond with other minerals, it is helpful in softening water. It is widely used by the laundry and cleaning industry to make good "natural" cleaners, although some may still contain chemicals that are not natural. Soaps and laundry detergents can be made more effective when citric acid is added to the formula. Once again the chelating aids in removing the hard mineral deposits in our hard water which makes our clothes dingy and breaks down the fibers.

Citric acid can be found in the canning section of your grocery store. It is also known as "Fruit Fresh." It can also be found in health food stores and purchased on line. You can also substitute lemon juice for the citric acid. For the correct substitute measurement of lemon juice to citric acid, 1 teaspoon of citric acid is equivalent to the juice of one lemon. One lemon produces about 1 1/4 ounces of juice, or 1/8 cup plus 1 teaspoon.

Uses of Citric Acid

Citric acid can be used in almost every recipe you would use lemon juice. It is a weak naturally occurring acid. Because it is a weak acid, citric acid has so many useful properties. It is safe for humans and animals to both ingest and touch. Its fragrance is clean and refreshing.

Laundry

Adding citric acid to your laundry will make your soaps and detergent more effective. The citric acid helps to remove the minerals from the water, soften the water as well as give your laundry a clean fresh scent.

Air Freshener

Citric acid is used to eliminate odors. Add to your air freshener recipes to mask and eliminate odors.

Bathroom

Citric acid is the active ingredient in some bathroom and kitchen cleaning solutions. A solution with a 6% concentration of citric acid will remove hard water stains from glass without scrubbing.

Rust Remover

You can use citric acid to dissolve rust from steel.

With the trends of environmentally friendly cleaning and laundry products, citric acid has emerged. It is a green natural cleaner at its best, because it attracts and extracts dirt. It is a powerful cleanser for stuck on dried messes.

Stainless Steel

Use citric acid mixed with the Basic Soft Scrubber and Stainless Steel Appliance Cleaner recipe.

The soft scrub cleaners are just as effective as harsher chemicals and much less hazardous. Citric acid is completely organic and found abundantly in lemons and limes.

Hard Water Deposits

Dissolve 3 to 6 tbsp. citric acid in about 1 quart of warm water. Dip the cloth into the solution. Wipe down the area you want cleaned. Rinse and dry. Rub with the cloth to shine surfaces.

Decalcification of Shower Heads and Faucets

Dissolve 2 to 5 tbsp. citric acid in 1 quart of warm water. Soak individual parts in the solution for two hours. Citric acid is safe to remove mineral deposits, but it is also among the slowest acting cleansers. Rinse well and wipe dry.

It's Not Just for Gravy and Pudding

Cornstarch

Corn starch, cornstarch, or corn flour in the United Kingdom, Ireland, New Zealand and Australia, is simply starch derived from corn. It is ground from the white heart of a kernel of corn.

Cornstarch is used as a thickening agent in cooking, soups, gravies, white sauce, pies, and puddings. It is also mixed with sugar to make powdered sugar.

Cornstarch is also a health-conscious alternative to talc and is the main ingredient in biodegradable plastic. Another interesting property of cornstarch is that it does not conduct static electricity. Therefore, cornstarch is used in the manufacturing of static free high density foam for the packing and shipping of electronics which would be damaged by contact with static electricity. We wish to thank Angelyn and Benyse for bringing this information to us.

Cornstarch can also be used in homemade household cleaning products.

A mixture of cornstarch and water make what is known as a suspension. When you squeeze a cornstarch suspension it really feels like a solid because its molecules line up. But it looks like a liquid and acts like a liquid when no one is pressing on it because the molecules relax. For this reason, the most interesting properties of cornstarch, is often demonstrated in the elementary classroom. Making a suspension out of cornstarch is a fun and easy experiment to try at home, especially if you can share it with young children.

Uses of Cornstarch

Furniture Polish Left on Wood Furniture

For an abundance of furniture polish on your wood, lightly sprinkle cornstarch on the oil. Wipe up the excess and buff the surface.

Carpet Ink Pen Stain Remover

To remove an ink stain from your carpet, make a paste of milk and cornstarch. Apply the paste to the ink stain and allow the paste to dry on the carpet. Make sure it is dry; allow 2 to 3 hours or more to dry before brushing off the dried paste. Vacuum the carpet as usual.

Carpet Freshener

To give your carpet a freshening, lightly sprinkle cornstarch on your carpet. Allow cornstarch to remain on carpet 30 minutes to an hour before vacuuming as normal.

Clean Stuffed Animals

If you need to clean a toy stuffed animal simply rub cornstarch onto the animal or toy. Wait a few minutes and brush clean. You can also place cornstarch in a bag or container and drop in stuffed toy animals. Close the bag or container tightly and shake the contents. Remove the toys and brush clean.

Scorch Mark Remover

If you need to remove a scorch mark, simply wet the scorched area and then cover it with cornstarch. Allow the area to dry then brush away the cornstarch and the scorch mark.

Clean Grease Spots on the Walls

To remove grease splatters on the walls, here is an easy and quick tip. Using a soft cloth and cornstarch, gently rub the grease spot until it disappears.

Remove Blood Stains

This requires fast action; the sooner the better. Make a paste of cornstarch and cold water. Cover the stain with the paste and rub into the fabric. Rub easy on delicate fabrics. Place in a sunny area to dry. When dry, brush off the dried cornstarch powder. If the stain remains repeat the process.

For Shinier Silver

To restore the sparkle and shine to your silverware, make a paste of water and cornstarch. Using a damp soft cloth, apply the paste to your silver pieces. Let the paste dry completely, before rubbing it off with a clean soft cloth to bring back the brilliant shine of silver.

Dry Grease, Oil Stain Remover from Satin

Treat the oil or grease stain with dry cornstarch. Gently rub the cornstarch on the stain. Leave on overnight. Brush cornstarch from the stain, then wash as usual.

Rubber Gloves Hard to Put On

For the ease of putting on or to reuse rubber gloves, just sprinkle gloves with cornstarch before putting them on.

Prevent or Kill Mildew in Damp Books

Sprinkle corn starch throughout the book to absorb the moisture from damp pages. Wait several hours, before brushing clean. If the pages are mildewed, brush the corn starch off outdoors to keep mildew spores out of the house.

Fun Science Experiment for Children

Mix one part water with one-and-a-half to two parts cornstarch, adding a bit of food color for fun if you wish. The cornstarch-water mixture, sometimes called Oobleck in reference to a Dr. Seuss book, acts as a thick liquid when allowed to sit, but as a solid when force is applied. One can sink a hand into the mixture slowly, but it will not give if one tries to punch it.

Clean a Carpet

For a quick carpet cleaner, sprinkle cornstarch on the carpet and wait thirty minutes, before vacuuming clean.

Clean Silver

Make a paste of cornstarch and water. Apply with a damp cloth and let dry. Rub off with clean soft cloth.

Substitute for Baby Powder and Talcum Powder

Apply corn starch sparingly when diapering a baby. Corn starch is more absorbent than talcum powder. Apply lightly since it does cake more readily.

Make White Clown Makeup

Mix two tablespoons corn starch with one tablespoon solid shortening. To add color, use drops of food coloring.

Snickerdoodles, Scones, and Scouring Oh My!

Cream of Tartar

We're convinced. There are two types of people in the world. Dog people and cat people, toilet paper rolling out or in, you ask; no, the snickerdoodle cookie lovers, and the snickerdoodle cookie haters. We're split evenly down the middle in our family. Not only is, cream of tartar a key ingredient in this cookie recipe, it is a fabulous cleanser for your home!

Cream of tartar is a common baking ingredient, found in almost every spice section in the grocery stores.

Cream of tartar is actually a byproduct of the process of wine making and is sometimes referred to as "crusty wine." The potassium bitartrate crystallizes in wine casks during the fermentation of grape juice and can precipitate out of wine in the bottle.

This crude form is collected and purified to produce the white, odorless, acidic powder used for many culinary and other household purposes.

When Cream of tartar is combined with baking soda, this creates baking powder.

Cream of tartar is also one of nature's best bleaching agents, which provides a safe and gentle alternative to using chlorine bleach to remove tough stains. This also makes it a most useful item in your collection of cleaning supply ingredients.

Uses of Cream of Tartar

Cleaning With Cream of Tartar

To create a powerful cleaning compound without toxic fumes, use cream of tartar to clean your home squeaky clean.

Soft Scrub

Cream of tartar removes stubborn stains without the need of harsh abrasive products.

Non Toxic Additive

Mix cream of tartar with a variety of other non toxic substances to clean grout to fabric stains.

Bleach Alternative

Cream of tartar provides safe and gentle alternatives to chlorine bleach. Also it removes tough stains from a variety of household surfaces.

Laundry

Removes rust stains
Gentle non chlorine bleach
Removes ring around the collar
Excellent stain remover

Non Abrasive Soft Scrub

Combine 2 teaspoons cream of tartar with 2 teaspoons of vinegar. This non-abrasive cleaner also attacks stains and successfully cleans nearly all surfaces.

Copper Cleaner

Combine 1 teaspoon cream of tartar with 1/2 teaspoon of lemon juice. Rub the copper item then rinse and polish to achieve the same result as with the commercial copper cleaner.

Kitchen Uses:

Baked-on Food Cleaner

Remove baked-on food from pots and pans, by using cream of tartar and vinegar.

Aluminum Pan Cleaner

Use a few tablespoons of cream of tartar with hot water or hydrogen peroxide and clean any aluminum pans which have discoloration. This can also be used on any rusty drains, pans, or stains.

Copper Kettle Cleaner

Do you have copper kettles? Mix cream of tartar with lemon juice and rub onto the copper, rinse well.

Bathroom

To clean the bathtub, make a paste by adding a small amount of hydrogen peroxide and cream of tartar. Spread the paste around the area to be cleaned. Scrub the tub with a brush and the paste, rinse well.

Grout Non Toxic Bleach

Remove mold and mildew from grout by making a paste of hydrogen peroxide and cream of tartar. Apply the paste to the grout. Allow to dry. Rinse the dried paste.

Porcelain Cleaner

To clean a porcelain sink, tub, commode, rub the porcelain surfaces with cream of tartar and watch the stains disappear.

Sweet, Simple, and Pure

Glycerin

Glycerin may come from vegetable oils such as soybean oil, canola oil, coconut oil, palm kernel oil and palm oils. The most commonly used are palm or coconut oils. It is one of the most versatile and valuable chemical substances known to man. It possesses a unique combination of physical and chemical properties that are utilized in a myriad of products.

Glycerin is a chemical compound which is known as glycerol. The word comes from the Greek word glykys and it means "sweet." Being a colorless, odorless, viscous, non-toxic liquid and having a very sweet taste, it has many uses.

Glycerin can be dissolved easily into alcohol and water but not into oils. Many more substances will dissolve into glycerin than will dissolve into water or alcohol. Therefore, glycerin is a very good solvent.

Glycerin is a natural by-product of the soap making process. Commercial manufacturers remove the glycerin to use in their more profitable lotions and creams. Handcrafted soap retains glycerin in every bar.

Glycerin has many known uses, such as an ingredient or processing aid in cosmetics, toiletries, personal care, drugs, and food products. In addition, glycerin is highly stable under typical storage conditions; it is compatible with many other chemical materials. It is virtually non-toxic and non-irritating in its varied uses and has no known negative environmental effects.

Glycerin is a humectant, meaning it attracts moisture to your skin. Humectants are used in skin and hair-care products to promote moisture retention. These hygroscopic compounds posses a chemical structure that attracts water from the atmosphere and binds it to various sites along the molecule.

In food products, glycerin is used as a texturizer or icing stabilizer in cake decorating and it is used in making some candies. It is also used to moisten, sweeten, and preserve such foods as meat, cake, cheese, and dry food products. It can also be used in pharmaceuticals.

For cleaning uses, it is a natural solvent; it is used to clean spilled sticky food that is stuck to your freezer and is a stain remover. Keep a bottle of glycerin handy in your cleaning arsenal. It cuts through grease easily and is especially effective on tar or oil stains.

Uses of Glycerin

Tar, Oil and Grease Stain Remover

Rub the stain with glycerin. Allow to sit for 30 minutes. This should easily lift out the stain, wash as usual.

Dried On Food Cleaner

Glycerin is also effective in cleaning dried on, frozen foods that have collected in the bottom of your fridge and freezer. Just apply a small amount and let it sit for a few moments before you lift the food away.

Soft Drink Stain Remover

Sponge the stain immediately with cold water. Apply a pre-wash stain remover and glycerin. Launder using non-chlorine bleach in hottest water safe for the fabric. Some soft drink stains are invisible after they dry, but turn yellow after aging or heating. This yellow stain may be impossible to remove. Try soaking in a solution of hydrogen peroxide and water. Soak overnight. For really stubborn stains you may need to soak in a strong solution for a few days.

Ink Stain Remover

To remove ball-point pen ink, sponge stain with rubbing alcohol. Apply glycerin and rinse thoroughly, rub with detergent, then launder. For drawing ink stain, rub absorbents, such as baking soda and salt into the stain. Apply hydrogen peroxide full strength if stain is unaffected, steam over teakettle. Rinse thoroughly, launder as usual. If this has failed to remove the ink stain, soak in an ammonia solution (4 tablespoons ammonia to 1 quart of water) for an extended period. For felt tip pen ink stains, rub household cleaner, or rubbing alcohol into stain. Rinse thoroughly and launder.

Mustard Stain Remover

Work glycerin into the stain. Using a paper towel, rub the area in a blot-and-lift motion. You can repeat this process two or three times to get the desired results. Be careful not to damage the fabric. Pre-treat with detergent and a stain remover, then launder using non-chlorine bleach. If stain persists, sponge the stain with rubbing alcohol. Launder as usual. If the stain is still present, drying in sunlight may help fade the mustard stain.

Caution: NEVER PLACE A STAINED GARMENT IN THE DRYER BEFORE REMOVING THE STAIN. THE HEAT FROM THE DRYER WILL MOST CERTAINLY SET THE STAIN PERMANENTLY.

Alcohol, Whiskey, and Vermouth, Stain Remover

Always treat these stains as soon as possible. Often times, stains are almost colorless at first, but turn brown on standing, washing and ironing. Fresh stains can be removed by sponging several times with warm water. If there is any mark left, pour glycerin on the dampened stain, rub lightly between the hands, and leave for half an hour. Rinse in warm water. Launder as usual.

Wool and Silk Stain Remover

Wool and silk or any fabric may be sponged with lukewarm water, then apply glycerin, rubbing lightly between the hands. Let stand for half an hour. Rinse with warm water. If a grease spot remains from cream, sponge with dry cleaning fluid.

Fruit and Berry Stain Remover

Old fruit and berry stains may be softened with glycerin. Dampen the stain with water, apply glycerin, and leave on 1 to 2 hours. Add a few drops of vinegar, leave on the stain 5 to 10 minutes and rinse well. For persistent stains, apply equal amounts of denatured alcohol and ammonia. Rinse well. This method is safe for all fabrics, except triacetate. Dilute mixture with an equal quantity of water for fabrics with unstable, non-colorfast, or “bleeding” dyes.

Paint Stain Remover

Paint varies greatly in composition and it is not possible to give one treatment for all types. As a guide, use the solvent suggested on the paint can label for thinning paint and cleaning brushes. Treat promptly, as set stains are very difficult to remove. If paint has dried, soften with glycerin before applying treatment of choice.

For oil paint, enamels, and alkyd type paints, scrape off as much as possible and spray with WD-40™ or soak in turpentine or kerosene. Wash as usual.

Latex and water-base paints will wash out easily with soapy water when fresh. Remove any remaining color stain with denatured alcohol. (Test first to see that acetate fabrics are not affected.) Once dry, these paints are virtually impossible to remove.

Tobacco Stain Remover

Pour glycerin over the tobacco stain. Rub lightly between the hands or pre-treat the dry fabric with a laundry pre-soak (spot stain remover), leave for half an hour then wash as usual. If stain persists, soak in a solution of hydrogen peroxide and water.

Tomato Stain Remover

Thoroughly wet the stain with cold water. Pour glycerin on the stain, rubbing lightly between the hands, and let sit half an hour. Or pre-treat the dry fabric with a laundry pre-soak (spot stain remover), leave for half an hour then wash as usual. Rinse in warm water. Remove any remaining stain with non-chlorinated laundry bleach.

Mother Nature's Bleach

Hydrogen Peroxide

Mother Nature or Mother Earth is a commonly known personification of nature. This exemplifies the life-giving and nurturing features of nature by embodying it in the form of the mother. Isn't it just like a mother to provide us with everything that we need in every circumstance? Mother Nature has given us a safe natural bleach to meet all of our needs. Hydrogen peroxide is a greener alternative to chlorine bleach.

It is simply water with an extra oxygen molecule (H_2O_2) and breaks down into oxygen and water, making it a good alternative to chlorine bleach.

Chlorine bleach is a chemical that almost everyone has and uses in their homes. Chlorine bleach (sodium hypochlorite) has the ability to form more toxic byproducts such as dioxin, furans, and other organ chlorines (an organic compound containing at least one bonded chlorine atom) when reacting with other elements. Many derivatives are controversial because of the effects of these compounds on the environment.

Hydrogen peroxide is produced by both animal and plant cells. It is formed naturally in the environment by sunlight acting on water. It's certainly kinder and better on the environment.

The benefits are deep and wide. It is good for the rivers and it is good for the plants. Most importantly, it replaces the hidden toxic chemicals such as chlorine bleach and other chemicals we are using that harm the rivers and the plant life.

When used responsibility, hydrogen peroxide's benefits are good for people, animals, plants, and rivers breaking down into **water and oxygen.** What could be more non-toxic?

Be careful when purchasing and handling this substance as some commercially available "food grade" hydrogen peroxide is

35% pure, highly corrosive, and can be toxic or fatal if ingested at that strength.

Hydrogen peroxide should be diluted down to 3% as a base for most applications. It's also readily available in 3% solution from your local pharmacy or drugstore.

If you choose to dilute a 35% solution, add the hydrogen peroxide to distilled water and wear gloves, body, and eye protection when doing so.

Uses of Hydrogen Peroxide

Hydrogen Peroxide is very practical to keep on hand for many reasons. Remember it is truly eco-friendly.

There are many uses for hydrogen peroxide:

Disinfect
Sanitize
Bleach and whiten clothes
Remove mold
Remove stains
Produce wash for fruits and vegetables
Wash carpets, floors, and windows

Hydrogen Peroxide is an inexpensive alternative to many cleaning products on the market today!

Coffee and Tea Stain Remover

Remove fresh stains from cotton and linen materials by first rinsing in warm water then pouring boiling water from a height of 2-3 feet onto the stain. Follow by washing in hot soapy water. If a trace remains, bleach white garments in the sun or hydrogen peroxide. Tea stains on cottons and linens can also be removed by soaking in Borax™ and water (1 Tbsp. Borax™ per cup of warm water).

Fruit and Berry Stain Remover

Fresh stains are easy to remove, but once dry, they are very stubborn. Treat immediately with cool water and follow up if necessary, by soaking in a non-chlorine laundry bleach or hydrogen peroxide solution. Rinse and launder as usual.

White cottons and linens may be stretched over a basin and boiling water poured through from a height. Any remaining stain may be removed with chlorinated laundry bleach.

Colored fabrics or washable silk, etc., may be soaked in a diaper wash/sanitizer container sodium percarbonate or a warm Borax™ solution (1 Tbsp. Per cup of water), or covered with a paste of cream of tartar and warm water. Leave on for 30 minutes or until stain is gone, then rinse well.

Perfume Stain Remover

Wet the affected area and apply glycerin. Rinse well, or sponge with equal parts of full-strength hydrogen peroxide (on whites) and water. If the color has already been removed from the fabric by the alcohol in the perfume, it may be helpful to add a few drops of denatured alcohol to a cheesecloth pad and sponge fabric lightly, working towards the center of the stain, thus distributing remaining color evenly.

Laundry Whitener

You can also add a cup of hydrogen peroxide instead of bleach to a load of whites in your laundry to whiten them. If there is blood on clothing, pour directly on the soiled spot. Let it sit for a minute, then rub it and rinse with cold water. Repeat if necessary.

Kill Germs on Toothbrushes

Soak your toothbrushes in 1 cup of hydrogen peroxide to keep them free of germs.

Countertop Cleanser

Clean your counters and table tops with hydrogen peroxide to kill germs and leave a fresh smell. Pour a little on your dish cloth to wipe or spray down the counters.

Cutting Board Anti-bacterial Cleaner

After rinsing off your wooden cutting board, pour hydrogen peroxide on it to kill salmonella and other bacteria.

Bathroom Disinfectant

Fill a spray bottle with a 50/50 mixture of hydrogen peroxide and water and keep it in every bathroom to disinfect without harming surfaces.

Fruit and Vegetable Wash

Use as a fruit and vegetable wash to kill bacteria and neutralize any chemicals.

Large Appliance Disinfectant

Disinfect your dishwasher or refrigerator with one of the hydrogen peroxide sprays.

Toxic Mold Cleaner

To clean your house once it has become a biohazard after invaded by toxic mold, such as those spores found after water damage, clean with hydrogen peroxide.

Give Your House a Shot of Clean

Isopropyl Rubbing Alcohol

My granddaughter is like so many children her age. She hates shots and doesn't forget the incident one year to the next! One day, right before her yearly checkup, as I was cleaning my silk plants with the **Silk Flower and Plant Saver**, she came to my house for visit. Immediately, upon her arrival, she displayed a great anxiety level, which continued to rise. As she walked over to me, I was greeted with a dismayed face, complete with scrunched up nose. She commented with great disdain, "It smells like a shot!" She has a highly sensitive nose and associates the scent of rubbing alcohol with the quick swab before getting an immunization. Thank goodness the alcohol evaporates quickly!

Isopropyl alcohol is a common name for the chemical compound known as rubbing alcohol. It is colorless and flammable with a strong odor. It is the simplest example of a secondary alcohol, where the alcohol carbon is combined with water and propylene. Isopropyl (rubbing) alcohol provides the base for an evaporating cleaner to rival commercial window and glass cleaning solutions.

Alcohol works just as well or even better than the brand name cleaners you are probably using, and it is much cheaper.

Isopropyl alcohol is effective for many cleaning projects. Put it in a small spray bottle and it works well for cleaning and shining chrome faucets. It also can be helpful when trying to remove ink stains from fabric and upholstery. Always pretest the alcohol in an inconspicuous spot before using on a stain. Isopropyl Alcohol can be purchased in the grocery store or the drug store. It's usually in the first aid aisle. Look for sales and save.

It is also a very good cleaning agent for cleaning electronic devices such as contact pins (like those on ROM cartridges), magnetic tape decks, floppy disk drive heads, the lenses of lasers in optical disc drives (CD, DVD), and removing thermal paste from CPUs. It can also be used to clean LCD and glass computer monitor screens (at some risk to the anti-reflection coating of the screen) and is used by many music shops to give second-hand or worn records newer looking sheens. It cleans white boards very well and other unwanted ink related marks. Isopropyl alcohol also works well at removing smudges, dirt and fingerprints from cell phones and PDAs. It is effective at removing residual glue from sticky labels.

Rubbing alcohol not only makes an amazingly simple cleaner, but it kills nasty germs around your house in the process. Rubbing alcohol is not just for medicinal purposes; it can be used in all sorts of practical and cleaning applications around the home.

Uses of Isopropyl Alcohol

Antiseptic Cleanser

Isopropyl (rubbing) alcohol kills germs around your house but it is also a fantastic simple cleaner. Alcohol removes grime from household fixtures, give your door knobs a quick antiseptic clean with a cloth dampened with alcohol.

Ink Stain Remover

Rubbing alcohol will remove fresh ink stains and some permanent marker stains on carpet. Just blot the stains with a soft cloth and alcohol.

To remove ink on your favorite shirt or dress, soak the spot in rubbing alcohol for a few minutes before putting the garment in the wash.

Streak Free Window Cleaner

Use alcohol in your window washing solutions for streak free shine.

Inexpensive Dry Erase Cleaner

Alcohol sprayed on dry erase boards cleans shadows from old stained dry erase boards.

Excellent Instant Table Shine

Alcohol removes dirt and dust that collects on tabletops and can uncover a beautiful shine.

Remove Hair Spray on Mirrors

When spraying your hair with hair spray, some will inevitably wind up on the mirror and surrounding surfaces. A quick wipe with rubbing alcohol on a soft cloth will whisk away that sticky residue and leave your mirror and surfaces sparkling clean.

Clean Venetian Blinds

Rubbing alcohol does a terrific job of cleaning the slats of venetian blinds. To make quick work of the job, wrap a flat tool, such as a spatula or maybe a 6-inch (15-centimeter) drywall knife, in a cloth and secure with a rubber band. Dip in alcohol and go to work.

Keep Windows Sparkling and Frost-free

To prevent your windows from frosting up in the wintertime, wash them with a solution of 1/2 cup rubbing alcohol to 1 quart (1 liter) water. Polish the windows with newspaper after you wash them to make them shine.

Dissolve Windshield Frost

Fill a spray bottle with rubbing alcohol and spray the car glass. You'll be able to wipe the frost right off. No more scraping frost off your car windows. Keep the spray bottle in your car for those times your car is exposed to the winter weather.

Prevent Ring Around the Collar Stains

To prevent your neck from staining your shirt collar, wipe your neck with rubbing alcohol each morning before you dress.

Clean Phone

To restore your phone to the clean state it once was, wipe it down with rubbing alcohol. It will remove the grime and disinfect the phone at the same time. Alcohol cleans phones, switch plates, and doorknobs.

Carpet Stain Remover

To remove some stains from your carpet, blot the stain with a soft cloth moistened with rubbing alcohol. Most stains can be lifted out and there is no need to rinse. The alcohol will evaporate without leaving any residue.

Erase Permanent Markers

Removing permanent marker from your countertop is not as problematic as one might think. Most countertops are made of a non-permeable (not permitting fluids to pass through it; or impenetrable) material such as plastic laminate or marble. Use rubbing alcohol to dissolve the marker into a liquid state so you can wipe it right off.

Get Rid of Fruit Flies

The next time you see fruit flies hovering in the kitchen, get out a fine-misting spray bottle and fill it with rubbing alcohol. Spraying the little flies knocks them out and makes them fall to the floor, where you can sweep them up. The alcohol is less effective than insecticide, but it's a lot safer than spraying poison around your kitchen.

Make a Shapeable Ice Pack

You can make a slushy, conformable pack by mixing 1 part rubbing alcohol with 3 parts water in a self-closing plastic bag. Place in freezer. When needed, remove from freezer, wrap the bag in a cloth, and apply it to the area. (If your children are anything like mine, you might consider double bagging the ice pack.)

Clean Bathroom Fixtures

Pour some rubbing alcohol straight from the bottle onto a soft, absorbent cloth and wipe down the fixtures. There is no need to rinse. The alcohol evaporates, leaving chrome sparkling and free of germs.

Pucker Power

Lemon

We love the invigorating scent of citrus! It says fresh and clean better than any scent out there. The cleaning products miss the mark on replicating this scent, don't they? Upon researching the benefits of citrus, we learned something. Not only does citrus smell wonderful, it has many properties that make it very valuable as a cleaning agent. Does the marketing or advertising tell us this? No, of course not! If they did, they would have to admit how simple the basics really are. So the next time you see a lemon or orange scented cleanser, remember that the scent is not because "they" want your house to smell lemony fresh; citrus is a cleanser in its own right.

The lemon is a small evergreen tree originally native to Asia and is also the name of the tree's oval yellow fruit. The fruit is used for culinary and non-culinary purposes throughout the world, primarily for its juice. The pulp and rind or zest is also used mainly in cooking and baking. Lemon juice is about 5% to 6% citric acid, which gives lemons a sour taste and a pH of 2 to 3.

Being readily available lemon juice is an inexpensive, acid for use in educational science experiments.

A wide variety of wonderful culinary delights come from lemons. Delicate pastries tout the delicious flavor of the lemon, as well as many main dishes.

Household uses for lemons go beyond utilizing them for preparing foods. Lemons provide anti-bacterial and antiseptic qualities that make them ideal for cleaning purposes. They are a refreshing fruit that naturally clean some of the toughest messes. It is a mild, yet effective green cleaner. Lemon juice can be used as a mild de-greaser and whitener.

It's interesting to note that lemon juice is one of the best liquids you can use to restore older pennies that have the dull gray or green look that comes from copper oxide.

The citric acid in lemon juice can dissolve the oxide that forms when the copper on the penny bonds with oxygen in the air.

A great and inexpensive copper cleaner is just a lemon away.

Caution: DON'T USE LEMON JUICE TO BLEACH ANY SILK FABRICS.

Uses for Lemon

Lemon cleaning is certainly a cleaner alternative to the toxic cleaners. Using fresh lemons and lemon juice to clean is certainly eco-friendly but the advantages don't stop there.

Laundry

Lemon juice can be added to a wash cycle for fresh smelling laundry and to brighten whites without using harsh bleaches. Lemon also cleans ink and other stains from clothing when applied directly to spots.

Bleach White Clothes

Mix 1/2 cup lemon juice (or use sliced lemons) and 1 gallon of very hot water together. Only use very hot water for fabrics that are safe to wash in hot water. Soak the clothes.

This is perfect for white socks and underwear. It can even be used on white polyester. Allow to soak an hour to overnight. This will depend on the bleaching needs. When satisfied, pour the mix and clothing into the washing machine, wash as usual. It is impossible to over-bleach using lemon juice.

Caution: NEVER USE LEMON JUICE ON SILK FABRICS.

Rust Remover

Lemon will remove rust from your clothes. Simply rub lemon juice on the rust and sprinkle cream of tartar on the top. Make a loose paste and very lightly tap the paste into the fabric until the stain is removed. Some stains may require up to 15 to 30 minutes to remove the stain. Wash as usual.

Garbage Disposal Freshener

Lemon peels ground in the garbage disposal freshens the drain and leaves a nice fresh lemon scent.

Plastic Storage Container Stain Remover

Use either fresh lemons or lemon juice and use baking soda as the cleaning agent. Let this sit overnight if needed.

Cutting Board Disinfectant

Lemon cleans and disinfects wooden cutting boards and removes the onion and garlic smells. You can also use lemon to clean wooden bowls and utensils. Cut a wedge of lemon and rub over the cutting board.

Lime Build-up Remover

Lemon removes lime buildup. You can use lemon juice to replace vinegar.

Sparkling Dishes

Lemon half placed in the dishwasher will leave sparkling and spot free clean scented dishes.

Air Freshener Fragrance

Add lemon juice to your homemade air freshener for a fresh lemony fragrance.

All-Purpose Cleanser Fragrance

Add lemon to the all-purpose cleaning recipes, if you desire a lemon fragrance.

Hard Water Deposit Remover

Lemon juice can be substituted for vinegar to remove soap scum and hard water deposits.

Lemon Furniture Polish

Add lemon juice to vegetable or olive oil for a great homemade furniture polish.

Counter Top Stain Remover

Remove stains on your laminate countertops by rubbing 1/2 cut lemon on the stain or squeeze juice and let sit. Lemon juice also works. The citric acid will remove the stain. You can also try this with vinegar.

Microwave Cleaner

Add lemon juice to water to boil in the microwave for a great scent and a quick cleanup. Just wipe down.

Copper, Brass, and Stainless Steel Cleaner

Lemon cleans copper, tarnished brass, and stainless steel. Cut the lemon into wedges and sprinkle salt onto the lemon. Rub the lemon wedge onto the brass and squeeze the juice until the tarnish is buffed off. Add more salt as needed to keep cleansing and removing the tarnish. Rinse well with water and let it dry. It is important to keep your copper bottom pans clean. Copper redistributes the heat according to how clean they are on the bottom. **Caution: TO CLEAN BRASS, ONLY USE LEMON ON SOLID BRASS PIECES.**

Brass Plated Cleaner

Brass plated should be cleaned very tenderly with oil soap. **Caution: BRASS PLATED IS BRASS ON ONE SIDE AND BLACK ON THE OPPOSITE SIDE.**

Joe DiMaggio, Homer, and Popeye

Olive Oil

Joe DiMaggio, Homer, and Popeye this is an interesting combination, don't you think? These three men have something uniquely in common. Maybe we should send this tidbit to Trivial Pursuit or the game show Jeopardy. If you have not already guessed, the answer or the question is "What is olive oil?"

Baseball legend and Hall of Famer, Joe DiMaggio began his baseball career with a team sponsored by Rossi Olive Oil. (www.joedimaggio.com) Perhaps this sponsorship led to his ritual of soaking his bats for 10 days in olive oil to give them more spring. (The Passionate Olive) Did it work, you ask? Will this give my child an added edge in Little League? We can't promise that you will be the parent of a baseball great if you soak your son's bat in olive oil (and it might be illegal, we don't know about Little League rules), but it worked for "Joltin' Joe."

Homer (no, not Homer of The Simpsons™) we are speaking of Homer of ancient Greece. He called olive oil "Liquid Gold" due to the enormous impact the olive had on the Greek economy and everyday life. Olive trees are said to have been a gift from the gods. When Zeus asked each god or goddess to present the best gift for mankind, his daughter Athena presented him the olive tree. Athens is named in her honor for the gift of the olive tree.

Spinach loving Popeye the Sailor Man's love interest was none other than Olive Oyl. Olive's name in Spanish was changed due to the fact that putting olive oil in a cartoon and treating it lightly was considered too frivolous. Moral of the story, even Popeye's sweetie is not important enough in Spanish speaking countries to hold the same prestige as olive oil.

There are many different beliefs surrounding olive oil. The earliest reports of the great benefits of olive oil are found in the Scriptures. We learned that it is used for food, anointing oil, lamp oil, and building material. It is also been believed to contain healing and mystical properties.

The olive fruit leaves and branches are also used as a symbol of abundance, glory, peace or goodwill and healing. This is evidenced by the use of the symbols by various governments as part of a country's map and or different seals of important government branches. Such examples include; the Great Seal of the United States, Seal of the United States Senate, or the flag of the United Nations.

Olive wreaths were also used as an adornment worn by brides. In ancient Greece during the Olympic Games a wreath of olive branches was placed on the winner's head.

Olive oil is widely used in Mediterranean cooking and growing in popularity in the United States. It is a must have in many kitchens. Many cookbooks tout the wonders of olive oil.

Olives are a small bitter and oval fruit which is green with unripe and when ripened black. It is used for food and for oil. The classifications of the oil are as follows:

Extra Virgin (EVOO so called by chefs and celebrity chefs): this is considered the finest of the oil. It is made from the first cold pressing of the olives. This gives a mild and delicate flavor. This is the most expensive of the olive oils. Save this grade of olive oil for salads, dipping breads, and for an added flavor on pasta. It is best that this fine grade of olive oil not be heated.

Virgin: this also comes from the first pressing, but this olive oil has a sharper flavor, the darker the oil the sharper the flavor. This can be used for brief cooking times for meats and vegetables.

Fino: This is a blend of extra virgin and virgin olive oils.

Pure: the mildest flavored olive oil comes from a combination or refined virgin and extra virgin oils. This is recommended for all purpose cooking.

Light: This does not refer to the amount of fat or of the number of calories in the olive oil. This rating refers to the color of the oil and is similar to the vegetable oils which are preferred for cooking when you don't want a strong olive flavor.

Uses of Olive Oil

Garden Tools

Spray olive or vegetable oil on your tools before using for easy clean up and to reduce dirt buildup.

Leather Conditioner

To condition leather furniture, rub olive oil into worn leather with a clean soft cloth and leave for 30 minutes. Remove any excess oil and buff with a soft clean cloth. This treatment can also be used on sports equipment such as baseball and softball gloves.

Wood Furniture Polish

To make your own polish, mix 1 cup olive or vegetable oil and the juice of a lemon or 1/2 cup lemon juice concentrate. Use a soft cloth to polish furniture. You can also smooth out small scratches in light colored wood by rubbing the wood with a solution of equal parts oil and lemon juice.

Wood Furniture Polish and Cleaner

Place a small amount of olive oil or vegetable oil on a soft clean cloth and wipe down furniture. By adding a small amount of lemon juice or white vinegar, you will experience a cleaning and polishing all in one and add a clean fresh scent.

Give Your Wood Hydration

Plant based oils (olive, sunflower, soy, and vegetable) oil combinations are quick and easy. By using the substitutions for the less beneficial furniture polishes. The plant based oils will loosen dirt and grime, protect and diminish scratches and imperfections, and hydrate wood that has dried out from age or overexposure to the sun.

Lubricate Measuring Cups and Spoons

This is so easy and so smart! Using a small amount of olive oil and a paper towel, oil your measuring cups and spoons when measuring any sticky ingredients such as syrup, honey. The sticky mess cleans up so easy!

Rattan and Wicker Furniture

To protect wicker and rattan furniture from drying out or cracking, use a light brushing of vegetable oil. By heating the oil on the stove to thin, it makes it easier to apply.

Caution: Do not over heat. You only want to heat until thin. Oil will heat rapidly and could cause physical harm if used while oil is too hot.

Fix a Stuck Zipper

Apply a tiny amount of olive or vegetable oil to a cotton swab and dab on the teeth of a stuck zipper. Gently ease the tab up and down to release the stubborn zipper.

Shine Stainless Steel

To shine up your stainless steel apply a small amount of olive oil on a clean cloth. Shine up those streaky dull stainless steel pots and pans. Applying the oil will keep them streak free and shiny.

Protective Coating for Brass

After cleaning your brass, to give it a protective barrier dampen a soft cotton cloth with olive oil and apply to your brass. Apply as lightly as possible. This will give you added protection and a lasting shine. This should also prevent tarnish and corrosion to your brass pieces.

Scrub and Rub Free Paint Remover

To prevent the harsh scrubbing that is required when removing paint from your hands, arms and face, gently rub olive oil onto paint splattered hands, arms or face. By allowing the olive oil to soak into the skin for five minutes, the paint will then rinse off easily with soap and water.

Fix a Squeaky Door

Use a rag or cotton swab to apply olive oil to the top of a problematic hinge in your home or automobile.

Shoe Polish

Wipe down your shoes with a damp cloth or sponge to remove any dirt residue. Apply a drop of oil to a soft cloth and rub the leather to remove scuff marks. Buff the shoes to shine. If you lightly spritz water on an old nylon stocking and buff your shoes, this gives a great deep shine.

Cast-iron pans

Make a scrubbing paste with vegetable oil and 1 teaspoon of coarse salt to combat cooked-on debris, rinse with hot water.

Car Interior Conditioner for Leather, Plastic, and Vinyl

1 cup olive oil
1/2 cup lemon juice

Combine olive oil and lemon juice in a spray bottle. Spray a small amount onto the dashboard and any other surface of leather, plastic or vinyl. Rub the mixture into the surface with a clean soft cloth. Use another clean soft cloth to wipe off the excess and buff.

Warning: Do not use this on the steering wheel, floor pedals or any other controls where slipperiness could pose a hazard. Also be careful not to get in on windows.

More Than a Savory Seasoning

Salt

There are days that only a salty potato chip fits the bill. Salt is extremely abundant, natural and dirt cheap. We think salt has gotten a bad rap these days. In excess in our diets, it can certainly be harmful, as we have learned. But for use around the house, it is an incredible staple, giving many benefits. We are in awe at the marvels of the natural world in providing everything we need. It is up to us to learn how to use them.

Salt is a mineral that is composed primarily of sodium chloride. It is essential for animal life in small quantities, but is harmful to animals and plants in excess. Salt flavor is one of the basic tastes, making salt one of the oldest, most ever-present food seasonings. Salting is an important method of food preservation.

Salt for human consumption is produced in different forms: unrefined salt (such as sea salt), refined salt (table salt) and iodized salt. It is a crystalline solid, white, pale pink or light gray in color, normally obtained from sea water or rock deposits. Edible rock salts may be slightly grayish in color because of mineral content.

For many centuries man has used salt and the uses continue to increase. This is an amazing substance and the uses are way beyond the kitchen spice rack.

Salt is a great natural cleaner and has a multitude of purposes. It is an alternative to the harsher chemicals we may be using.

Salt is cheap, easy to find and is safe for the environment.

If your state does not tax food items purchased from the grocery stores, you are in for an added bonus. Each time you make cleaning products with food items such as salt, vinegar, baking soda, cream of tartar, lemons or lemon juice, you will not be taxed as you would on cleaning products.

Since salt is most plentiful, it is also inexpensive. Any table salt sold in supermarkets or other food shops will do perfectly well, whether iodized or not.

Uses of Salt

Cleaning with Salt

Salt dissolves in water and can be mixed with several other natural cleaners. Vinegar, lemon juice and washing soda all combine safely with salt for various cleaning tasks. Borax™ can be used with salt for cleaning carpets and other tasks.

Cleaning Sponges

The perfect breeding ground for nasty bacteria is the kitchen sponge. Soak the sponge in a heavy salt brine (water saturated with or containing large amounts of a salt) to kill the bacteria.

Remove Smells from Cutting Boards

The bad smell in cutting boards means the presence of bacteria. Salt kills bacteria when you rub it into the board and let sit. Rinse for a clean and healthy cutting board.

Remove the Onion Smell from Your Hands

Rub your hands with salt and vinegar and rinse with cold water. This should eliminate the entire odor.

Clean Greasy Cookware

Pour rock salt on greasy cookware before scrubbing to cut through the grease.

General Household Cleaning

Salt helps makes cleaning in the bathroom, laundry, kitchen, carpets, floors, and general cleaning a lot easier. Give it a try to increase your cleaning power and decrease your costs.

Silk Flower and Delicate Items Cleaner

Salt can also be sprinkled on some (dry) materials to clean off dust and dirt. For example, if you have delicate cloth items or artificial flowers which have dust embedded in the folds, a sprinkling of salt will gather the dust and it can be carefully shaken out of the item.

Fire Extinguisher

Keep a container of salt handy while cooking with grease. This should not be used as a replacement for a fire extinguisher, but it is a great backup. Should you experience a grease fire, pour salt directly at the bottom or base of the fire to smother the flames.

Easy Clean-up of Spilled Oil and Eggs

To clean up oil and egg spills, cover the spill with salt. It makes this messy spill quick and easy to clean.

Frost-Free Windows and Windshields

Salt greatly decreases the temperature at which ice freezes. To keep the windows in your home frost-free, wipe them with a sponge dipped in salt water and let dry. In the winter, keep a small cloth bag of salt in your car. When the windshield and other windows are wet, rub them with the bag. Your car windows won't be covered with ice or snow.

Easy Oven Spill Clean-up

Pour salt on oven spills for easy clean up. Wipe off with a warm wet cloth after oven has cooled.

The Simple Staple

Soap

Ever wonder when soap and water were replaced by all these chemicals that we can't even pronounce? A staple in every home was soap and water. Now we have as many choices of specialized products to clean every surface in our home as there are types of attorneys in the yellow pages! Everything is compartmentalized and specialized. Do they need to be though? No, not really. We have a 21st Century News Flash for you. Soap still cleans.

Then why are we using so many chemicals to clean? We have replaced the simplicity of soap with so many high tech advertized products that make wonderful claims to do the work for us. What we have forgotten is how simple soap can be and more importantly it still gets the job done.

The difference between soap and detergent needs some defining. Soap is a cleansing agent made from the salts of vegetable or animal fats. Detergents are a cleansing agent made from chemical compounds. These chemicals can cause drying, irritation, inflammation, itching and burning of our skin; and are found in the products that we use many times in our daily lives.

These chemicals are in our everyday world and what we are using to surround our families with the added benefit of the great enhanced fragrance. The most common of "fragrances" used are also synthetic petrochemicals. These chemicals can trigger allergic reactions in many. Now they mix in the toxic colorants and other substances such as fillers and preservatives and we just might say they have made us a petrochemical cocktail. This isn't what we thought we were purchasing!

Although both the soap and detergents perform the same task, cleansing, a significant difference exists between them. In order to differentiate between the soaps and detergents, we need to understand the properties of each such as the ingredients.

Soap cleanses by lowering the surface tension of water, emulsifying or dissolving grease and by absorbing dirt into the foam.

Soaps are manufactured using natural materials such as the oils of plants and or animals, lye and water. Oil and water normally do not mix, but when mixed together with lye, a washing and cleaning agent is produced.

Soap is widely used in washing, laundry, dishwashing liquids, hand soaps, shampoos and cleaning products.

Soaps come in various forms of consistency such as bars, powders, flakes and liquids.

Detergents are generally synthetic, made from petroleum products with surfactants, foaming agents and alcohol being their primary constituent. To remove the disagreeable odor of these chemicals, detergents can be heavily scented with cheap, synthetic and artificial fragrances.

Soap and Hard Water

The most important difference between a soap and detergent is their behavior in water. There is a big drawback of washing with soap, it forms a scum in hard water, which is not easy to rinse away and is known to tint laundry, a grayish hue. The insoluble film that soap leaves can leave a residue on the laundry much like one would see in a shower stall where hard water is present.

On the other hand, detergents react less to minerals in water hence does not leave this residue. In case you are living in an area, where the water is soft, soap will work satisfactorily, but even then a gradual build-up of calcium and magnesium ions (also called 'curd') will be left on the fabric.

Another important difference between soaps and detergents, is the sensitivity of soaps to acidic conditions. Soap and lye require less energy in the manufacturing process. It is possible to make soaps without having leftover by-products, which tend to go to the landfill and the soap, which flows down the drain, is biodegradable. These soaps have a pH of 9.5 to 10 (alkaline) that makes them effective cleansing agents and eliminates the requirement for harmful antibacterial chemicals and preservatives.

Superior quality soaps are produced with oils; from palm, castor, coconut or olive oils and retain the natural glycerin, rather than removing it and selling it for profit, which bulk manufacturers generally do.

Uses of Soap

All Natural Air Freshener

Unwrap soap bars and place around your home for a nice fragrance. Your house will smell clean and fresh. The drier the soap, the longer it will last.

Stuck Zipper?

If you have a stuck zipper, rub the teeth with a bar of soap to lubricate the zipper teeth to get the zipper moving easily again.

Sticky Drawers

To fix stuck drawers rub the top and bottom of the drawers and the supports they rest upon with a bar of soap. Soap lubricates and once again drawers slide with ease.

Help for Power Tools

Use soap on the metal blades of power tools to allow them to move through wood with ease. Also use a bar of soap to twist screws and nails into prior to securing down. This will make the task easier.

Remove a Broken Light Bulb

Turn off the power and insert a corner of a large bar of soap into the light socket. Turn until the base unscrews. You will be able to remove the broken bulb safely.

Deodorizer

To deodorize your car or truck, place a small piece of your favorite soap in a mesh bag and hang it from your rearview mirror.

Hem Marker

If you need to mark a hem and you don't have tailors chalk, use a thin piece of soap to mark your hem. The soap marking will wash right out.

Pin and Needle Lubricant

To lubricate pins and needles, stick them into a bar of soap for easy use.

Cast Iron Pot Cleaner

For easy clean up of cast iron pots, rub with a bar of soap on the bottom of the pots before cooking over sooty open flames.

Luggage Storage Freshener

If you store clothes or luggage, add a bar of your favorite soap. This will keep your clothes or your luggage fresh from season to season.

If You Like Little Orange, You Will Love Big Yellow

Washing Soda

Little Orange? Big Yellow? What are we talking about now, right? Let's try an experiment. We'd like to invite you to do an experiment with us. Close your eyes and think of a package of baking soda. We're pretty sure you thought of a little orange box, didn't you? The little orange box has become an icon for baking soda, hasn't it? You may or may not buy the brand in that little orange box, but you think of it as baking soda. We're introducing you to the big brother of the little orange box, Washing Soda. To our knowledge, you can only find in a big yellow box.

Washing soda is a highly alkaline chemical compound, which can be used to remove stubborn stains from laundry. It also has numerous uses around the house.

The chemical formula for washing soda is Na_2CO_3 and it is also known as sodium carbonate. It is a salt of carbonic acid, a chemical that produces a wide range of salts collectively known as carbonates. One common source of washing soda is the ashes of plants and it is sometimes called soda ash. Sodium carbonate can also be created from sodium chloride, also known as table salt.

Washing soda should not be confused with washing powder, which is a powdered soap used as a detergent. It is also not the same thing as baking soda, although the two compounds are closely related.

In laundry, washing soda accomplishes several things. The high alkalinity of washing soda helps it act as a solvent to remove a range of stains.

Wear gloves when cleaning with washing soda, because it is very caustic and it can cause severe skin damage.

Many markets carry washing soda, typically with other laundry products.

Caution: NOT RECOMMENDED FOR ALUMINUM SURFACES; MAY CAUSE DISCOLORATION. NOT RECOMMENDED FOR NO-WAX FLOORS. AVOID CONTACT WITH EYES.

Uses of Washing Soda

One of the domestic uses of washing soda is for the purpose of softening hard water. Hard water contains calcium and magnesium ions which react with the soaps and detergents. These chemicals change the properties of soap and prevent the formation of soap lather or suds, which affects the soap's ability to clean. More detergent is required to make the suds or lather. Adding washing soda prevents the ions of hard water from forming these chemical bonds. This allows the detergent to clean the dirt from the clothes.

Uses in the Laundry Room

Gets out greasy dirt stains
Perspiration
Collar and Cuff Stains

Food Stains

Mustard
Chocolate
Blueberry
Cola
Meat
Grease
Olive Oil
Make-up
Blood
Grass
Clay

Uses for Cleaning in the Bathroom

Tiles
Sinks

Tubs
Showers
Toilet bowls
Cleans drains

Uses for Cleaning in the Kitchen

Walls
Countertops
Refrigerators
Appliances
Cleans drains

General Household Cleaning

Washing soda cleans both indoor and outdoor grease surfaces all around your home. It is non-foaming so it rinses easily. Washing soda will work for all your tough cleaning problems.

Washing soda is also a cleansing agent to remove dirt from the surface of silver.

Washing soda when dissolved in water is used as a fungicide to kill molds.

Use washing soda for cleaning up engine oil and any other tough materials that generally require the use of solvents.

Washing soda cuts grease, cleans petroleum oil, removes wax, removes lipstick and neutralizes odors in the same way that baking soda does.

Caution: Don't use it on fiberglass, aluminum or waxed floors—unless you intend to remove the wax.

You'll be Buyin' by the Gallon at the Store!

Vinegar

Corny sing-a-longs?!? What next? Confession time. I went through about a small quart of vinegar every few years before embarking on our workshops; Cheaper Greener Cleaner Ceiling to Floor Savings in 30 Minutes or Less. Now I buy it by the gallons! Try club stores for bulk packaging (yes bulk packaged vinegar) to save even more. If someone asks why you are buying vinegar by the gross, answer them in one of two ways: give them our website address, or tell them that you are the Easter Bunny and have a lot of eggs to dye. Twitch your nose, rub your ears and hop down the aisle towards the carrots. Wagging your bunny tail is optional.

Mildly acidic, white vinegar dissolves dirt, soap scum, and hard water deposits from smooth surfaces, yet it is gentle enough to use in a solution to clean hardwood flooring.

White vinegar is a natural deodorizer, absorbing odors instead of covering them up. Any vinegar aroma disappears when dry. With no coloring agents, white vinegar won't stain grout on tiled surfaces. Because it cuts detergent residue, white vinegar makes a great fabric softener substitute for families with sensitive skin.

As a cleaning substance, white vinegar can provide an excellent and eco-friendly alternative to chemical substances. Many people swear by using white vinegar to clean windows.

Apple Cider Vinegar, White Distilled Vinegar

Is vinegar really wine gone badly? From the Old French *VIN aigre* translates into "sour wine." It is believed that in the beginning it was a barrel of wine past its prime. Either by a mistake or a forgotten barrel of wine, we don't know if this is really true but by whatever means a valuable treasure was created.

So we found our answer to the age old question, is vinegar, wine that has gone bad? Maybe long ago, but no, not today, vinegar is a wine that is altered by a yeast based and a form of acetic acid substance called Mother of Vinegar or Vinegar Mother. Mother of Vinegar or Vinegar Mother or the sludge is formed during the fermentation process. (This is the mucky residue at the bottom of a bottle of older vinegar.) It is the acetic acid that gives vinegar its distinguishing flavor and sets it apart from wine.

As we have travelled through the centuries, vinegar has been produced from a wide variety of things. It can be made from a variety of sources that contain sugar or starch. These ingredients range from beer, berries, beets, coconut, dates, fruits, grains, honey, malt, maple syrup, melons, molasses, potatoes, sorghum (grain), whey and wood.

While researching vinegar it reminded me of stories from my great grandmother and her starter dough for her bread making. This was a coveted staple in times long ago. Without the starter dough or in this case the Vinegar Mother there would be no future bread or vinegar to be made. Great care was given to protect and preserve the starter for future use. Many stories have been shared of starters going bad and the need to travel to another farm in hopes of borrowing a small portion of a neighbor's starter.

I can just imagine the same types of stories and needs when it came to the making and keeping the Vinegar Mother.

Vinegar has long been a staple used in cooking, cleaning and for medicinal uses.

The main question surrounding the difference between apple cider vinegar and white vinegar and which to use where is simple. We all know that the specialized vinegars have their own unique uses in the culinary field. Now to the real question we need answered for cleaning purposes, apple cider vinegar is generally used in cooking and white vinegar is used for cleaning.

Apple cider vinegar comes from the fermentation from apple mash. The cider vinegars will come from whatever the type of vinegar it is, such as rice vinegar, red raspberry vinegar, and the like. White distilled vinegar usually comes from converting the sugar into alcohol and the alcohol into vinegar.

We use white distilled vinegar in our cleaning but I did use the apple cider vinegar in the recipe for the terrible stench in my kitchen. (See Chapter 5 **Quick and Convenient MIY Kitchen Cleaners, Air Fresheners, Serious Odor Eliminator**)

For experimentation, we have found both work great in creating volcanoes but the cider vinegar gives off a light brown color unlike white distilled vinegar volcanoes.

Caution: NEVER USE WHITE DISTILLED VINEGAR ON MARBLE. THE ACID CAN DAMAGE THE SURFACE.

Uses of Vinegar

White vinegar is a popular household cleanser. It is effective for killing most mold, bacteria, and germs because of its acidity.

Cleaning with white distilled vinegar is a smart and easy way to avoid using harsh chemicals. White vinegar is also environmentally friendly and very economical.

Remove White Water Rings

To remove white water rings from wood, use a solution of equal parts white distilled vinegar and olive oil or vegetable oil. Always rub with the grain of the wood.

Safe Disinfectant

To safely disinfect and clean baby toys use white distilled vinegar in a soapy water solution. Rinse well and allow to dry.

Clean Vinyl Baby Books or Board Books

To clean vinyl baby books or board books, wipe down with white distilled vinegar. Wipe clean with a damp sponge or cloth.

Clean and Deodorize Urine on a Mattress

To clean and deodorize urine on a mattress, make a solution with white distilled vinegar and water. Sprinkle the area with baking soda and let dry. Brush or vacuum the residue after it has dried.

Clean Computers

To clean your computer, printer, fax machine and other office gear use vinegar and water.

Turn off all the components before cleaning.

Mix a solution of equal parts of vinegar and water. Wet a soft cloth in the solution and wring it out very well.

Make sure that the cloth is not overly wet and water is not dripping from the cloth. Do not let any water fall into your keyboard or computer. This could damage your electronics.

Wipe all the surfaces of your electronics and get them shining clean. Use cotton swabs around small or tough to reach areas, for example, in between the keys of the keyboard.

Clean Window Blinds

Vinegar works well to clean your window blinds. Make a solution of equal parts of white vinegar and water. Wearing white cotton gloves dip your fingers in the solution and slide your fingers across the blinds, with fingers on each side of the slats. Be sure to get both sides of each blind. Rinse with clean water.

Remove Mildew Stains

Apply full strength white vinegar to heavy mildew stains. For light stains dilute half and half with water. No ventilation is required and you can apply white vinegar to nearly any surface without worry. To prevent mildew from forming on rugs and carpets mist the back of the rug with full strength white vinegar in a spray bottle. Let dry for a few minutes.

Shine Silverware or Silver Jewelry

Make a solution of one half cup of white vinegar and two tablespoons of baking soda. Soak the silverware or jewelry for a couple of hours. Rinse with cold water and dry thoroughly with a soft cloth. Return to solution if all tarnish has not been removed. They will sparkle and shine without any hard rubbing and messy creams.

Remove Ink Pen Marks

To remove pen marks use white vinegar on a sponge and blot the marks. Keep using until the marks are gone.

Remove Sticker Residue

To remove a sticker or decal that is on a painted surface, saturate the corners and edges with white vinegar. Scrape it off with a plastic card. The sticky glue can also be removed by soaking it with white vinegar and then wiping clean. This will remove the sticker or price tag from just about any surface using white vinegar.

Shine Chrome and Stainless Steel

Spray full strength vinegar to clean chrome or stainless steel. Buff to a shine with a soft cloth.

Clean Piano Keys

To clean piano keys, use a solution of equal parts vinegar and water. Dip a soft cloth into the solution and wring out as much as liquid as you can. Gently wipe each key. Use a soft cloth, dry as you go. **Leave the keyboard uncovered for 24 hours after cleaning.**

Clean and Brighten Bricks

To clean and brighten bricks for floors or brick fireplaces, make a solution of one cup of vinegar per gallon of hot water. Spray with the mixture and scrub with a brush if needed. There is no need to rinse. This solution works for cleaning brick inside and outside your home.

Brighten Wood Paneling

Mix 1 pint of warm water, 2 tablespoons of olive oil and 4 tablespoons of white vinegar in a small sealable container. Seal and shake the container to mix thoroughly. Apply to the paneling with a clean cloth. Allow the mixture to soak into the paneling for a few minutes then polish with a clean, dry cloth.

Clean Carpet or Rug without a Steam Cleaner

Make a solution of one gallon of water and one cup of white vinegar. Dip a broom into the solution and brush your carpet to bring back the life and color. This is quick and easy and you do not need to rinse. The vinegar smell vanishes as it dries.

Remove Carpet Stains

To get carpet stains out use 1/2 cup of white vinegar and 2 tablespoons of salt. For tough carpet stains, add 2 tablespoons of Borax™ to the mixture.

Remove Grease

To remove grease from any kitchen surface, use a solution consisting of equal parts white vinegar and water.

Spray-on Carpet Stain Remover

Put 1 part vinegar and 5 parts water into a spray bottle. In a second spray bottle, mix five parts water with one part non-sudsy ammonia. Spray the stain with vinegar solution to saturate it and allow it to soak into the stain. Blot the stain with a clean cloth. Spray with the ammonia mixture and blot up excess wetness and stain. Repeat the process until the stain is gone.

Leather Cleaning

To clean leather articles, use a mixture of white distilled vinegar and olive oil. Rub the mixture into the leather and then polish with a soft cloth.

Windows Will Sparkle

To make windows really shine, spray any cleaner onto windows and wipe with newspaper. You will be amazed. Wear gloves if you don't want to get any ink on your hands.

Kitchen Countertop Spray Cleaner

In the kitchen, use vinegar-and-water spray to clean countertops, lightly soiled range surfaces and backsplash areas.

Bathroom All Purpose Spray Cleaner

In the bathroom, use a vinegar spray cleaner to clean countertops, floors and exterior surfaces of the toilet.

For really tough bathroom surfaces such as shower walls, pump up the cleaning power by removing the sprayer element from the spray bottle and heat the solution in the microwave until barely hot. Generously spray shower walls with the warmed solution, wait 10 to 15 minutes, then scrub and rinse. The heat helps soften stubborn soap scum and loosens hard water deposits.

Uses for White Vinegar in the Kitchen:

To shine chrome sink fixtures
Scouring cleanser
Clean counter tops
Clean and deodorize a drain
Deodorize and clean the garbage disposal
Clean the microwave
Clean the shelves and walls of the refrigerator
Cut the grime on the top of the refrigerator
Wipe down a newly cleaned oven
Clean grease splattered oven door window
Remove soap buildup and odors from the dishwasher
Prevent etching on glassware in the dishwasher
Restore cloudy glassware
Get rid of lime deposits in a tea kettle
Remove mineral deposits from coffee makers
Remove stains from coffee and coffee cups
Remove stains and smells from plastic food containers
Remove odors from a lunch box
Clean tarnished brass, copper and pewter
Clean metal
Polish brass and copper
Get rid of calcium deposits on faucets
Remove soap buildup from faucets
Rid a faucet of lime deposits

Uses for White Vinegar in the Bathroom:

Air Freshener
Clean Spray shower doors
Deodorize the toilet bowl
Clean toilet bowl
Disinfectant
Mold Remover
Chrome Fixture Cleaner and Shiner
Tile Cleaner
Bathtub and Sink Cleaner
Shine colored porcelain sink

White Vinegar Uses for General Household Cleaning:

Shining finish on a no-wax vinyl or linoleum floor
Tough linoleum stains floor cleaner
Eco- Friendly floor cleaner
Carpet stains removed
Color Brightener in carpet
To reduce soap bubbles in a steam cleaner
Indoor/outdoor carpet cleaner
Window cleaner
Woodwork and wall cleaner
Wood paneling cleaner
Unclog drains and deodorize
Remove smoky smell

"The habit of thrift is simply the habit which dictates that you shall earn more than you spend. In other words, thrift is the habit that provides that you shall spend less than you earn. Take your choice."

Elbert Hubbard
(American writer, publisher, artist, and philosopher.
He and his wife were lost at sea, May 7, 1915, while travelling
to England aboard the ill-fated Lusitania.)

Chapter Nine

A Treasured Legacy

My pretty patchwork quilt.

MY PRETTY PATCHWORK QUILT

Yes, it surely seems a crime
Thus to spend such precious time,
Piecing silks and satins gay
Night and morning, all the day,
Just to make a cover fine
For that old-style bed of mine;
Pieces all of **this** and **that**
Placed to fit so nice and pat.
My pretty patchwork quilt.

Cutting, basting, fitting all
Into space that seems too small,
But they all are placed at last
On the block secure and fast
Strips of yellow, band of green
Held by stitches quite unseen;
'Till I think I'll surely wilt
Working on this patchwork quilt.
My pretty patchwork quilt.

But each piece a story tells,

Buddy's blouse—a dress of Nell's;
And this pretty ribbon scrap
Was from Grandma's Sunday cap.
Of someone dear, someone kind,
Some-one far, and some-one near
Some-one gone and some-one here.
My pretty patchwork quilt.

So, I sit and piece the while
Sometimes sad, sometimes I smile;
Memories of things that were
All my thoughts and feelings stir
But altho' I **do** get tired
With ambition I'm still fired
Just to see my work complete
And all finished nice and neat
My pretty patchwork quilt.

Ada Dilworth Tracey Wootton

One's Life Story Found in a Patchwork Quilt

We found the preceding poem "My Pretty Patchwork Quilt," by my husband's grandmother, Ada Dilworth Tracey Wootton among the many boxes we were gifted. (This is the same grandmother we refer to in **Chapter One, "Trash or Treasure."**) This particular poem was published in a ladies society anthology of verse in 1941.

We wish one of the many quilts made by Grandmother Ada survived the passage of time to accompany her poem. Although, among our treasures we have the next best thing, quilts from my Grandma Bessie. Bringing together the combined items from both sides of our families we wish to honor these industrious women. What a perfect blend of treasures from the past!

We didn't find any stories of Grandmother Ada and her quilting other than her poem so we speculate she had the same practices of using up what she had as she refers to "pieces of this and that." My heart is heavy and tears soon fill my eyes as she continues..."each piece a story tells, Buddy's blouse—a dress of Nell's;" these were two of her children whom she lost at such a young age. She continues on, "Of someone dear, someone kind, Some-one far, and some-one near, Some-one gone and some-one here." She gives us only glimpses of her memories of all those that she held dear.

Grandmother Ada wrote many poems. She wrote about their life changing when times turned from relative ease to hardship. Finding themselves in a desperate situation during the Great Depression it became necessary to leave the city and return back into their very basic and small farm house. There were not any modern features to this little house, yet she writes of her fond memories of her starting off her marriage in that little house. She writes that as they turned onto the little lane that led to the house it was like greeting an old and trusted friend. She found peace and appreciation, even within the circumstances they were experiencing for the shelter that the little farmhouse provided.

She found her life harder, yet she records her gratitude for her surroundings. She expresses her circumstances being far better off than most during this time. They had a house and farm land in which they would plant and grow their food. These were resourceful and industrious people, who faced their struggles head on.

She so eloquently composes her thoughts on various topics such as her faith, grief, and beauty of the world, love of family, and especially a devoted husband and the principals of life. Her steadfast attributes are intertwined within her poetry, each taking their place to recreate a life unknown to us. Her verse gives us the insight to know who she was, what she stood for and how she regarded life's challenges. She seemed to have excelled in all areas. We have taken these pieces (poems) to complete her patchwork quilt called life.

Learning the lessons of life from Grandma Bessie was more easily recognizable for some of us. Some of her children and grandchildren always realized her strength of character; others might only have seen her as the wife of a farmer. We had our personal time with her as we lived life's experiences with her.

Always having a special, soft spot in connecting to the past; in a secure portion in the closet my greatest treasures from my past, are some of the patchwork quilts made by Grandma Bessie.

In my memories I recall her quilting year-round. She firmly believed and lived by the philosophy that idle hands were a deep disgrace. Her quilts were piled on every bed and stored in a chest bursting at the hinges! Every year we would get a package of quilts or other homemade gifts from her. I have a few of her quilts, worn with age and bursting with Grandma's life lessons.

Long before yard sales, garage sales, and thrift stores became an accepted mode of savings, Grandma would go to rummage sales, church bazaars and such to find her treasures. She purchased any number of things that she needed at a greatly reduced price. She reduced, reused, recycled, revalued as much as she could and then improvised when needed.

She bought bags of clothes for mere pennies to supply fabric for her quilt making or for rags to use on the farm. On rainy days she would sit on the floor to sort through what would be cut into pieces for quilting. She also removed buttons to place in her vast button tin.

As a child it was so much fun to sort through Grandma's buttons to see all the many different types, colors, and kinds she had. She never bought buttons for any of her many needs she had in her sewing. Whatever she needed she found in her tin.

Remembering my first sewing project as a young mother, I missed Grandma's button tin. Having to purchase buttons made a huge impression on me. Grandma's button tin was another overlooked treasure. I started my own collection of buttons, which my granddaughters love to sort through just as I did as a child. Funny, even in the fast paced world of computers, DVD's, internet games, MP3 players and the like, my little granddaughters love to get into their own collection of scrap fabric and sort through my button tin.

Grandma liked to sew and really loved to quilt. These quilts were well made, but nothing that would win quilt shows. They did not have batting, for batting was expensive, and she pieced fabric as a substitute for batting to place between the quilted layers. They were simple patterns and sewed upon her old treadle sewing machine.

The amazing thing to me has always been how they were pieced. She used small pieces that she sewed together to make up a complete quilt piece. She would sew pieces of fabric from scraps to make a tiny piece that was missing when she cut out her quilt pieces.

Once when I was young, I sat at Grandma's side as she worked, fascinated as only the young are at tasks that seem mundane to the adults completing them. While I sat in awe beside her, she accidently snipped a small corner off a small patchwork piece. She shook her head, and reached casually over into her basket. She selected a small piece of fabric to sew on the piece to make it complete. When I inquired why she didn't just make a new piece to replace the one ruined, she taught me that there is something of use in everything. Just because it had an extra piece, it made the two pieces come together to become complete. She explained it might not have won a prize ribbon at the fair but it certainly served the purpose for which it was created.

I don't think she ever really had a particular color scheme in mind as she worked her quilting pieces. She saw first the necessity the pieces were providing and the beauty of the colors, textures and designs would follow. I only know of two quilts that she made with exactness. One was a double wedding ring quilt and the other was a gift for Granddad on his birthday. She chose the theme for his quilt in his favorite color, green. What a great treasure I received when she gave me his quilt. It means so much more than any words could ever express.

She taught me character, principles, and values in all aspects of life. She taught me the lessons in life in everything that she did. She worked from sun up to after sun down. She always made sure that her family had the essentials they needed. Her treats came in the way of desserts. She didn't like to cook and preferred to work outdoors, yet whenever we would come for a visit she would have her baked goodies on her work table waiting for us.

When given a task, I wanted to work just as hard and constant as she did. I wanted to walk right beside her, stride for stride, chore by chore. She was a woman of great cheer. No matter what life presented, she made the best of everything.

She worked all day, every day rain or shine. She cooked, cleaned, canned, quilted, gardened, helped Granddad when he needed her. She worked right beside him during harvesting, and even drove the tractor when needed.

We remember the times helping Grandma Bessie with her daily chores. Some chores were truly enjoyable while others simply had to be done. Never was a chore left undone or incomplete; that was unthinkable. Few ever wanted to be thought of as lazy. She taught us a great work ethic at a very young age, for which we are most grateful.

On a visit, I discovered that my packed clothes didn't match. Thinking this rather unacceptable, she easily dismissed the stripes and floral or non matching colors by simply explaining the farm animals don't care what we wear, they just wanted their food and water. My dismay ended as we began our day working together without the matching ensemble I thought I needed.

Grandma Bessie came to care for us when my little sister was very ill. She taught us self reliance at a very young and tender age. She set the example of a disciplined character. She was the same steadfast woman in the big city as she was on her farm. When life's circumstances presented grief she showed me the courage needed to accept what which had been given. She did not let me see her cry, but she held me as I wept and gave me her kind and loving strength of character to face my biggest challenge thus far in my early years. By her unfailing example and great strength of character I strived to be as she had taught.

Our Grandma Bessie was a short little thing but she was a very strong woman, to us she was the icon for courage, integrity, honesty and, loyalty. She had a way of making even the worst of times a fun adventure.

To honor my grandmother, I too took up quilting. I followed her example and used my daughter's discarded clothes she especially acquired for her 18 months living abroad in France. As a special memento, I made her a patchwork quilt to always remember her experiences. As I placed the pieces together I always thought of Grandma Bessie.

All through the years, we have appreciated Grandma Bessie's quilts. As we have worked on this book we have come to realize that her quilts symbolize her life. As each piece of the quilt is placed to make a colorful design, so is each deed in one's life. She lived a simple life well within her means and was always steadfast to meet whatever life presented. So were her quilts, simple in design, colorful in pattern, and ever present to meet whatever the need of comfort and warmth. The beauty was not in the complexity of the quilt pieces but rather in the dedication she put forth. Upon close inspection, one might find many imperfections; we only see her love and life's lessons.

And so to Grandmother Ada, Grandma Bessie, and all our grandmothers we thank you for your example of living life to the fullest. Teaching by example, giving us a strong foundation to help define who we are and what we can do and how to leave the world a better place.

Wisdom from the Past

Honoring the women from our past.

Our treasured legacy to us is of great and intrinsic value. We honor the women from our past for their great contribution of passing down their time honored traditions and wisdom. Their children's and their grandchildren's memories and stories serve as a testament to the principles by which they lived their lives.

After all this reminiscing, we realize we have become who we are by way of a sheer genetic accident or a treasured legacy.

We choose to believe we win on either count. Our grandmothers that we had the incredible blessing of knowing; and the newly discovered grandmothers were incredible women. These great women lived life to their fullest. They showed their family love in everything that they did. They gave more service to not only family members but others who were in need. They never failed to show up with a meal to a neighbor when there was the need.

These wonderful women from our past have given us more than we had ever realized. By writing this book, we have explored their lives, discovered their secrets, shared their trials and shed tears for their grief. We have learned far more about these unselfish women than just their cleaning tips and tricks.

We found women with the strength and courage to look deep into their souls, to face their faults by striving to make themselves better. Women of great strength and courage that faced their greatest fears head on. Women who gave all they had to give and then gave more to everyone around them. Women, who did not complain about their circumstances, accepted whatever came their way and recognized the blessings. They not only saw to the needs of their families but they gave to many others even when they had so little. They knew that asking for help was not a sign of weakness but a show of strength. They each possessed dignity and grace that showed upon their faces even in trying times their strength helped them to stand straight and tall. Each one of our mothers and grandmothers which we honor were women of strength who had the faith to travel the journey of life making the world a better place than when they arrived. Each one of these amazing women has each left a treasured legacy.

Conclusion

We are certainly fortunate that we were gifted boxes of undiscovered treasures. We not only learned a great deal about the simplicity of making our own homemade laundry and cleaning items; we also became acquainted with past family members we knew next to nothing about. This has been a marvelous experience!

When we began experimenting, we were so astonished how uncomplicated the entire process of removing hidden toxic chemicals turned out to be. We imagined a stressful total waste of time, energy and money. Wow, were we in for a new awakening, we started with a bias and ended enriched in knowledge, monetarily, and a healthier home, reduction in allergies, migraines and an all around physical improvement.

The amount of money that we were saving each time we cleaned or did laundry was a great incentive and we did it without paying for those extremely high priced "green" products. Now we were doing something for our environment that was once out of our budget or so we thought.

You will be amazed how much this will impact your budget without extra work or a real change in your habits. Making it yourself is truly quick and easy. You will be surprised with the effortlessness. We just can't seem to truly express how great it feels to completely pass the cleaning and laundry aisles in the store. We feel completely empowered it is as if we are boycotting the industry giants without the conflicts of picketing.

It is our hope to teach consumers that they can decide for themselves whether or not they want to pay the prices that have been set by the cleaning industry giants. By freeing ourselves from the bonds of high priced products without giving up quality and convenience, we are making a difference in our homes, for our loved ones and for the environment.

The health benefits are enormous for our family. Removing the hidden toxic chemicals and the fragrances from many products once used, we have drastically reduced our allergies and migraine headaches induced by chemicals. Added fragrances have been eliminated. Having suffered from chronic bronchitis, this has been reduced to a minimum by removing the harsh cleansers in our homes.

Health issues still exist, we were not looking for a "cure all," we just wanted our daily lives to be more tolerable. In the process we have come much further than we ever even imagined.

We have discovered the enormous impact that chemicals play in our daily lives. We were naïve to think we did not have a choice or a difference course to take. We were spending so much more money than we thought we needed to for the "green" products, never thinking we could make these ourselves. This has been a marvelous journey removing the chemicals from our lives.

We finally have come to the end of our labor of love. We sincerely hope we have given the right encouragement to entice you to start saving money and help anyone interested in going green without paying the high prices. We have loved every minute we have spent preparing for our workshops and researching for this book.

About the Authors

Carolyn Wootton and Dena Wootton are a mother and daughter writing, research and speaking team teaching the simple and inexpensive way to keep costs down in various aspects of your life.

Dena presented the idea of reducing their laundry expense to Carolyn. After much coaxing (pestering), she won and the research began. After running out of excuses, Carolyn relented and began researching, perfecting and creating recipes with Dena.

They realized that they just might save money making their own laundry soap. The results thrilled them so much that they plunged in and began a quest to save even more money and make their homes a safer environment. The more learned the more money saved, they became "make it yourself" laundry and cleaning products enthusiasts.

When the word got out, they were asked to give a workshop to their church's ladies auxiliary. From that first workshop they were hooked. They truly enjoy helping and teaching others their secrets, hints and tips.

The workshops teach how to make laundry and cleaning product replacements for pennies versus spending dollars. The women at the workshops encouraged them to write a book so they could take Carolyn and Dena home with them.

Carolyn worked as an artist endorsement director and professional research/script writer for a media production company for many years. Carolyn and her husband, collectively have five daughters and twelve grandchildren. She enjoys spending time with her family, being a grandmother and actively serving in her church. She also likes to serve as a volunteer coordinator for various community service projects and charitable organizations.

Carolyn lives in Centennial, Colorado with her husband and two standard poodles.

Dena received her B.A. from the University of Northern Colorado in speech pathology and audiology. She served in the France Marseille Mission for her church. Dena has taught French to elementary students as well as to adults at the Arapahoe Community College, in Littleton, Colorado.

She actively serves in her church, is a Girl Scout leader, a homeschooler, and actively involved in community service. She is an advocate of empowering women and children of abuse; participating through various organizations that improve the lives of women and children suffering from or healing from abuse. Dena also lives in Centennial, Colorado with her two children, Angelyn and Benyse.

Carolyn and Dena continue to give Cheaper Greener Cleaner Workshops.

They have come together to conduct workshops to promote a safer less costly way to meet all the household cleaning needs.

Visit our website at www.cheapergreenercleaner.com.

Bibliography

Agency for Toxic Substances and Disease Registry, 2002. "ToxFAQs™ for Sodium Hydroxide." http://www.atsdr.cdc.gov /tfactsx8.html. (accessed August 19, 2010.)

American Lung Association. Indoor Air Quality http://www.lungusa.org/associations/charters/mid-atlantic/air-quality/indoor-air-quality.html. (accessed November 12, 2010).

American Tartaric Products, Inc. 2004. "Sodium Citrate MSDS Number: S3386." http://www.americantartaric.com/pdf/SODIUM_CITRATE_MSDS.pdf. (accessed April 12, 2010).

Armstrong, Pablo Demetrio Scapinachis. Green House Concept photograph. File # 8957706 www.istockphoto.com/stock-photo-8957706-green-house-concept.php. (accessed March 23 2010).

Armstrong, Pablo Demetrio Scapinachis. White and red Christmas fireplace interior photograph. File # 14692453 www.istockphoto.com /stock-photo-14692453-white-and-red-christmas-fireplace-interior. php. (accessed March 22, 2011).

Bardelline, Jonathan. 2011. Congress renews Debate Over U.S. Chemical Policy Reform. http://www.greenbiz.com/news/2011/04/14/congress-renews-debate-over-us-chemical-policy-reform. (accessed October 23, 2011).

Bojaršinov, Arkadi, Change Ahead Sign photograph. File # 14081605. www.istockphoto.com /stock-photo-14081605-change-ahead-sign.php. (accessed March 22, 2011).

Bond, Annie Berthold. 1999. *Better Basics for the Home*, by New York: Three Rivers Press.

Bonincontro, Aldo. "Borax™: A classic cleaning product still useful today."
http://www.helium.com/items/377503- Borax™ -a-classic-cleaning-product-still-useful-today. (accessed May 6, 2010).

Bower, Lynn Marie. 2000. *Creating a Healthy Household: The Ultimate Guide for Healthier, Safer, Less-Toxic Living.* Indiana: Healthy House Institute.

Brady, George S; et al. 2002. *Borax™" Materials Handbook 15 Ed.* New York: McGraw Hill.

Breyer, Melissa. 2010. "Clean Clothes, Happier Planet." Healthy and Green Living."
http://www.care2.com/ greenliving/clean-clothes-happier-planet. html#. (accessed November 9, 2010).

Breyer, Melissa. 2009. "7 Sources of Scary Indoor Air Pollution, Healthy and Green Livin."
http://www.care2.com/greenliving/7-sources-of-indoor-air-pollution.htm. (accessed November 9, 2010).

Byron, Ellen "The Great American Soap Overdose." *Wall Street Journal*, January 25, 2010.

The Clorox Company. 2010. "Ingredients Inside Product Information." TheCloroxCompany.com.
http://investors.thecloroxcompany.com/releasedetail. cfm?ReleaseID=441522. *(*accessed April 12, 2010*).*

Colburn, Theo, Dianne Dumanoski, and John Peterson Myers. 1997. *Our Stolen Future*. New York: Plume/Penguin.

Cook, Michelle Schoffro. 2010. "Natural Alternatives to Toxic Fabric Softeners." http://green.yahoo.com/blog/care2/45/ natural-alternatives-to-toxic-fabric-softeners.html. (accessed August 6, 2010).

Covey, Stephen R., A. Roger Merrill, Rebecca R. Merrill. 1994. *First Things First: To Live, to Love, to Learn, to Leave a Legacy.* New York: Simon & Schuster.

Dadd, Debra Lynn and Jeremy Tarcher 1997. *Harmful Household Products.* Pennsylvania: Putman Publishing.

Dadd, Debra Lynn.and Jeremy Tarcher. 1997 *Home Safe Home: Protecting Yourself and Your Family From Everyday Toxics.* Pennsylvania: Putnam Publishing.

Davis, Devra. 2004. *When Smoke Ran Like Water – Tales of Environmental Deception and the Battle Against Pollution.* New York: Basic Books.

Diggs, Lawrence.1996. *Vinegar.* Ohio: Tresco Publishers.

Duggan, Ken. 2010. Is Your Toilet Bowl Cleaner Killing You? Apr 01. http://www.articlesbase.com/allergies-articles /is-your-toilet-bowl-cleaner-killing-you-2086536.html#ixzz15yW1xGPO 2010. (accessed May 29, 2010).

Environmental Working Group's Skin Deep Cosmetic Safety Database, 2010, "Coceth-7." cosmeticsdatabase.com. http://www.cosmeticsdatabase.com/ingredient.php?ingred06=701530. (accessed August 6, 2010).

Fagin, Dan, Marianne Lavelle and the Center for Science in the Public Interest. 1996.*Toxic Deception: How the Chemical Industry Manipulates Science, Bends the Law and Endangers Your Health.* New York: Birch Lane Press.

First Research, 2008, "Soap and Detergent Manufacture." Hoover's, Inc. https://www.mccadataport.com/pdfs/First_Research_Industry_Profiles.pdf. (accessed October 28, 2010).

Freedman, Donna. 2009. "5 Life Skills You Can Learn for Free." MSN Money, Sept. 2. http://articles.moneycentral.msn.com/SavingandDebt/SaveMoney/5-life-skills-you-can-learn-for-free.aspx. (accessed August 6, 2010).

Firenze, Carol. 2005. *The Passionate Olive; 101 Things to Do with Olive Oil.* New York: Ballantine Books, Random House Publishing Group.

Green Seal's. 2004. "Choose Green Report." Whole Building Design Guide, National Institute of Building Sciences. http://www.wbdg.org/ccb/GREEN/REPORTS/cgrfloorcare.pdf. (accessed September 3, 2010).

Greenfield, Ellen J. 1991. *Healthy House Institute, House Dangerous, Indoor Pollution in Your Home and Office and What You Can Do About It*. Massachusetts: Interlink Books.

Greensfelder, Liese. 2006. Study warns of cleaning product risks. *University of California, Berkeley News*, May 22. http://berkeley.edu/news/media/releases/2006/05/22_householdchemicals.shtml (accessed April 23, 2010).

Harte, John, Cheryl Holdren, Richard Schneider and Christine Shirley 1991.*Toxics A- Z: A Guide to Everyday Pollution Hazards.* California: University of California Press.

Hasan, Fariha, Aamer Ali Shah*, Sundus Javed and Abdul Hameed. 2010. Enzymes used in detergents: Lipases. *African Journal of Biotechnology* 9, no. 31, (August 2, 2010): 4836-4844, http://www.academicjournals.org/AJB/PDF /pdf2010/ 2Aug/Hasan%20et%20al.pdf (accessed November 9, 2010).

Health Canada. 2010. "Proposed Re-evaluation Decision PRVD2010-06, Hexahydro-1,3,5-*tris*(2-hydroxyethyl)-s-triazine (hexahydrotriazine)."
http://www.hcsc.gc.ca/cps-spc/pest/part/consultations /_ prvd2010-06/prvd2010-06-eng.php. (accessed April 12, 2010).

Holland, S. 2010. "She-conomy: Marketing to Women."
http://she-conomy.com/report/ facts-on-women/. (accessed September 5, 2010).

Hollender, Jeffrey, Geoff Davis with Meika Hollender and Reed Doyle. 2006. *Naturally Clean* Canada: New Society Publishers.

Huffman, Belinda. 2010. "Green" Cleaning to Minimize Asthma Triggers."
http://www.lungusa.org/associations/charters/midland-states/program-information/asthma/ct5are/news/asthma-and-your-child-summer-issue.pdf. (accessed July 6, 2010).

International Occupational Safety and Health Information Centre. International Labour Organization. 1995. "Calcium Chlorine (Anhydrous) ICSC: 1184."
http://www.ilo.org/legacy/english/protection/safework/cis/products/icsc/dtasht/_icsc11/icsc1184.htm. (accessed August 6, 2010).

Johnson, Stacy. 2010. "Do-It-Yourself Laundry Detergent."
Money Talks News April 20.
http://finance.yahoo.com/family-home/article/109349/do-it-yourself-laundry-detergent. (accessed October 26, 2010).

Kiefer, David M. 2002. Today's Chemist at Work, "It was all about alkali," Vol. 11, Oxford University Press.

Kristof, Nichola D. 2010. New Alarm Bells About Chemicals and Cancer. *The New York Times*, May 5.

Lawless, Julia. 2001. *Essential Oils: An Illustrated Guide.* Massachusetts: Element Books Ltd.

Lawless, Julia 1995. *Encyclopedia of Essential Oils.* Massachusetts: Element Books Ltd.; 2nd edition

Lawless, Julia. 1995. *The Illustrated Encyclopedia of Essential Oils: The Complete Guide to the Use of Oils in Aromatherapy & Herbalism.* Massachusetts: Element Books Ltd.

Lawson, Lynn. 2000. *Staying Well in a Toxic World: Understanding Environmental Illness, Multiple Chemical Sensitivities and Sick Building Syndrome.* Illinois: Lynnword Press.

Lowry, Adam. 2010. "Laundry's Dirty Secret: The Overdose Dilemma." http://geteconow.com/ laundrys-dirty-secret-the-overdose-dilemma/. (accessed April12, 2010).

McMurry, J. E. and R. C. *Fay*, 2008. *General, Organic, and Biological Chemistry*, *5th* edition. New Jersey: *Prentice–Hall.*

National Resources Defense Council, *Clearing the Air: Hidden Hazards of Air Fresheners.* September 2007.

National Health Information Centre. 2002-2008. "Sodium Laureth Sulfate (SLES). What it is, where to find it and how to avoid it." http://www.natural-health-information-centre.com/sodium-laureth-sulfate.html. (accessed April 12, 2010).

Nazaroff, William W., and Charles J. Weschler. 2004. Cleaning Products and Air Fresheners: Exposure to Primary and Secondary Air Pollutants. *Atmospheric Environment* 38: 2841-2865.

New York State Department of Health, Center for Environmental Health. *Reducing Environmental Exposures.* New York. 2010.

New York State Department of Health, Center for Environmental Health. *An Introduction to Toxic Substances, Glossary of Environmental Health Terms.* New York. 2006.

New York State Department of Health, Center for Environmental Health. *A Guide to Reference Materials on Toxic Substance. New York.* 2004.

New York State Department of Health, Center for Environmental Health. *The Facts About Chlorine.* New York. 2004.

The New York University Medical Center. 1993. *Family Guide to Staying Healthy in a Risky Environment*, edited by Arthur C. Upton and Eden Graber, New York: Simon and Schuster.

Packaged Facts. 2010. U.S. Market for Green Household Cleaning Products Enters Forefront of Consumer Consciousness with Shift toward More Eco-Friendly and Sustainable Lifestyles, Packagedfacts.com. http://www.packagedfacts.com/about/release.asp?id=1635 (accessed August 6, 2010).

Packaged Facts. 2010. "'Green Household Cleaning Products in the U.S.: Bathroom Cleaners, Laundry Care and Dish Detergents and Household Cleaners."Packagedfacts.com. http://www.packagedfacts.com/about/release.asp?id=1673 (accessed August 6, 2010).

Pellerano, Maria. 1995. *How To Research Chemicals: A Resource Guide.* Environmental Research Foundation: Annapolis, Maryland.

The Personal Care Products Council, "Glyceryl Oleate." cosmeticsinfo.org http://www.cosmeticsinfo.org/ ingredient_more_details.php?ingredient_id=297. (accessed October 23, 2010).

Outwater, Alice. 1996. *Water: A Natural History.* New York: Basic Books.

Rider, Kimberly. 2006. *The Healthy Home Workbook: Easy Steps for Eco-Friendly Living.* California: Chronicle Books.

Rob, Matthew. 2005, Indoor Air Quality Is a Top Health Risk Pollen-Choked Spring Only Makes It Worse. *The Washington Post*, April *9, 2005.*
http://www.arapahost.com/yahoo_site_admin/assets/docs/Indoor_Air_Quality_Is_a_Top_Health_Risk_washingtonpost.160130755.pd (accessed April 12, 2010).

Schettler, M.D., Ted, Gina Solomon, M.D., Maria Valenti and Annette Huddle. 1999. *Generations at Risk.* Massachusetts: MIT Press.

Science Daily. 2010. "Scented Consumer Products Shown to Emit Many Unlisted Chemicals,"
http://www.sciencedaily.com/releases/2010/10/101026091559.htm (Oct. 26, 2010)

Scranton, Alexandra, 2010. "What's That Smell" Women's Voices for the Earth,
http://www.greenbiz.com/sites/default/files/Whats_That_Smell.pdf. (accessed August 6, 2010).

Seventh Generation Chlorine Free Bleach. "Reviews, Specs Ratings and Prices." 2008. Green Options Community
http://www.greenoptions.com/products/seventh-generation-chlorine-free-bleach-detergent. (accessed January6, 2010).

Steingrabe, Sandra. 1997. *Living Downstream: An Ecologist Looks At Cancer and the Environment.* Massachusetts: Addison Wesley Publishing.

Steinman, David and Michael R. Wisner. 1996. *Living Healthy in a Toxic World.* New York: Perigee.

Steinemann, Anne C. 2009, "Fragranced consumer products and undisclosed ingredients" Environmental Impact Assessment Review 29 (1) 32-38.

Steinemann, Anne C. University of Washington (2008, July 24). “Toxic Chemicals Found In Common Scented Laundry Products, Air Fresheners.”

*ScienceDaily.*2008. “Toxic Chemicals Found In Common Scented Laundry Products, Air Fresheners.” http://www.sciencedaily.com/releases/2008/07/080723134438.htm. (accessed September 15, 2010).

Steinemann, Anne C., Ian M. MacGregor, Sydney M. Gordon, Lisa G. Gallagher, Amy L. Davis, Daniel S. Ribeiro and Lance A. Wallace. 2010. “Fragranced Consumer Products: Chemicals Emitted, Ingredients Unlisted.” *Environmental Impact Assessment Review* 2010 DOI:10.1016/j.eiar. 2010.08.002

Steinman, David and Samuel S. Epstein, M.D.,1995. *Safe Shopper's Bible: A Consumer's Guide to Non-Toxic Household Products, Cosmetics and Food.* New York: Wiley Publishing, Inc.

Switalski, Erin. 2010 “Tell the American Cleaning Institute You Want SAFE Cleaning Product Ingredients!” Women's Voices for the Earth. http://www.womensvoices.org/2010/page/5/. (accessed September 15, 2010).

Tatum, Malcolm. “Is Ammonia a Safe Cleaning Agent?” Edited by: Bronwyn Harris. 2003-2011 Conjecture Corporation. www.wisegeek.com/is-ammonia-a-safe-cleaning-agent.htm. (accessed October 23, 2011).

TerraChoice Environmental Marketing. 2010. “Sins of Greenwashing Study Finds Misleading Green Claims on 95 Per Cent of Home and Family Products.” http://www.terrachoice.com/files/ TerraChoice%02010%20Sins%20of%20Greenwashing%20Release%20-%20Oct%2026 %202010%20-%20ENG.pdf (accessed August 6, 2010).

TerraChoice Environmental Marketing. 2009. "Greenwashing Affects 98% of Products Including Toys, Baby Products and Cosmetics. Study Finds New Greenwashing Sin: 'Worshiping False Labels." http://www.terrachoice.com/images/Seven%20Sins%20of%20Greenwashing%20Release%20%20April%2015%202009%20-%20US.pdf (accessed April 12, 2010).

Thornton, Joe. 2000. *Pandora's Poison: Chlorine, Health and a New Environmental Strategy*, Massachusetts: MIT Press.

"Too Many Buns." Frances Goodrich, Albert Hackett, Nancy Meyers, Charles Shyer. *Father of the Bride*. DVD. Directed by Charles Shyer. Burbank, CA: Buena Vista, 1991.

Tryon, Lillian Hart. 1916. *Speaking of Home: Being Essays of a Contented Woman*. Boston and New York Houghton Mifflin, The Riverside Press. (174).

U.S. Centers for Disease Control and Prevention. *Protect the ones you love Poisonings*. Washington, D.C.: Government Printing Office, 2009. http://www.cdc.gov/safechild/Fact_Sheets/Poisoning-Fact-Sheet-a.pdf (accessed November 9, 2010).

U.S. Department of Energy, Brookhaven National Laboratory. *Scientists Report on a Natural Cleanup Solution for Polluted Soil and Incinerator Ash*. Washington, D.C.: Government Printing Office, 1998. (128-98).

U.S. Department of Health and Human Services, Public Health Service Agency for Toxic Substances and Disease Registry (ATSDR). *Toxicological Profile for Ammonia*. Atlanta, GA: 2011 (CAS# 7664-41-7). http://www.atsdr.cdc.gov/ToxProfiles/TP.asp?id=11&tid=2(accessed October 23, 2011).

U.S. Department of Health and Human Services, Division of Toxicology. *ToxFAQs for Chlorine*. Washington, D.C.: Government Printing Office. 2002.

U.S. Environmental Protection Agency. *Technical Background Document to Support Rulemaking Pursuant to the Clean Air Act, Section 112(g), Ranking of Pollutants with Respect to Hazard to Human Health.* By Kenkel, J. Caldwell, and C. S. Scott. Washington, D.C.: Government Printing Office, 1994. (EPA-450/3-92-010).

U.S. Environmental Protection Agency. *Guidelines for Carcinogen Risk Assessment.*, Washington, D.C.: Government Printing Office, 2005. (EPA/630/P-03/001F).

U.S. Environmental Protection Agency, U.S. Public Health Service, National Environmental Health Association. *Introduction to Indoor Air Quality: A Reference Manual.* Washington, D.C.: Government Printing Office, 2010.

U.S. Environmental Protection Agency, U.S. Public Health Service, National Environmental Health Association. *Introduction to Indoor Air Quality: A Self-Paced Learning Module.* Washington, D.C.: Government Printing Office, 1992.

U.S. Environmental Protection Agency, Office of Air and Radiation, U.S. Consumer Product Safety Commission, *The Inside Story: A Guide to Indoor Air Quality.* Washington, D.C.: Government Printing Office. 1995 (EPA 402-K-93-007).

U.S. Environmental Protection Agency, Office of Toxic Substances, *Indoor Air Pollutants from Household Product Sources.* By Thomas Sack and David Steele. Washington, D.C.: Government Printing Office. 1991 (EPA 600/4- 91/025).

The Vinegar Institute. 2010 "Vinegar Lore". http://www.versatilevinegar.org/vinegarlore.html (accessed December 3, 2010).

Wallheimer, Brian and Purdue University. 2010. E. coli Thrives Near Plant Roots, Can Contaminate Young Produce Crops. *ScienceDaily*.com. http://www.sciencedaily.com/release/2010/11/101103135340.htm. (accessed November 4, 2010).

Washington Toxics Coalition, and Washington State University. *Phase One Report A Home Tour for Toxic Products*. By Philip Dickey. *Seattle, Washington. 1991*

Washington Toxics Coalition, and Washington State University *Phase Two Report* Hazardous Household Products and Alternatives. By Philip Dickey, Seattle, Washington. 1991.

Washington Toxics Coalition. *Buy Smarter Buy Safe: A Consumer's Guide to Less-Toxic Products*. By Philip Dickey, Seattle, Washington. 1994

Winter, Ruth. 1992. *A Consumer's Dictionary of Household, Yard and Office Chemicals*. New York: Crown Publishing.

Wootton, Ada Dilworth Tracey. "My Pretty Patchwork Quilt." In *Our Legacy: Relief Society Centennial Anthology of Verse by Latter-Day Saint Women, 1835-1942,* edited by Annie Wells Cannon, 239-240. Salt Lake City, Utah; General Board of Relief Society, Church of Jesus Christ of Latter-Day Saints, 1941.

Wootton, Dena R. 2011 "Letters of Old, Soap Suds, Girls DNA Cleaning, Fantastically Frugal Fifteen, What Does Green Mean to You? 30 Minutes or Less, One Billion Dollars Down the Drain, Laundry ingredients, Laundry room, Girls Making Their Cleaning Supplies, Clean down to your kids toes, Kitchen, Bathroom, A Little Drop Will Do Ya,' Doodles, Dreams and Dilemmas, My Pretty Patchwork Quilt, Wisdom from our Grandmothers a Family Collage. Centennial, Colorado. www.cheapergreenercleaner.com

WVE (Women's Voices for the Earth). 2007. "Household Hazards: Potential Hazards of Home Cleaning Products." http://www.womensvoices.org/our-work/safe-cleaning-products/learn-more/disinfectant-overkill/chart/ (accessed April 12, 2010).

Yaws, C.L. 1999. *Chemical Properties Handbook.* New York: McGraw-Hill.

JP, "et al." 2007. The Use of Household Cleaning Sprays and ult Asthma. American Journal of Respiratory and Critical Care edicine. 176 (8): 735-741.

Zogorski, J.S., Carter, J.M., Ivahnenko, T., Lapham, W.W., Moran, M.J., Rowe, B.L., Squillace, P.J., and Toccalino, P.L., 2006, The quality of our nation's waters--Volatile organic compounds in the nation's ground water and drinking-water supply wells: U.S. Geological Survey Circular 1292, 101 p.